Ethics and Law

Can someone be a good person yet act in a professional role that may involve deception, procedural trickery, withholding information, and working on behalf of terrible people and institutions? This question is at the heart of legal ethics. Using cases from around the common-law world, W. Bradley Wendel looks at issues including confidentiality, the moral responsibility of lawyers, and truth and deception in advocacy. He then examines the classic questions of philosophy of law, including the nature of law, positivism, natural law, the relationship between law and morality, unjust legal systems, and the obligation to obey the law. Finally, he considers the ethical issues surrounding the role of lawyers, including criminal defense and prosecution, civil litigation, counseling clients on the law, and representing corporations. Combining the theoretical, philosophical, and practical, his book will be of vital interest to students of law, the philosophy of law, ethics, and political philosophy.

W. BRADLEY WENDEL is Professor of Law at Cornell Law School. He is the author of *Lawyers and Fidelity to Law* (2010) and *Professional Responsibility: Examples and Explanations, 4th Edition* (2013), and co-editor of *The Law and Ethics of Lawyering, 5th Edition* (with Geoffrey C. Hazard, Jr., et al., 2010).

Cambridge Applied Ethics

Titles published in this series

ETHICS AND BUSINESS *Kevin Gibson*
ETHICS AND CRIMINAL JUSTICE *John Kleinig*
ETHICS AND ANIMALS *Lori Gruen*
ETHICS AND THE ENVIRONMENT *Dale Jamieson*
ETHICS AND THE MEDIA *Stephen J. A. Ward*
ETHICS AND WAR *Steven P. Lee*
THE ETHICS OF SPECIES *Ronald L. Sandler*
ETHICS AND SCIENCE *Adam Briggle and Carl Mitcham*
ETHICS AND FINANCE *John Hendry*
ETHICS AND LAW *W. Bradley Wendel*

Ethics and Law

An Introduction

W. BRADLEY WENDEL

Cornell University

CAMBRIDGE
UNIVERSITY PRESS

CAMBRIDGE
UNIVERSITY PRESS

University Printing House, Cambridge CB2 8BS, United Kingdom

Cambridge University Press is part of the University of Cambridge.

It furthers the University's mission by disseminating knowledge in the pursuit of education, learning and research at the highest international levels of excellence.

www.cambridge.org
Information on this title: www.cambridge.org/9781107617247

© W. Bradley Wendel 2014

First published 2014

Printed in the United Kingdom by Clays, St Ives plc

A catalogue record for this publication is available from the British Library

Library of Congress Cataloging in Publication Data
Wendel, W. Bradley, 1969– author.
Ethics and law : an introduction / W. Bradley Wendel, Cornell University, New York.
    pages   cm – (Cambridge applied ethics)
Includes bibliographical references and index.
ISBN 978-1-107-04256-8 (hardback)
1. Legal ethics.   I. Title.
K123.W46   2014
174′.3–dc23

2014029266

ISBN 978-1-107-04256-8 Hardback
ISBN 978-1-107-61724-7 Paperback

Contents

Preface

This book is about the ethical principles that govern the professional activities of lawyers and the relationship of lawyers' ethics to two important normative domains: first, general moral considerations that apply to all of us, as moral agents; and second, to the law, with its characteristic ways of making and justifying demands on citizens of a society. In a modern, complex society in which people disagree about morality and justice, the law is an important source of social stability and solidarity. The law sets limits on what the government can do to its citizens and what citizens can do to each other. It gives people the right to establish the terms of relationships with others through contracts, wills, and trusts, and the form of various forms of property ownership. Criminal prosecutions and civil lawsuits provide a means for expressing collective disapproval of antisocial conduct and can empower far-reaching social change. But the law can also be an instrument of oppression, entrenching the privileges of powerful individuals and corporations and perpetuating injustices against marginalized individuals and groups. The law has protected the rights of slaveholders and established the principle of "separate but equal." The law can be used to harass or impose costs on others, and, instead of contributing to social solidarity, it can create a sense of individualism and disputatiousness. The law is neither inherently good nor inherently bad but is instead a tool that can be used for good or bad ends.

Although one commonly personifies "the law," the institutions and procedures of the legal system cannot exist apart from the people who administer them. Lawyers (subdivided in some countries into barristers and solicitors) are the means through which the law acts through the representation of clients – from individuals to corporations to "the people" or "the Crown." In a society characterized by a complex, highly technical system of laws, ordinary citizens may take up a variety of ethical attitudes toward the law (including approval, support, resentment, resistance, indifference, etc.), but when they act with respect to the law, they generally do so with the assistance of legal professionals. Very few nonlawyers have the ability to do something as basic as prepare a will or residential lease document without potentially making serious mistakes and harming their legal interests. Whether lawyers are merely hired guns who cannot be blamed for representing nasty clients or doing nasty things for them or whether instead they should be held personally morally responsible for their actions is one of the great questions of practical ethics. The academic discipline of philosophical legal ethics seeks to use the tools of moral and political philosophy to analyze the responsibilities of those professionals who represent clients inside and outside the courtroom. Because citizens rarely encounter the law without professional assistance, the ethical problems facing lawyers are a helpful lens through which to view the more general issue of the nature of the relationships among law, state, and citizens.

Throughout the book, we will look at cases, most of which are based on actual events. The cases differ from those in many practical ethics textbooks in being fairly detailed. Legal and philosophical reasoning have a lot in common, but one crucial difference is that lawyers know the importance of facts. Cases in philosophical ethics are often outlandish ("you can push a fat man off the bridge to stop the speeding trolley"[1]), remote from the experience of most people ("you and two companions are adrift in a lifeboat in the middle of the Pacific Ocean and are running out of food"[2]), or lacking in crucial details (why in the world would an insurgent let his captive free if he shot a randomly selected hostage?[3]). If there is anything lawyers believe deeply in their bones, however, it is that the facts matter a great deal to the resolution of cases, and, as someone trained in both law and philosophy, I hope to bring the distinctive techniques of both disciplines to bear on the problems of legal ethics.

Although I am an American legal scholar, I have tried to include cases from other common law jurisdictions, including Canada, New Zealand, Australia, the United Kingdom, and Israel. I loathe "American exceptionalism" and

---

[1] Judith Jarvis Thomson, "The Trolley Problem," *Yale Law Journal* 94: 1395–1415 (1985).

[2] The famous "lifeboat case," *R v. Dudley & Stephens*, 14 Q.B.D. 273 (1884).

[3] See Bernard Williams, "A Critique of Utilitarianism," in J. J. C. Smart and Bernard Williams, *Utilitarianism: For and Against* (Cambridge: Cambridge University Press 1973), pp. 98–99.

would like this book to be accessible to lawyers around the world. For example, many difficult legal ethics issues for American lawyers arise in the context of pretrial discovery in civil litigation, but because most other nations have had the good sense not to adopt American-style discovery rules, these issues would not arise in the same way. Nevertheless, many of the classic cases that are frequently discussed in the English-speaking legal ethics literature are from the United States, in part because it is a litigious society, but also because many of the first generation of theoretical legal ethics scholars were Americans, including Richard Wasserstrom, Deborah Rhode, Stephen Pepper, David Luban, Gerald Postema, William Simon, and Thomas Shaffer. The early prominence of American scholarship in legal ethics may simply be a historical accident owing to legal ethics having been made a compulsory subject in US law schools after the Watergate scandal in the early 1970s. The discussion here will not assume any knowledge of US law or any other jurisdiction's law for that matter. The point of the cases is to illustrate ethical issues, not legal ones. Lawyers in common law systems are regulated by some combination of the organized bar, the judiciary, legislative enactments, and administrative agency regulation. As a result, in each jurisdiction, there is a body of law governing lawyers, which is a fascinating subject in its own right. The cases in this book, however, have been written around the law as much as possible and do not presuppose any familiarity with the law.

This book is not intended as a contribution to an academic debate. I have said my piece in a book called *Lawyers and Fidelity to Law*. The aim here is to present the field of philosophical legal ethics fairly, to treat the contending positions sympathetically, and to let readers make up their own minds about who is right. At the same time, I will sometimes criticize and always engage with the participants in these debates. Nothing could be more dreary than going through a back-and-forth, he-says, she-responds presentation of the positions. Some of the analysis here is very much my own, and readers may disagree with it. I have tried to make clear where I am acting as an advocate for a position and to keep that advocacy to a minimum. In the end, there are significant questions that have no easy answers. I hope readers come away having formed views about what the right answers are, even if we may not agree.

I am grateful to the students I have taught over the years in seminars on philosophical legal ethics. The experience of teaching these readings and cases has done more than anything else to sharpen my own understanding of the subject. I did substantial work on this book while teaching legal ethics at Tel Aviv University in May 2013, so discussions with those students played a particularly important role in defining the form in which the analysis is presented here. Similarly, my experience teaching legal philosophy at the University of Auckland in January 2012 was helpful in thinking through the discussion of jurisprudence in Chapter 4. Thanks to Tim Dare for sharing that course with me, for ongoing conversations about jurisprudence and legal ethics, and for work-related excuses to visit New Zealand. The book benefited immeasurably from the extensive comments provided by Dana Remus on each draft chapter, for which I am most thankful. Special thanks are due to Hilary Gaskin and three anonymous reviewers for the Press, as well as to David Luban for recommending me for this project. As always, I am grateful to my wife, Elizabeth Peck, and our children, Ben and Hannah, for putting up with the collateral damage of the writing process.

Part I

Lawyers, ethics, and the law

1 Defining the problem

1.1 Role-differentiated morality

A security guard was murdered and another guard seriously injured during the robbery of a store in a big city – it could be Manchester, Auckland, Calgary, Los Angeles, Johannesburg – anywhere in the common law world.[1] The surviving guard identified two men, Logan and Hope, as the perpetrators. A week later, a man named Wilson was arrested for an unrelated crime, the murder of two police officers in the same city. Hope heard through jailhouse gossip about the arrest of Wilson and told his lawyer that he had committed the robbery with Wilson, not Logan. Hope's lawyer communicated this information to Wilson's lawyers, who went to see Wilson at the jail. Wilson confessed to his lawyers that he had committed the robbery with Hope and that he had in fact shot the security guards. Wilson declined to make a statement to the police, but the lawyers prepared an affidavit (a sworn statement) summarizing his statement, which they kept in a locked safe. Meanwhile, not knowing of Wilson's admission of responsibility, prosecutors filed murder charges against Logan and Hope. Based on the testimony of the surviving guard, both were convicted and sentenced to lengthy prison terms. (Eyewitness identification is notoriously unreliable; the defense lawyer tried to establish this point, but the jury convicted the defendants anyway.) Wilson was convicted in a separate trial of murdering

---

[1] The actual case took place in Chicago. See, e.g., Fran Spielman, "Chicago to Pay $10.25 Million in Another Burge Case," *Chicago Sun-Times* (January 14, 2013); "After 26 Years, 2 Lawyers Reveal a Killer's Secret," *USA Today* (April 13, 2008). Logan was released from prison in 2007, after Wilson died and his lawyers disclosed their affidavit. Logan filed a lawsuit claiming that evidence of his innocence had been covered up by state prosecutors. Wilson's lawyers were not charged with any wrongdoing in connection with the case.

the two police officers and was sentenced to two life sentences without possibility of parole.

Imagine that you are one of the lawyers representing Wilson. What do you do with the knowledge that an innocent person will be spending the rest of his life in prison for a crime committed by your client? Perhaps the answer is to be found in a code of professional ethics, applicable to lawyers representing clients in a situation like this one. You consult the rules in your jurisdiction and read the following:

> A lawyer shall not reveal information relating to the representation of a client unless the client consents after consultation ... A lawyer may reveal such information to the extent the lawyer reasonably believes necessary (1) to prevent reasonably certain death or substantial bodily harm.[2]

You have made repeated attempts to convince Wilson to consent to disclosure of the affidavit containing his statement that he committed the restaurant robbery and murders, but he has consistently refused to provide it. Now what do you do?

Students are often keen to "fight the hypothetical" and try to argue that a lawyer's obligations in this case, as a matter of professional ethics, permit you to disclose the statement by Wilson. Although it would be nice if this were the case, the professional rule of confidentiality and the exception just quoted do not permit disclosure. The communication from Wilson is "information relating to the representation" because you learned it in the course of defending Wilson in the separate murder case; it does not matter that the communication relates to a separate crime. You might argue that Logan's continued imprisonment constitutes "substantial bodily harm" because he is quite corporeally stuck in prison. That is not a bad argument, but the authority responsible for interpreting the ethical rules in your jurisdiction has rejected it in a similar case. You might then reason that the duty does not apply because disclosing Wilson's communication cannot possibly harm him because he is already serving two life sentences for the other

---

[2] American Bar Association Model Rules of Professional Conduct, Rule 1.6(b). Some version of this rule is in effect in all US jurisdictions. Similar rules can be found in the codes of professional responsibility of other common law jurisdictions. See, e.g., Solicitors Regulation Authority (England and Wales) Code of Conduct 2011, chapter 4; Federation of Law Societies of Canada, Model Code of Professional Conduct, Rule 3.3-3; Australian Solicitors Conduct Rules 2012, Rule 9.1; New Zealand Lawyers Conduct and Client Care Rules 2008, Rule 8.

murders. The rule defining the duty of confidentiality does not make reference to harm to the client, however, and, upon reflection, you realize that
there might be harm to Wilson if you disclose. What would happen, for
example, if his convictions for the other murders were reversed on appeal?
He might then face prosecution for the robbery of the store and the murder
of the security guard. In the end, you recognize that the duty of confidentiality is interpreted very strictly, and exceptions are narrowly construed. As
a matter of professional ethics, your duty is clear: You must not disclose
Wilson's statement even if it would result in freeing an innocent man from
prison.

If this seems wrong to you, or if you at least feel a tension between what is
required as a lawyer and what otherwise you might believe you ought to do,
then you recognize the problem of *role-differentiated morality*. A lawyer is
obligated by rules of professional ethics to do something – to keep
Wilson's secret even though disclosing it would free an innocent person –
that appears unjust from the point of view of ordinary, common, everyday
morality. The lawyer occupies a social role with specific obligations attach-
ing to it – hence the term "role-differentiated." In one way, nothing could be
more familiar than duties that vary according to the role one plays. As a
parent, I have an obligation to show special care and concern for my own
children, above and beyond the duties I owe to children generally (e.g., to
refrain from harming them and to help them if they are in distress). As a
teacher, I am bound by the ethics of that role to evaluate the performance of
students impartially and not be influenced by irrelevant factors. Most of the
time, these role-differentiated obligations appear as unproblematic aspects
of a life in which one has a variety of relationships of different sorts with
friends, family members, strangers, and institutions. Frequently, these special obligations are easily harmonized with duties owed more generally. In
most cases, I can show special care and concern for my children without
harming anyone else. The wrongful conviction case just described, however, is an instance of a role-based obligation clashing with something we
believe to be more basic – namely, the duties that apply to us universally,
simply by virtue of our being moral agents. How is it possible that a general
moral duty no longer applies just because a person is acting in a professional capacity?

Whether and to what extent moral obligations can vary according to the
social role one occupies is one of the major issues in practical ethics

generally, including the ethics of government officials, law enforcement personnel, soldiers, and business managers.[3] Before considering the issue more systematically, however, it may be helpful to begin with some more intuitive and impressionistic reactions to the wrongful conviction case. In the real case, Wilson's lawyers have steadfastly maintained that they did nothing wrong, but there was a massive public outcry when the case was reported in the media. Suppose now that you are not one of the lawyers in the case but an interested observer – a lawyer or law student, let's say – who is participating in a conversation about the case. You are attempting to defend the lawyers' conduct to someone who is outraged by it. What are some of the arguments you might make?

In many years of teaching legal ethics, I have found that these arguments tend to fall into patterns. (At this point, I am not necessarily endorsing any of these arguments, only setting them out.) Some of the most common moral defenses of Wilson's lawyers might include the following.

1.1.1   Division of labor

The legal system is just that – a system – and no one person is solely responsible for its functioning. Rather, different actors play assigned roles: prosecutor, defense lawyer, judge, juror, court clerk, and so on. The system functions best if everyone plays his or her assigned role. In fact, the system may break down if an actor steps out of her role and does something that is within someone else's job description. If defense lawyers took it upon themselves to disclose information that would be helpful to the prosecution, their clients would stop trusting them, and it would be difficult to provide effective representation to defendants. In the wrongful conviction case, Wilson's lawyers played their role by representing him effectively and keeping his secrets. Logan's lawyer had the job of preventing him from being convicted, and the prosecutor had the responsibility to disclose any evidence subsequently discovered indicating that Logan had been wrongfully convicted. If there is some malfunction, it should be blamed on the actor responsible for that aspect of

---

[3] For a lively introduction to the problem of role-differentiated morality in the form of an imagined dialogue between a writer and Charles-Henri Sanson, the executioner who served under Louis XVI and later detached heads during the Reign of Terror, see Arthur Isak Applbaum, "Professional Detachment: The Executioner of Paris," in *Ethics for Adversaries* (Princeton: Princeton University Press 1999), ch. 2.

the system. Because safeguarding against the possibility of wrongful convictions is not the job of a lawyer for a different defendant in a separate case, it is inappropriate to blame Wilson's lawyers for the harm experienced by Logan.

1.1.2   Rules of the game

Wilson's lawyers did nothing wrong according to the rules of evidence and procedure, substantive criminal law, and the code of professional ethics that applies to them. In short, they followed the rules. The system may be flawed and may on occasion result in unjust convictions, but Wilson's lawyers cannot be blamed as long as they stayed within the rules. As the saying goes, don't hate the play[er], hate the game.[4] This argument is related to the division of labor within a system, but more explicitly it attempts to displace evaluation from individuals to the system as a whole. If the result of a game is lousy, perhaps the rules should be changed, but the only responsibility a player has is to play by those rules. What happened to Logan is an extreme injustice, but rather than blaming the defense lawyers, it would be better in the long run to seek to reform the criminal justice system, perhaps by recognizing heightened duties on the part of prosecutors to investigate when there is evidence of a wrongful conviction.

1.1.3   Hired guns, mouthpieces, instruments, or tools

Lawyers are sometimes called all of these things, and they are not meant as compliments. There is a sense, however, in which lawyers are quite properly regarded as instruments of their clients. In legal terms, lawyers are *agents*. Agency law governs the relationships whereby one person, the agent, has the power to act on behalf of another, the principal. The agent is an extension of the principal, acts to effectuate the principal's instructions, and has power no greater than the principal herself. As an agent of the client, the lawyer speaks for the client, is empowered to enter into binding agreements on behalf of the client, and can commit the client to certain courses of action. In every instance, the lawyer's actions are done *for* the client; the client is the driving force, so to speak. Wilson's lawyers in this case were instruments of Wilson's will – nothing more, nothing less. If

---

[4] After the song, "Don't Hate the Playa," by Ice-T.

Wilson instructed them not to disclose his communication, then they were legally and ethically bound to follow his instructions because ultimately any authority they have is derived from Wilson and from the attorney-client relationship. Furthermore, it is inappropriate to attach moral blame to mere instruments. It may be appropriate to blame the government of a country for starting a war, but, as long as they comply with the laws of war, it is inappropriate to blame soldiers in that country's military for their actions. Similarly, whereas one might blame Wilson for not confessing to the murder of the security guard, one can hardly blame his lawyers for following his lawful instructions to keep his statement confidential.

1.1.4   How do we know?

You might have noticed me trying to slip something past you in the first question asked earlier: "What do you do with the *knowledge* that an innocent person will be spending the rest of his life in prison for a crime committed by your client?" "But wait," you might have said, "Wilson's lawyers do not *know* he committed the crime. Wilson said he did, but he may have been lying, or crazy, or messing around with his lawyers." At most, what the lawyers have is evidence tending to prove that Logan is innocent, not conclusive proof. In a hypothetical invented by an ethics professor, some fact may be specified as true, or an actor may be said to know something. In the real world, however, things are considerably murkier, and real-world norms must be adapted to situations involving uncertainty. There may be good reasons for lawyers not to act on the basis of even well-founded beliefs if they do not rise to the level of actual knowledge. Of course, those of you with a background in philosophy will cite Descartes and ask how we ever know anything with certainty. But one does not have to be a committed Cartesian skeptic to acknowledge that there are many cases in which conflicting evidence, unreliable witnesses, and motivations to lie or tell half-truths can make it difficult for a lawyer to have a firm basis for believing in the truth of some proposition.

1.1.5   Incentive effects

Suppose Wilson's lawyers did disclose the communication – what would happen in future cases? Defendants might worry that their lawyers will "rat them out" and disclose incriminating facts to the prosecutor or the judge.

They will protect themselves by either lying or withholding information that the lawyer might need to know in order to provide an effective defense. The American legal ethicist Monroe Freedman, who is also a practicing criminal defense attorney, tells the story of representing a woman charged with murdering her husband.[5] At first, she insisted that she had been at her sister's house at the time of the killing, but when Freedman talked to the sister, she did not confirm this alibi, so he asked the client again what had occurred. She stuck with her implausible story until Freedman reassured her, in the strongest possible terms, that nothing she told him would ever be disclosed to anyone, under any circumstances. The client then revealed that her husband had physically and emotionally abused her for years, was a mean drunk, and, on the night of the murder, had come home intoxicated and enraged. He had his hands around her neck and was beginning to strangle her when, in desperation, she grabbed a kitchen knife and stabbed him. This account, of course, constituted a complete defense to the murder charge, but the client would not have revealed it without an ironclad promise of confidentiality. What this story shows is that a result that appears just *ex post*, meaning as between the parties to the case, might create incentives that lead to injustice *ex ante*; that is, in future cases in which the precedent of the prior result is applicable. If disclosing Wilson's communication creates mistrust among defense lawyers and clients in the future (*ex ante*), that should be a reason that counts against disclosure in this case (*ex post*).

Notice something about all of these arguments: They appeal to considerations of ordinary morality and the circumstances of the real world in which professionals practice. They do not simply fall back on the separateness or special quality of professional ethics, but seek to explain why, in moral terms, lawyers have the duties they do. For example, the argument from the *ex ante* point of view appeals to the interests of future clients seeking legal advice who need reassurance that their lawyers can be trusted not to reveal confidential communication. The values of loyalty and trust are certainly moral reasons counting in favor of a conclusion; moreover, they are general reasons, not appeals to the self-interest of lawyers. Here is a metaphor that may be helpful in understanding the issues regarding

---

[5] See Monroe Freedman and Abbe Smith, *Understanding Lawyers' Ethics* (New Providence, N.J.: Lexis-Nexis, 4th edn., 2010) § 6.02, at 152.

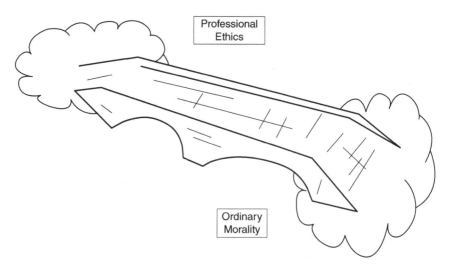

Figure 1.1   The Bridge Between Ordinary Morality and Professional Ethics

role-differentiated morality.[6] Imagine two different "lands" or domains of value, connected by a bridge, as in Figure 1.1.

This image emphasizes that the lands are separate, but there is – and indeed there must be – a connection between them. The arguments given by defenders of Wilson's lawyers are about building a bridge between ordinary morality and professional ethics. They reach out from the domain of professional ethics and appeal to considerations that are intelligible within the domain of ordinary morality. If there were no bridge, then these two worlds would be totally separated, normatively speaking. In that case, there would be no reason why society as a whole would tolerate the profession, no matter how rigorously it was governed by a code of "ethics." Lawyers would be, in essence, repeating the defense forever discredited by the Nuremberg trials, that one may be excused from responsibility for wrongdoing for merely doing his or her job or "only following orders." The bridge ensures that the principles of ethics by which professionals conduct themselves are acceptable to the wider society of which the profession is a part.

At the risk of overtaxing the metaphor, we can think about some of the issues to be considered in this book as pertaining to how much traffic has to flow across the bridge or how tight or direct the connection has to be

[6] Thanks to the students in my 2013 legal ethics seminar at Tel Aviv University for helping me come up with this way of representing the basic issue.

between professional ethics and ordinary morality. One of the issues dividing proponents of the so-called Standard Conception of legal ethics and its critics has to do with the closeness of the connection between these two domains of value. Many defenders of the Standard Conception argue for a relatively indirect bridge between ordinary morality and professional ethics, while critics argue that this attenuation is unjustified. A different way to consider the question might be to ask how frequently a professional must cross back over the bridge into the land of ordinary morality to ensure that her conduct is acceptable by general ethical standards. Sometimes theorists talk as though a person crosses the bridge once, becomes a professional, and then no longer has to go back to the land of ordinary morality. Others have pointed out, however, that people literally and metaphorically move between different roles frequently in their lives. A lawyer comes home and becomes a spouse, parent, neighbor, friend, member of a softball team, and the like. It may be psychologically taxing to switch back and forth frequently between different domains of value if they differ to any significant extent. One response might therefore be to adopt a stance of detachment with respect to both worlds, which is not a particularly attractive vision of the ethical life.[7]

We return to the metaphor of the two worlds connected by a bridge throughout the first half of this book. The next section of this chapter briefly discusses the terrain on the ordinary morality side of the bridge. The concluding section introduces the world of legal ethics, with its distinct priority to the values of loyalty, confidentiality, client service, and respect for the rule of law.

1.2   A note on ethics and morality

One aim of this book is to be accessible to students of practical ethics in undergraduate or graduate law school programs who may not have extensive background in academic moral philosophy. At any rate, we can set aside many of the issues that preoccupy academic ethicists. In particular, we can remain unconcerned, for our purposes, with issues of *metaethics*. Metaethics concerns such matters as the justification of ethical principles (are they

---

[7] This argument was made brilliantly in Gerald J. Postema, "Moral Responsibility and Professional Ethics," *New York University Law Review* 55: 63–89 (1980).

grounded in rationality, the character of a person, a divine command, widely shared sentiments, or something else?); the right way to understand moral utterances such as "slavery is wrong" (do they express truth-functional propositions, the attitude of the speaker, or something else?); the relationship between values and facts about the natural world (are values part of the furniture of the universe, do they supervene on natural properties, or are they projected onto the natural world by human subjects?); the relationship between justification and motivation; and so on. These are extremely interesting questions, but the debates in legal ethics have by and large proceeded independently of metaethics. Legal ethics proceeds by assuming that all of these issues have been worked out or can be worked out on the ordinary morality side of the bridge, and the hard question is whether and how they apply to people acting in a professional capacity. Thus, this book mostly avoids questions such as "how do we *really* know that lying is wrong?" We will assume lying is wrong and concentrate instead on questions such as whether presenting evidence inconsistent with a client's guilt, known by the lawyer to be false, is subject to the same moral stigma as lying. Another way of putting this point is to say that legal ethics belongs to the branch of moral philosophy called *normative* ethics.[8]

You have probably noticed the words "ethics" and "morality" used interchangeably. This is a common practice in academic ethics, although a few philosophers draw a distinction between ethics and morality. The late English ethicist Bernard Williams, for example, has argued that there are many interesting questions of ethics, understood as how one ought to live, but he was a severe critic of a particular way of thinking about ethics, which he referred to as "morality" and which is preoccupied with the notion of obligation and of narrowing the range of considerations that bear on what

---

[8] The word "normative" sometimes causes confusion. In philosophical usage, its antonym is "descriptive," "positive," or "empirical" – that is, concerned with what is. Normative questions are concerned with what *ought* to be. The confusion arises from the use of normative in a wider, more sociological sense in contexts other than ethics. There are norms of rationality, grammar, and etiquette, for example. Games and sports have norms beyond the formal rules, such as those governing when it is permissible for a baseball pitcher to hit the batter. There are cultural norms, such as how close people stand together when they talk. These are all norms in that they are concerned with what one has a reason to do, but they are not norms of ethics.

one has reason to do.[9] I am not relying on a distinction between ethics and morality, but one might still ask what we mean by ethics (or morality). Speaking fairly generally, I understand ethics as having to do with *what we owe to each other*.[10] When we act, we sometimes do things that implicate the interests of others. Someone may say, "hey, you can't do that to me!", and it is the task of ethics to articulate reasons that justify actions to others who are affected by them. Those reasons have to be shared or be, at least in principle, shareable – that is, they must refer to considerations that the affected person can endorse. Being able to justify our conduct to others is what it means to act ethically. On this view, ethics is not about something purely theoretical, like promoting the good, but is concerned with concrete relationships among people and the way we regulate our interactions with others to take account of their interests.

Despite its connection with relationships among people, ethical reasoning is necessarily abstract and general in several ways. The process of giving reasons in justification of one's actions may be hypothetical only. In the wrongful conviction case, Logan never confronted Wilson's lawyers and asked, "why didn't you disclose the information?" Nevertheless, acting ethically requires Wilson's lawyers to consider what they would say if they did have to justify their decision to Logan. Furthermore, ethical reasons are necessarily *impartial*, in that they apply to all similarly situated actors. This means, in connection with the process of justification, that we have to imagine an affected person being able to stand apart from his or her own situation and reason from the point of view of all similarly situated people. If Wilson's lawyers had actually asked Logan if he wanted them to disclose the information, he would have said, "of course!" The question, however, is whether a person falling within a general category – say, defendants in criminal prosecutions – would want the information to be disclosed. In the

---

[9] Bernard Williams, *Ethics and the Limits of Philosophy* (Cambridge, Mass.: Harvard University Press 1985). For a more standard usage see, e.g., William K. Frankena, *Ethics* (Englewood Cliffs, N.J.: Prentice-Hall 1963), p. 3 ("Ethics is a branch of philosophy; it is moral philosophy or philosophical thinking about morality, moral problems, and moral judgments.").

[10] I am borrowing this phrase from T. M. Scanlon, *What We Owe to Each Other* (Cambridge: Harvard University Press 1998), but do not intend to invoke Scanlon's contractarianism, his account of reasons, or any other technical aspect of the book. I am borrowing the phrase to emphasize, as Scanlon does, that ethics is about giving reasons that others can share.

context of political philosophy, John Rawls has used the thought experiment of a "veil of ignorance" to dramatize the constraint of impartiality.[11] Rawls asks the reader to imagine people getting together to settle on rules for the constitution of a society in which the decision makers know very little about themselves and particularly do not know characteristics such as whether they are rich or poor, men or women, members of a minority ethnic or religious group, disabled, young, old, and so on. Ethical reasoning must be similarly impartial, so the person to whom the lawyers' decision must be justified is not Logan himself but a hypothetical criminal defendant. Wrongfully convicted prisoners would all want disclosure, but criminal defendants generally might prefer a strict rule of confidentiality. Alternatively, one might argue, on ethical grounds, for a confidentiality rule that has a narrow, carefully defined exception for disclosures that are necessary to rectify wrongful convictions (perhaps where no other source of evidence is available or where the convicted person is facing a long prison sentence).

The abstraction inherent in ethical reasoning may make it seem incapable of producing standards of conduct in actual cases. It might seem that anything can be justified if we are sufficiently clever in coming up with reasons or perhaps manipulating the categories of similarly situated subjects (why talk about "criminal defendants" and not "innocent people" or some other category?). Indeed, there is widespread concern that ethical reasoning is *indeterminate* – that is, it does not yield standards that are specific enough to tell an actor what to do in a situation of real perplexity. Certainly, there are clear cases – no one questions that slavery is wrong – but ethics should have something to say about hard cases, too. There are two different responses one could give to this concern. The first is that, at least in professional ethics, there is not that much indeterminacy in the ordinary moral evaluation of conduct. If someone learned information suggesting that an innocent person was serving a lengthy prison sentence, absent special circumstances, there is really no question that he or she would have to do something with that information. Many of the interesting issues in professional ethics come within the qualification to the previous sentence: "absent special circumstances." The circumstance of being a lawyer, representing a criminal defendant, plausibly changes the evaluation, but this is not a sign of indeterminacy in moral reasoning.

[11] John Rawls, *A Theory of Justice* (Cambridge, Mass.: Harvard University Press 1971).

The second response regarding the indeterminacy of ethical reasoning is that, to the extent that there is indeterminacy, it reveals something deep and important about the nature of human values, namely, that there is more than one way of leading an authentically good human life and, accordingly, that there are a diversity of principles and values that bear on ethical conduct. Consider an example from Jean-Paul Sartre.[12] A young man's brother was killed in the war in 1940. Wishing to avenge his brother's death and to fight the occupying German army, the man considers joining the Resistance but, as the sole source of consolation to his mother after the death of her other son, the man also feels an obligation to remain at home and care for his mother. This illustration is generally taken to show that there may be cases in which one has good moral reasons to do one thing (resist an unjust occupation) and good moral reasons to do another (take care of his mother) in circumstances in which it is impossible to do both. Both of these proposed courses of action are admirable; we recognize within each of them important human ideals and aspirations. Neither can be ruled out as contrary to the obligations that the young man owes to others, such as his mother or his fellow citizens.

The dilemma facing Sartre's young man becomes particularly acute when we consider decisions that have to be made not as individuals but on behalf of an entire political community. One of the characteristics of modern societies is ethical pluralism. Citizens of modern liberal democracies such as Canada, the United Kingdom, and Australia are committed to a wide range of moral viewpoints, both religious and secular. They are committed to very different ethical positions with respect to the role of religion in public life, the proper scope of the criminal law, the relative priority of environmental values and economic development, the right balance between neutrality and consciousness of the different perspectives of minority and indigenous groups, the role of men and women in the workplace and at home, the rights of animals, and numerous other issues. This kind of ethical pluralism is not the same as relativism: One need not affirm (and, in fact, probably would deny) that propositions about ethics can be determined to be true or false only relative to the values and commitments of a given culture or society. Rather, pluralists assert *nonrelative* claims about

---

[12] Jean-Paul Sartre, "Existentialism Is a Humanism" (Philip Mairet, trans.) in Walter Kaufmann, ed., *Existentialism from Dostoevsky to Sartre* (New York: Meridian 1957).

the nature of human goods and interests. A pluralist may assert, as did the political thinker Isaiah Berlin, that the lives of a monk and a soldier both represent authentic human ideals, and the goods inherent in each life cannot be reduced to those of the other.[13] Liberal democracies seek to accommodate pluralism by providing space for citizens to lead lives according to principles and values that they themselves endorse, until the actions of one member of the society cause harm to another. Of course, what constitutes harm, and what may justify something that otherwise counts as a harm, are themselves contested issues. One role for the law in a liberal society is therefore to regulate the boundaries between one person's asserted freedom to act and another person's right to noninterference.

If one function of the law is to settle issues that arise when people with different moral values and commitments live together in society, then it may follow that the ethical standards applicable to lawyers are derived in some way from the function of law. John Rawls has argued that a political conception of justice ought to be independent to some extent of what he calls "comprehensive doctrines." A comprehensive doctrine is one that "includes conceptions of what is of value in human life, and ideals of personal character, as well as ideals of friendship and of familial and associational relationships, and much else that is to inform our conduct."[14] In a liberal society, citizens affirm different religious, moral, or philosophical comprehensive doctrines. Thus, it would be impossible to ground principles of *political* justice, which apply to all citizens in a society, on one of these contested comprehensive doctrines. Rawls argues that political conceptions of justice may be justified if there is an overlapping consensus among citizens who subscribe to different comprehensive doctrines.[15] For example, both Catholics and Protestants may agree that toleration of citizens with different religious views is an important principle of justice.[16] They do not have to agree with each other about everything, only that toleration is a reasonable principle for both groups of religious believers to affirm. One possibility to be considered in this book is that principles of legal ethics may be political in this sense. They may be grounded in an

---

[13] For example, Isaiah Berlin, "The Pursuit of the Ideal," in Henry Hardy, ed., *The Crooked Timber of Humanity* (Princeton: Princeton University Press 1990).

[14] John Rawls, *Political Liberalism* (New York: Columbia University Press 1993), p. 13.

[15] Ibid., pp. 144–50.   [16] Ibid., p. 148.

overlapping consensus on a principle of justice – for example, the value of the rule of law – and not on comprehensive doctrines of morality.

1.3   Legal ethics and the law governing lawyers

Now we are on the professional ethics side of the bridge. What is required of lawyers *as lawyers* by their professional role? Practicing lawyers sometimes have a tendency to identify ethics with only the authoritative rules govern- ing their conduct. These generally take the form of codes of professional responsibility established by a bar association, law society, or court setting forth rules respecting matters such as competent representation, keeping client confidences, refraining from representing clients with conflicting interests, charging reasonable fees, not introducing false evidence at trial, and not communicating with the opposing party outside the presence of her lawyer.[17] These codes of "ethics" are perfectly unobjectionable – indeed, they are a good thing to the extent that they define and enforce the obliga- tions of lawyers with respect to clients and the legal system. But, strictly speaking, they are part of the domain of positive law, not ethics. Positive law here means simply that these rules are enacted pursuant to an official process of defining norms, the violation of which may subject the violator to sanctions.[18] By contrast, principles of ethics, as that term is used here, are applicable without being officially promulgated as law. A lawyer has a *legal* obligation to safeguard confidential client information and will be subject to penalties such as loss of her law license or a lawsuit by the client for breach of this duty. In addition, a lawyer may have a professional *ethical* obligation to keep a secret if it was entrusted to the lawyer by the client

---

[17] There is considerable variation in the common law world in the structure of the regulation of the legal profession. In Canada, "arguably, the last bastion of unfettered self-regulation of the legal profession in the common law world," provincial law societies (i.e., associations of lawyers) adopt, interpret, and enforce rules of professional ethics. Alice Woolley, *Understanding Lawyers' Ethics in Canada* (Markham, Ont.: LexisNexis 2011), p. 4. In the United States, state appellate courts promulgate the rules based closely on model standards prepared by the American Bar Association which, although lacking official regulatory authority, has considerable experience with issues relating to the regulation of lawyers.

[18] Legal positivism is quite a bit more subtle than this crude statement suggests. We return to questions concerning the nature of law in subsequent chapters, and we will work with a more rigorous definition of legal positivism where necessary.

under circumstances in which the client justifiably trusted the lawyer to protect his interests, which would apply even if there were no officially enacted rule of professional conduct requiring confidentiality. The client's trust and reliance on the lawyer is a sufficient moral reason to keep the client's secret, at least in the absence of any countervailing reason to disclose the information. Legal and ethical professional obligations may overlap, and in fact often do, but they are analytically distinct.

As part of the process of becoming a lawyer in many common law jurisdictions, a student must take a course on a subject called legal ethics or professional responsibility.[19] In the United States, this subject became compulsory in law schools following the Watergate scandal and the revelation that many of the government officials who participated in the cover-up of wrongdoing had been trained as lawyers. John Dean, who went to prison for his role in the cover-up, said that his education in legal ethics had been inadequate:

> "In 1972, legal ethics boiled down to 'don't lie, don't cheat, don't steal and don't advertise,'" says Dean. "When I took the elective course in ethics at law school, it was one-quarter of a credit. Legal ethics and professionalism played almost no role in any lawyer's mind, including mine. Watergate changed that – for me and every other lawyer."[20]

Dean and Watergate co-conspirator Egil "Bud" Krogh say they would have done things differently if they had known more about the law governing the conduct of lawyers, such as the priority of the duty to avoid illegal conduct over other obligations such as confidentiality. They also say, however, that knowing the content of the rules is not enough. As Krogh put it, "The sad thing is, I never asked the most basic question in 1971 and 1972: 'Is this right? Am I doing the right thing?'"[21] That question – *is this*

---

[19] Useful introductory textbooks on legal ethics in the legal sense are [United Kingdom] Andrew Boon and Jennifer Levin, *The Ethics and Conduct of Lawyers in England and Wales* (Oxford: Hart, 2nd edn., 2008); [Canada] Alice Woolley, et al., *Lawyers' Ethics and Professional Regulation* (Markham, Ont.: LexisNexis 2008); [Australia] Ysaiah Ross, *Ethics in Law: Lawyers' Responsibility and Accountability in Australia* (Chatswood, N.S.W.: Butterworths, 10th edn., 2010); [New Zealand] Duncan Webb, *Ethics, Professional Responsibility and the Lawyer* (Wellington: Butterworths 2000).

[20] Quoted in Mark Curriden, "The Lawyers of Watergate: How a '3rd-Rate Burglary' Provoked New Standards for Lawyer Ethics," *ABA Journal* (June 1, 2012).

[21] Ibid.

right? – is the basic ethical issue we will consider here, and part of answering it will be understanding the relationship between the law governing lawyers and more general principles of right and wrong. One may also ask whether conduct is right or wrong as considered solely by the standards of professional ethics. As it happens, not surprisingly, conduct such as actively participating in a client's cover-up of a crime is a violation of professional ethics, as well as being wrong in ordinary moral terms. There are many cases in which ordinary morality and professional ethics come into conflict, but do not be too quick to assume that every instance of wrongdoing is like this. A great deal of conduct that is morally wrong, such as lying, is also a violation of law, and it is wrong *in professional ethics terms* to violate the law or to assist one's client in violating it.

The examples considered in practical ethics courses tend to be those in which there is a conflict, at least an apparent conflict, between the ethical norms of some profession or social practice and the requirements of ordinary morality. Thus, most of the cases discussed in this book cannot be resolved by law alone. Either the law does not determine the result one way or the other, or, if the result is clear as a matter of law, there is still a difficult ethical issue. The wrongful conviction case that started this chapter involves a perfectly clear legal obligation: The lawyers representing Wilson may not reveal his confession that he, not Logan, was involved in the murders without Wilson's permission. At least in most American jurisdictions, and certainly in Illinois at the time, there are no exceptions to this strict duty of confidentiality. (Inventive students troubled by the case often try to come up with creative ways to read in an exception to the rule, but trust me on this one: There is a solid wall of legal authority prohibiting disclosure.) Still, this is only the resolution to the question as a matter of law. There is still the moral question: Even though the law says "do not disclose," should Wilson's lawyers nonetheless disclose? Maybe they'll be subject to professional discipline for doing so, but if it means an innocent person will be released from prison, should they not disclose and try to defend themselves later to the professional disciplinary authorities? Turning the question around, if the lawyers do not disclose, are they justified as a moral matter? Is the *legal* duty of confidentiality a sufficient *moral* justification for keeping their client's secret?

These are the questions that will be taken up in the remainder of the book. Roughly, the layout of the discussion to follow is this: Chapters 2–6 will consider theoretical questions about the relationship between morality and ethics and between law, morality, and justice. Then, Chapters 7–11 will apply the theoretical concepts we have developed to specific areas of legal practice, such as criminal defense and client advising. The next chapter takes up the basic structure of justification that Wilson's lawyers would use to avoid moral criticism for keeping their client's secret.

2 Justifying principles of professional ethics

2.1 Can a good lawyer be a good person?

In a classic 1976 paper, Charles Fried asked whether a good lawyer can be a good person.[1] By this he meant to assert that principles of professional ethics – whether embodied in codes of professional conduct or propagated as informal norms through professional socialization and folklore – stand in need of justification in moral terms. A principle of professional ethics, such as the duty of confidentiality or the norm of zealous representation at trial, has to be shown to have the appropriate kind of connection with ordinary moral considerations. Otherwise, people will quite properly conclude that lawyers are a nasty bunch, deserving of moral condemnation. Of course, public criticism of the legal profession and lawyer jokes have been around as long as there have been lawyers. Lawyers therefore have many stock answers to the criticism they encounter, many of which were considered in a preliminary and impressionistic way in Chapter 1. The task of this chapter is to start to make these defenses more rigorous by examining the structure of some of the best known arguments offered by lawyers and scholars to show that the moral criticism they receive is unwarranted. Some of these arguments conclude that the principles of professional ethics by which lawyers practice are morally justified, at least for the most part. Others reach the very different conclusion that significant aspects of what practicing lawyers do fail the test of moral justification. To evaluate these contending positions, it will be helpful to look at how the arguments proceed, step by step. Before doing that, though, we should first consider a more general theoretical approach to the structure of ethical arguments, the method of seeking reflective equilibrium.

---

[1] Charles Fried, "The Lawyer as Friend: The Moral Foundations of the Lawyer-Client Relation," *Yale Law Journal* 85: 1060–89 (1976).

2.2   Reflective equilibrium

Reflective equilibrium in ethics involves going back and forth between our beliefs in the form of carefully considered judgments in response to a range of cases, the ethical principles that underlie those judgments, and the general theoretical considerations that support the ethical principles.[2] The goal of the process is to reach an acceptable coherence among our beliefs, principles, and theory. Reflective equilibrium is a dynamic process, so if the theoretical analysis of a case yields a result that is at odds with our considered judgment, a theorist may go back and tinker with the theory, with the aim of improving it to better account for the beliefs we hold. Alternatively, we may find that our considered judgment must be rejected in light of the theoretical reasoning. Both theory and beliefs are revisable, and the interplay between theoretical considerations and considered judgments across a variety of cases ensures that theory does not simply take existing beliefs (which may be erroneous) as given, but serves to challenge these beliefs in the course of systematizing and explaining them.

Practicing lawyers tend to have fairly strong, settled views about what their duties should be. They see themselves as being primarily obligated by an ethic of loyal client service. That means the client gets to define the goals and objectives of the representation, and the lawyer's job is to be the means to that end. The one important limitation is that the means employed by the lawyer may not violate the law, and the lawyer may not counsel or assist the client in violating the law. Otherwise, however, many lawyers would assert that they have no obligation to take into account the public interest, avoid inflicting harm on others, or be concerned if the client's goals are morally questionable. A lawyer would respond to the wrongful conviction case in Chapter 1 by emphasizing her duty to the client, Wilson, and her obligation not to consider the harm of Logan's continuing, and wrongful, imprisonment. No law requires disclosure of Wilson's confession, and Wilson has refused to consent to disclosure; thus, his lawyers are bound by the duty of confidentiality. Although this result is disquieting, most practicing lawyers would agree that it correctly states their ethical obligation.

Now consider a theoretical approach to legal ethics that instructs a lawyer that her fundamental duty is as follows: "The lawyer should take

---

[2] See Norman Daniels, "Reflective Equilibrium," *Stanford Encyclopedia of Philosophy*.

those actions that, considering the relevant circumstances of the particular case, seem most likely to promote justice."[3] The theory elaborates on this general maxim by instructing lawyers that they should consider how their decisions contribute to an allocation of scarce legal resources in society and whether their actions promote resolution of disputes on their merits.[4] A lawyer who observed these principles in her practice would ask whether justice was best promoted by keeping Wilson's secret. A resolution of Logan's case on the merits would require a court to at least consider evidence that another person had admitted to involvement in the crime and had exonerated Logan. The theory further tells the lawyer to "make her best effort to achieve the appropriate resolution in each case."[5] Although the institutions and procedures of the adversary system can be relied on in many cases to yield a just resolution of disputes, there may be cases in which, due to an institutional malfunction or incapacity, the procedures will not result in justice; in that case, a lawyer must "assume direct responsibility for the substantive validity of the decision."[6] This ethical theory also notes that, although disclosure of confidential information may impose costs on clients, these costs must be balanced against the costs imposed on nonclients as a result of maintaining confidentiality.[7] A utilitarian calculation would certainly favor disclosure, since Wilson is already serving a life sentence for the separate murder and is therefore unlikely to suffer any detriment as a result of the disclosure, whereas the benefit to the nonclient, Logan, is immense. A lawyer following this theory would therefore believe that it was ethically wrong to keep the secret.

Practicing lawyers recognize that the Logan case is agonizing, but I believe, after talking with countless lawyers about ethics, that virtually all of them would maintain their position that confidentiality is required. The theory briefly summarized in the preceding paragraph, and defended by William Simon, would require disclosure. The method of reflective equilibrium in legal ethics seeks to achieve coherence between the considered judgments of experienced practitioners regarding this case (and many others) and a theoretical account of the principles that should govern the actions of lawyers. The fact that Simon's theory does not fit well with the considered judgments of lawyers shows either that lawyers are reasoning

---

[3] William H. Simon, "Ethical Discretion in Lawyering," *Harvard Law Review* 101: 1083–1145 (1988), p. 1090.

[4] Id. at 1093.   [5] Id. at 1096.   [6] Id. at 1098.   [7] Id. at 1143.

erroneously about their ethical obligations, or that the theory needs to be modified in some way. Lawyers may find Simon's position bizarre, but he does have a point: The role of lawyer depends on a system of institutions and procedures that has been constituted for the purpose of resolving disputes on the merits; if a lawyer acts in ways that contribute to a failure of the system to achieve resolution on the merits, then the lawyer cannot consistently appeal to the social value of the system as a justification of her actions. Lawyers justify their actions with reference to an ideal system of procedures that reliably produce decisions on the merits, but that pattern of justification does not apply to a case in which, by its very terms, the system has failed to yield a just result.[8] Perhaps the majority of practicing lawyers are, in fact, in error. It would not be the first time that a large number of people were massively wrong about something – after all, everyone used to believe that the sun revolved around the earth until Galileo and Copernicus came along and proved them wrong. No one believes that considered judgments have the last word in determining whether a theory is correct, but perhaps they are not entitled even to presumptive or initial weight.

On the other hand, a theory of *practical* ethics that yields conclusions so at odds with the conventional wisdom is likely to have little impact on the professionals it is meant to address. This is not just a point about rhetoric, the likelihood of persuasion, or the contempt that some practitioners have for academics locked in their ivory towers. Rather, it is a thesis about what is likely to make the conclusion of an ethical argument more reliable. Reasoning from highly abstract, a priori principles to conclusions about what professionals should do in practice is likely to miss some of the considerations that make a significant difference to experienced practitioners. For example, one thing practicing lawyers know is that there is a difference between evidence and facts. A witness may say something – that is evidence – but how do we know the witness is not lying or mistaken? Most lawyers who handle litigated disputes have had the experience of beginning a case with an assumption about what was true only to be surprised by new evidence that came to light during the course of the proceedings. Lawyers accordingly develop a habit of withholding judgment on the truth of a matter, knowing that they can reach mistaken conclusions based on partial evidence. As his lawyers may see it, Wilson said he did the crime, but maybe

---

[8] Id. at 1102.

he is simply showboating to seem tough in prison or is temporarily insane. Experienced lawyers who have a feel for the uncertainty of facts in practice may rightly be skeptical of an ethical theory that calls on lawyers to assume direct responsibility for the validity of a decision. The considered judgments of experienced practitioners carry some weight, although even their judgments are revisable.

This book uses the method of reflective equilibrium rather than relying on either abstract theoretical ideas (such as justice, rights, or utility) or the results in specific cases as a starting point. Reflective equilibrium does not simply ping-pong back and forth between the general and the particular but seeks a dynamic process of justification. In some cases an ethical theory may begin with an intuition or considered judgment and seek a theoretical justification for it. For example, one might observe that lawyers in an adversary system believe themselves to have duties of loyalty that run primarily to their clients, permitting them to disregard the interests of nonclients. A theorist may then seek to understand what might be the ethical principles that support such a preference for one person over the interests of others. Working in the other direction, a theorist may begin with a general consideration, such as justice or truth, and use it to test or critique the existing practices of lawyers. A well-constructed theory will hold up to both directions of inquiry. It should account for many considered judgments about cases, but it should also be capable of grounding a critique of practices that lack ethical justification. The following discussion shows how many of the traditional arguments in the legal ethics debate are structured. As we will see, theorists implicitly accept the method of reflective equilibrium and seek coherence between judgments regarding cases and more general theoretical considerations.

2.3   The three-step model of justification

Recall Fried's question: Can a good lawyer be a good person? An answer to that question should show that good lawyers – that is, those who follow the duties set forth in codes of ethics and the traditions of the profession – are good people in the sense that they are responding to or respecting values that are important to people as such, not just professionals. To return to the metaphor from Chapter 1, there is a "land" or domain of moral values to which people appeal when deliberating about what to do or seeking to justify their actions to others. Suppose I promise my daughter that I will go to her hockey game on the weekend. Later, I remember that I had accepted an invitation to go out for beers with some friends. The promise to my daughter gives me a strong reason to decline the invitation even if it means not doing something I would have enjoyed doing. In other words, the promise changes the normative situation of the promise; the reasons counting in favor of doing some other action (going out with friends) no longer apply with the same force because of the promise. As a matter of morality, one can ask why promises have this force. On one account of the nature of promissory obligation, promises create duties because other people form expectations based on them; a promise invites the trust of others, and betrayal of that trust constitutes a harm to the promisee.[9] I induced my daughter's trust that I would be at her game by promising to be there. In this example, the moral ideas of reasonable expectations, trust, betrayal, and harm are used to explain a more complex practice, promising, which depends on these underlying moral concepts to ground duties. In other words, the practice of promising is analyzed in terms of more basic moral concepts.

Promises and basic values such as trust are both part of ordinary, everyday moral life, but the same pattern of analysis works with professional duties as well. We can ask what justifies a lawyer in following a professional obligation such as confidentiality or being single-mindedly dedicated to a client's interests, notwithstanding foreseeable harm to others. The answer will be in terms of considerations that can be endorsed by the people who are affected, directly or indirectly, by the lawyer's actions. By "endorse" here I do not mean anything technical, only that people who might have been inclined to criticize the lawyer will be capable of saying something along the lines of, "I can see why she did that, and while it initially seemed troubling, now that I understand better I believe the lawyer acted rightly." Significantly, the people to whom this justification is directed are outside the profession. A justification is not sufficient if it only relies on duties and concepts that are specific to a profession. Merely reciting that Rule XYZ of the code of ethics of a jurisdiction requires some conduct is insufficient from the point of view of someone who is asking, in effect, why anyone should care what Rule XYZ says when following it seems to result in harm to others.

---

[9] There are many competing explanations for the normative force of promises. See, for example, Seana Valentine Shiffrin, "Promising, Intimate Relationships, and Conventionalism," *Philosophical Review* 117: 481–524 (2008).

Legal ethics scholars have offered numerous justifications, appealing to various moral considerations that can be endorsed by nonlawyers, for what lawyers do as a matter of professional ethics. The constructive arguments, and the critiques offered by other scholars, tend to fall into a pattern. The basic structure is to identify a moral value, such as dignity, autonomy, trust, or truth, which is served by the legal system and the legal profession. Alternatively, it could be to identify a type of ethical wrongdoing that appears to be implicated by the professional duties of lawyers. A case may appear to be an instance of lying or cheating, for example.[10] After elaborating on how the relevant ethical value or principle should best be understood as a theoretical matter, the next step is to show that it entails certain principles within professional ethics. For example, if a theory emphasizes autonomy, an implication for legal ethics might be that lawyers should not refuse to assist clients with morally dubious but lawful projects.[11] The value may also provide grounds for a critical stance toward professional ethics, for instance by showing that excessively adversarial conduct is wrong because it assaults human dignity (the moral foundational value) rather than supporting it.[12] It may be necessary to show that the value is served in a special way within professional ethics. The implication from the ordinary value may be, for example, not that the lawyer straightforwardly acts on the value but participates in a process that respects the value indirectly. (The case considered next will be an example of that type of relationship between ordinary and professional values.) Finally, the method of reflective equilibrium tests the results of this theorizing by comparing it with considered judgments in response to cases. Cases can be presented at the beginning of a theoretical argument, yielding judgments that the theory must account for, or can be discussed in the middle or the end as a way of checking the conclusions of the argument. The aim of an argument is always to find a satisfying fit between theory and practice.

---

[10] Along these lines, Daniel Markovits argues that representing clients *comprehensively* involves what would be deemed lying and cheating in moral terms. See Daniel Markovits, *A Modern Legal Ethics* (Princeton: Princeton University Press 2008).

[11] This is one of the implications of Stephen L. Pepper, "The Lawyer's Amoral Ethical Role: A Defense, A Problem, and Some Possibilities," *American Bar Foundation Research Journal* 1986: 613–35.

[12] See David Luban, "Lawyers as Upholders of Human Dignity (When They Aren't Busy Assaulting It)," in *Legal Ethics and Human Dignity* (Cambridge: Cambridge University Press 2007), p. 66.

To summarize, arguments aiming to show that a good lawyer can be a good person generally follow this structure:

1. Define, specify, and if necessary explain the significance of a moral value.
2. Show that the value in step 1 entails a principle of professional ethics.
3. Test the resulting theory against cases.

As a student and critic of legal ethics, you can enter into the argument at any of these steps. For example, you might believe a theorist has identified the wrong foundational value. Why dignity and not, say, equality? Alternatively, the theorist may have the right value but may have specified or applied it incorrectly. Autonomy, for example, is a plausible foundational value for a theory of legal ethics, but there are many different senses or "conceptions" of autonomy.[13] It may mean freedom of choice or, in its Kantian sense, it may refer to being governed according to rational laws that one wills for oneself.[14] Which conception of autonomy is used as the foundational value may end up making a great deal of difference to a theory of professional ethics. A theorist may also not be clear, or may be inconsistent, about the relationship between the foundational value in step 1 and the professional duties it supposedly entails in step 2. Or, the foundational value may not entail the duty the theorist is aiming for. For example, a duty of zealous advocacy that is purportedly grounded on the value of loyalty to one's friends is vulnerable to the criticism that we are not privileged to do anything at all for our friends, including inflicting harm on others.[15] Thus, although the value of loyalty may be a plausible foundational moral value, it does not provide the support the theorist needs in the domain of

[13] Rawls uses the concept/conception distinction in *A Theory of Justice*, and it was made prominent in legal theory by Ronald Dworkin. See Ronald Dworkin, *Law's Empire* (Cambridge, Mass.: Harvard University Press 1986). In one of Dworkin's examples, his ideal judge Hercules has to interpret the right in the US Constitution to "equal protection of the laws" in order to determine whether an affirmative action program is constitutional. Hercules realizes that the *concept* of equality contains numerous, potentially inconsistent *conceptions* of equality. For example, a right to equality of opportunities is different from a right to equality of outcomes, and race-conscious remedial action may conflict with an ideal of color-blindness, both of which are rooted in the concept of equality. One of the labors of Hercules is therefore to determine which conception of equality best fits and justifies our existing practices.

[14] See Luban, *supra*, pp. 75–76.

[15] See Edward A. Dauer and Arthur Allen Leff, "Correspondence: The Lawyer as Friend," *Yale Law Journal* 86: 573–84 (1976).

professional ethics. Becoming proficient with these types of argumentative moves is the key to understanding the central problem in legal ethics, the relationship between morality and the obligations of a professional role.

The following overview of the three-step model of justification will begin with a case (so step 3 of the argument comes first, which is not unusual). This one – another classic from the legal ethics literature – comes from an ethics opinion by the Michigan State Bar Association,[16] but the events described could have occurred anywhere, and the lawyer's responsibilities would be substantially the same in other common law jurisdictions.

A man is charged with assault based on the victim's report that he was hit over the head with a blunt object and robbed at midnight near an automated teller machine. The accused retains an attorney and admits to the attorney that he committed the robbery. In a twist, however, the defendant tells his lawyer that the robbery occurred at 2:00 a.m. The victim apparently was mixed up about the time since, after all, the defendant hit him over the head and stole his watch. As luck would have it, the defendant was playing poker at midnight with a priest, a rabbi, and the president of the local bank, all of whom have an unblemished reputation in the community for honesty and integrity. The attorney's investigator talked to all three poker buddies, and they were all certain that they were playing poker at midnight with the defendant. The attorney believes that if she introduces the testimony of the three friends, the jury will believe them and conclude that the prosecution has not proved its case beyond a reasonable doubt. Is it ethical to put the friends on the stand to testify, the defendant having admitted that he committed the robbery?

What do you think? Almost every practicing lawyer with whom I have discussed this case believes there would be nothing wrong with putting the friends on the stand, even though the purpose of their testimony is to persuade the jury of something inconsistent with the guilt of the defendant. (In terms of the method of reflective equilibrium, this is a very strong and widely shared considered judgment.) How can it be that there is nothing wrong with introducing this testimony, given the moral value of truth? The criminal justice system in general, and the trial process in particular, is aimed at least in part at finding out the truth about a basic question: Did the defendant commit the crime of which he was accused? And although the

---

[16] Michigan Bar Association Ethics Opinion CI-1164 (1987).

testimony of the poker buddies may be true, it supports an inference that the lawyer knows to be false. Many years ago, one of my students gave me a wonderful analogy for this case from his childhood. When he was in high school, one of his chores was to take out the garbage. One night, he was feeling lazy so he threatened to beat up his younger brother unless he took out the trash. When his mother later asked him if he had taken out the trash, he replied, "It's on the sidewalk, mom." That statement was true on its face, but it was either nonresponsive or an outright lie relative to the question, "did *you* take out the trash?" The student's mother would have been outraged if she had found out the truth about how the trash got taken out. Similarly, the fact that the defendant was playing poker with his buddies at midnight is true but irrelevant to the question, "did the defendant commit the assault?" Even if introducing the testimony of the friends is not an outright lie because their testimony is truthful, it is at the very least an act of deception, which is inconsistent with the moral value of truth.

On the other hand, the criminal justice system cannot resort to any means to ascertain the truth. Even if torture were a reliable method of getting at truth, a decent society would not permit the police to put a suspect on the rack to find out the truth about a crime. Although torture is an extreme example, other practices suggest that truth is not the only value that matters in the criminal justice system. In most common law countries, the accused cannot be compelled to take the stand and testify against himself.[17] The prosecution has the burden of proof, which means that the state bears the risk of nonpersuasion – if the prosecution does not introduce sufficient evidence of guilt, the defendant is acquitted. In the United States, the burden of proof is set at a very high threshold, "beyond a reasonable doubt." All of these procedural protections, which ensure that the government does not abuse its power, that innocent people are not wrongfully convicted of crimes, and that persons accused of crimes are treated fairly and with dignity, do not exist in a vacuum. Abstract rights require flesh-and-blood people to administer them. Judges and jurors make decisions about the law and the facts, respectively, but defense lawyers are also required to assert the defendant's rights. (As we will see in Chapter 8, prosecutors also have special responsibilities related to their distinctive role

---

[17] For example, this right is guaranteed by the Fifth Amendment to the US Constitution; Section 11 of the Canadian Charter of Rights and Freedoms; Section 25(d) of the New Zealand Bill of Rights Act of 1990; and at common law in the United Kingdom.

in the criminal justice system.) How better in this case to assert the defendant's right to hold the state to its high burden of proof than to introduce evidence inconsistent with guilt?

The institutional setting of the case, with the defendant's rights and the requirement that the state prove its case beyond a reasonable doubt, distinguishes it from the case in which the student lied to his mother about taking out the trash. It therefore provides the lawyer with a way to redescribe the case as "not lying, but protecting the defendant's rights through legally permissible means." This justification of the defense lawyer's role does not permit a lawyer to do anything at all. It is quite clear that lawyers may not participate in introducing false evidence or making false statements to the court. Applicable rules provide, for example, that "[a] lawyer shall not falsify evidence [or] counsel or assist a witness to testify falsely"[18] and "[a] lawyer shall not knowingly make a false statement of fact or law to a tribunal."[19] In this case, however, the defendant's lawyer would argue that she is not trying to establish the truth of this proposition:

> My client did not commit the robbery.

Rather, the lawyer is trying to persuade the jury of the truth of this proposition:

> The prosecutor did not prove beyond a reasonable doubt that my client committed the robbery.

The defense lawyer will not state in her closing argument that her client did not commit the robbery, only that the prosecution's evidence does not suffice to prove the defendant's guilt beyond a reasonable doubt. (Indeed, the lawyer would be prohibited from arguing to the jury that the client was not guilty, given the client's admission of guilt to the lawyer.) As long as the lawyer only puts on the testimony of the poker buddies, however, the rules of professional conduct permit her to do so even if it would lead the jury to draw a false inference. The context in which the lawyer acts therefore changes the relevant description of the situation from lie or deception to "protecting the defendant's rights."[20] As we will see in later chapters, the context in which a lawyer acts

---

[18] American Bar Association, Model Rules of Professional Conduct, Rule 3.4(b).

[19] ABA Model Rules, *supra*, Rule 3.3(a)(1).

[20] See Arthur Isak Applbaum, *Ethics for Adversaries* (Princeton: Princeton University Press 1999), for an analysis of the argument from redescription.

makes a great deal of difference to the ethical analysis. Some of the actions that are permissible for criminal defense attorneys would be wrong, in professional ethical terms, if done by prosecutors or lawyers representing parties in civil litigation. An issue to consider as we work through those chapters is whether the context makes a difference to the moral analysis as well.

If this redescription works, it is because nonlawyers thinking about the case can understand how, first, there is an important moral value at stake, such as fairness or dignity, and second, how that value underwrites a duty on the part of a lawyer to act in a particular way. The redescription must therefore be in terms of ethical considerations that justify the lawyer's conduct. If successful, this type of explanation accounts in ethical terms for the fairly well-settled judgment that lawyers should be permitted to introduce the testimony of the poker buddies. It answers Fried's question by showing that a good lawyer – that is, one who follows the requirements of professional ethics to put on an effective defense for the client – can be a good person.

2.4   The model in action: two moral conceptions of the lawyer's role

The example of the poker game alibi and the role of the criminal defense attorney should give you a feel for the basic structure of the argument to justify a lawyer's professional ethical obligations in "good person" terms. This section employs this structure to consider two sophisticated theoretical accounts of the relationship between morality and professional ethics: David Luban's reliance on human dignity and Charles Fried's defense of the lawyer's role in terms of the value of close personal relationship.

2.4.1   Luban: lawyers and human dignity

Step 1: define and specify the moral value

Human dignity is a moral value with a close connection to the institutions of a liberal democratic state.[21] It therefore would appear to be a plausible

---

[21] The Preamble to the Charter of the United Nations states that one of the purposes of the organization is "to reaffirm faith in fundamental human rights, in the dignity and worth of the human person, in the equal rights of men and women and of nations large and small." One of the Basic Laws of Israel, which comprise its national constitution, is

candidate for a foundational value that supports a theory of professional ethics. David Luban has argued that what makes the practice of law morally worthwhile is upholding human dignity, and what makes certain actions by lawyers wrong in moral terms is that they attack human dignity rather than upholding it.[22] He recognizes immediately that it is vital to get the concept right before applying it willy-nilly to law, and he goes through some familiar philosophical accounts of the sources of human dignity, including humanity having been created in the image of God and possessing a soul as well as a body. He rejects these, however, in favor of a conception of dignity that is ultimately relational rather than metaphysical. Dignity is not a property of persons, but a way of being a person. It is related to having a story of one's own, to the ineffable experience of human subjectivity as the limit of one's word, of being an "I" in relations with others.[23] It is not the same thing as autonomy, although the concepts are closely related. Autonomy, from the sublime (Kant) to the ridiculous (the "don't tread on me" flags popular at American political rallies), identifies the value of persons with the capacity to will principles of action and to make choices; dignity, by contrast, is a property of someone's whole being, not merely choosing. "Honoring someone's human dignity means honoring their being, not merely their willing."[24] To honor dignity means taking one's cares and commitments seriously.

Step 2: show that the value in step 1 entails a principle of professional ethics

If dignity is about having a story to tell, having cares and commitments that deserve to be taken seriously, and having a whole way of being in the world that is fundamentally subjective, it follows that lawyers can honor human dignity by providing the tools clients need to tell their stories, to make them intelligible to persons and institutions in a position of power over them, and hopefully to persuade others to act in some way. Ignoring a person and the story she has to tell and presuming that she has no point of view worth

entitled Dignity and Liberty, and states in Section 4 that "[a]ll persons are entitled to protection of their life, body and dignity." The German Constitution, in Article 1, paragraph 1, states: "Human dignity shall be inviolable. To respect and protect it shall be the duty of all state authority."

[22] Luban, *supra*, p. 66.   [23] Id. at 70–71.   [24] Id. at 76.

paying attention to amounts to a humiliation of the person, a violation of her dignity.[25] Therefore one relatively general principle of professional ethics follows from the value of dignity: A lawyer ought to be a means for the client to tell her story, a mouthpiece or a voice. More specific duties follow from this general principle. For example, lawyers should not substitute their own judgment for the client's with respect to the legal arguments the client wishes to present in an appeal of his conviction.[26] They also should not dupe a client into giving up a defense that is consistent with the client's own commitments, even if there would be other ways to defend the case that would likely lead to a better outcome.[27] In addition to implying ethical duties for individual lawyers, the pattern of argument considered here can support legal principles or doctrines, such as the privilege against self-incrimination or the attorney–client privilege. Compelled self-incrimination, for example, humiliates a person by "enlisting a person's own will in the process of punishing her, splitting her against herself."[28]

Notice that these duties follow from a specific conception of human dignity, one that emphasizes subjectivity and having a story of one's own

[25] Id. at 71–72.

[26] Id. at 74. Luban dislikes the US Supreme Court case of *Jones v. Barnes*, 436 U.S. 745 (1983), but in my view pays insufficient attention to the allocation of decision-making authority in the lawyer–client relationship, recognized in ABA Model Rules, *supra*, Rule 1.2(a). Entrusting decisions about tactical or technical matters to lawyers reflects the opacity of professional knowledge and expertise to nonlawyers. The lawyer–client relationship is structured not only by contract (in which the client's specific instructions should be honored) but also by fiduciary duties, so that the lawyer, as the party with superior expertise, must use it always in the client's best interests. *Jones v. Barnes* merely recognizes that in some cases there is an objective sense of "the client's best interests," and lawyers as fiduciaries of clients may disregard their client's stated, subjective preferences where it is reasonably likely that the outcome would be a fiasco for the client.

[27] Id. at 76–79. While conceding that they were very effective, Luban criticizes the lawyers who defended the Unabomber, Ted Kaczynski, for tricking him into pleading guilty by relentlessly trying to persuade him to defend the case by claiming to be mentally ill. The problem with that strategy from Kaczynski's point of view was that it would require him to disavow the lengthy screed against modern society he had demanded to be published as a condition for no longer blowing up scientists. As Luban puts it, "The mental defense would discredit what [Kaczynski] regarded as his life's principal contribution to human welfare, the manifesto that he had killed to get into print. If the manifesto were discredited, then [Kaczynski's] intellectual justification for terrorism would evaporate." Id. at 78. Although the lawyers' actions spared Kaczynski the death penalty, they also "demolished his human dignity." Id. at 79.

[28] Id. at 83.

that deserves to be taken seriously. A different conception of dignity would support different professional duties. For example, a closer identification of dignity with autonomy would shift the focus to the capacity of clients to make choices without unwarranted interference by others. Stephen Pepper's theory, for example, emphasizes the relationship in a complex, highly regulated society between the exercise of autonomy and having access to information about the law and the technical expertise needed to structure one's affairs with reference to the law. It follows from this conception of dignity that lawyers should not "ration" or "filter" access to law on the ground that the client's goals are immoral.[29] Luban is not worried so much about access to law because his conception of dignity emphasizes telling the client's story. Thus, even theories that begin at roughly the same point may diverge as duties are connected with the specific conception of the foundational value.

Step 3: test the resulting theory against cases

One of the test cases for a dignity-based conception of legal ethics is fairly simple. Suppose the lawyer tells a story that varies from the client's story in crucial respects but is not literally false. The poker game case in this chapter is one example, and Luban uses a similar case (borrowed from William Simon)[30]: The client was arrested while placing a stolen television in the back seat of his car and charged with possession of stolen property. An element of the crime, which the prosecution would have to prove in order to convict the defendant, is *mens rea*, that is, a mental state of knowing the television was stolen. The lawyer argued to the jury that someone who knew the television to be stolen would have put it in the trunk, rather than driving around with stolen property in plain view in the back seat. The lawyer knew, however, that the defendant did not have a key to the trunk. The fact that the defendant put the television in the back seat actually had nothing to do with his *mens rea*, but it helped make a strong case for acquittal.

The issue in step 3 is not whether a case could be made for the ethical permissibility of arguing the story in the way the lawyer did. As Luban

---

[29] See Pepper, *supra*, pp. 617–19.

[30] Luban, *supra*, p. 72, citing William H. Simon, *The Practice of Justice* (Cambridge, Mass.: Harvard University Press 1998), pp. 171–72.

notes, most lawyers would justify the conduct here by pointing out that if there is evidence supporting an innocent explanation of the defendant's actions, then there is reasonable doubt and the defendant is entitled to an acquittal:

> All the lawyer has done is dramatize the reasonable doubt instead of arguing for it in an abstract manner. That seems like an entirely legitimate way to make the case for reasonable doubt. Every litigator knows that it takes a story to beat a story. Arguing abstractly for reasonable doubt will never shake a jury's preconceptions.[31]

This argument is quite powerful (I am in complete agreement with it), but here is the crucial question: Does it follow from the conception of the moral value identified in step 1 and the specific professional duties identified in step 2? Remember that, for Luban, the essence of human dignity is subjectivity – having a story of one's own to tell. The defendant's actual story is that he did not have a key to the trunk. The lawyer's embellishment, arguing that the defendant must not have known the television was stolen because otherwise he would have put it in the trunk, is a great story but it is not *the defendant's* story. It is a story that could be told by someone about the defendant, but Luban's dignity-based account of the value of legal representation emphasizes what people would actually say if they were sufficiently articulate and well informed to know how to speak to powerful actors and institutions. If the defendant told his story himself, not through a lawyer, he either would have lied about his reasons for putting the television in the back seat or he would have told the truth and been convicted. The argument given here in defense of the lawyer's conduct is a good one, but it does not ultimately trace back to the conception of the value of dignity identified as the foundation.

Here is where reflective equilibrium assumes a dynamic quality. A theorist is not necessarily stuck with a bad result. It may be possible to tweak the theory in some way to account for the result of a test case without having to revise it thoroughly. Luban tries such a modification by arguing that defense lawyers respect human dignity indirectly as well as directly. Direct respect for the value of dignity, as he has defined it, requires being a voice for the client's actual story. Indirect respect, on the other hand, means participating in a process that presumes innocence and sets a high burden that the

---

[31] Id. at 72–73.

prosecution must meet to obtain a conviction. "[T]he advocate defends her client's human dignity either directly, by telling his story, or indirectly, by demonstrating that a good faith story of innocence could be constructed from the evidence."[32] How close a connection must there be between the foundational value and the lawyer's obligations as a matter of professional ethics? There is no simple answer to that question. Here, it seems plausible to appeal to an institutional mechanism. Criminal defendants can be convicted only after compliance with procedures designed to protect their dignity, and it makes sense to understand the lawyer's ethical obligations within that system, not directly with reference to a fairly abstract moral value. If the connection is too attenuated, however, it may be the case that there is a better explanation for the content of a lawyer's ethical obligations; a theorist may be trying too hard to shoehorn a case into an explanation based on a particular foundational value. The next theory considered here may be an example of that problem – see what you think.

2.4.2   Fried: the lawyer as friend

Step 1: define and specify the moral value

Fried begins with a premise remarkably similar to Luban's, that is, the centrality of human subjectivity, with echoes of Pepper's emphasis on autonomy. "Before there is morality there must be the person. We must attain and maintain in our morality a concept of personality such that it makes sense to posit choosing, valuing entities – free, moral beings."[33] From our unique, subjective perspective, our interests are not the same as the interests of humanity as a whole. That does not mean we are selfish; rather, it means that morality begins with a recognition that others are in the same predicament – they view the world from their own subjective point of view and have interests that are intelligible from that perspective. Of all of the "others" who could conceivably be part of a person's moral concern, certain individuals – family members and close friends – become important, constitutive aspects of a person's life. Seeing the world from one's subjective perspective includes having concern for people with whom we stand in individualized (i.e. thick, historical) relations of love and friendship. It follows from the centrality of subjectivity and the importance to persons

---

[32] Id. at 73.   [33] Fried, *supra*, pp. 1068–69.

of individualized relationships that it may be permissible to favor the interests of those with whom we are in particularly close, personal relationships over the well-being of humanity as a whole:

> [I]t is not only consonant with, but also required by, an ethics for human beings that one be entitled first of all to reserve an area of concern for oneself and then to move out freely from that area if one wishes to lavish that concern on others to whom one stands in concrete, personal relations.[34]

Spending one's resources on after-school enrichment activities for one's children, for example, is morally permitted even though it would be possible to use the money spent on horseback riding lessons and dance classes to effect dramatic improvements in the well-being of people in the developing world who lack access to basic needs such as clean water.[35]

It is important to notice that, for Fried, the moral value of relationships with friends and family members has to do with their special connection with the person. Fried strongly resists a conception of morality "in which my own interests disappear and are merged into the totality of humanity"[36] – in other words, the classical utilitarian view that individuals are something over which some quantity is to be maximized. The concrete "other" who is the object of a person's concern is someone close enough so that his or her interests are also, in some sense, the interests of the actor. "[T]he individualized relations of love and friendship ... have a different, more intense aspect than do the cooler, more abstract relations of love and service to humanity in general."[37] This is because the interests of the friend or loved one have become intertwined with the actor's interests through a shared history together. People do not become friends in Fried's sense overnight because the sharing of interests he requires as a justification for special moral concern can develop only over time.

As a critical student of legal ethics, you should have already spotted a problem developing for Fried's theory. He pretty clearly is going to want to analogize the relationship between friends to the lawyer–client relationship and argue that the special moral permission to prefer the interests of one's friends to the interests of "the totality of humanity" has a parallel in

---

[34] Id. at 1070.

[35] This particular moral problem was famously raised by Peter Singer in "Famine, Affluence, and Morality," *Philosophy and Public Affairs* 1: 229–43 (1972).

[36] Fried, *supra*, at 1069.   [37] Id. at 1070.

professional life in the principle of single-minded loyalty to one's client, no matter what the effect on nonclients. Pay attention to the characteristics of friendship that Fried thinks ground the moral permission to favor the interests of one person over others or over the interests of humanity as a whole. Ask yourself whether they are also features of the relationship between a lawyer and a client. There may be a long, shared history in some professional relationships, but many of them are apt to be relatively impersonal, one-off transactions, with no experience of intimacy or sharing. Moreover, what about institutional clients? Can anyone have a personally meaningful relationship with Barclays Bank? (Maybe with an *employee* of Barclays, but a lawyer for an organization is deemed to represent the organization itself as a client, not individual officers or employees.[38]) You might also want to ask yourself now, in the domain of morality – we haven't gotten to professional ethics yet – what are friends allowed to do for each other? Anything at all? Not on a plausible conception of friendship.[39] There are moral limits to favoritism and partiality. I might keep many secrets for my friends, but if I learned that one of my friends was planning to set off homemade bombs full of shrapnel at the Boston Marathon, I would have a moral obligation to go to the police with this information. Fried's friendship analogy may not get him as much in the domain of professional ethics as he would like it to.

Step 2: show that the value in step 1 entails a principle of professional ethics

A lawyer is a "special-purpose friend." She is a friend for the purposes of legal representation. Like a friend, she prioritizes the client's needs above those of others, either known third parties or the diffuse aggregation of individuals and interests known as "society" or "the public interest," and she shows loyalty to the client and devotion to her interests.[40] The lawyer is not "morally reprehensible to the extent that he lavishes undue concern on some particular person"[41]; that's what friends do, so lawyers should be able to advocate exclusively for the interests of their clients without worrying

---

[38] In the US, see ABA Model Rules, *supra*, Rule 1.13(a).

[39] Although I can't resist a joke from Tom and Ray on the National Public Radio show *Car Talk*: A friend will help you move. A good friend will help you move a dead body.

[40] Fried, *supra*, at 1071–74.   [41] Id. at 1074.

about the claims of others, however pressing. When Wilson's lawyers in the wrongful conviction case kept his secret, even though disclosing it could have freed an innocent person, they were acting as true and faithful friends to their client. When the lawyer in the poker game case persuaded a jury that there was a reasonable doubt as to whether the defendant could have committed the crime, the lawyer was doing what friends always do – helping out a friend in need. Confidentiality, zealous representation, and single-minded devotion to the client's cause are all principles of professional ethics that are derived from the value of friendship.

Many of Fried's critics find this argument simply preposterous.[42] Two law professors writing in response to Fried's article asked acerbically,

> A lawyer is a person who, without expecting any reciprocal activity or inclination thereto, will attempt to forward or protect the interests of a client, within the rules of a legal system, so long as he is paid a sufficient amount to do so, and so long as doing so does not inflict any material unforeseen personal costs. That's "friendship"?[43]

There are too many relevant distinctions between natural friendship and professional, "special-purpose" friendship. Some of the most obvious include the lack of a shared history between the parties that leads them to regard themselves as having mutually shared interests; the frankly commercial nature of the lawyer–client relationship; the transactional nature of many lawyer–client relationships, which involve only one matter (a divorce, a criminal charge, or an accident) as opposed to a more holistic concern for all aspects of the other's well-being; the claim of permission to be special-purpose friends with odious people; and the claim of permission to violate the rights of others in service of the friendship. The lawyer–client relationship is actually, in many cases, characterized by its very *impersonality*; one person pays another to handle some complicated or meddlesome problem. There is nothing wrong with this sort of transaction, but it is the very antithesis of a natural friendship.

Fried appears to sense this problem, for he subtly shifts the terms of the justification for the lawyer's preference for her client's interests. He writes:

---

[42] See, e.g., Dauer and Leff, *supra*; William H. Simon, "The Ideology of Advocacy: Procedural Justice and Professional Ethics," *Wisconsin Law Review* 1978: 29–144.

[43] Dauer and Leff, *supra*, at 579.

We need only concede that at the very least the law must leave us a measure of autonomy, whether or not it is in the social interest to do so. Individuals have rights over and against the collectivity ... It is because the law must respect the rights of individuals that the law must also create and support the specific role of legal friend.[44]

It is apparent here that what really matters to Fried is not the friendship metaphor but the underlying idea that individuals have autonomy and should be able to assert rights that may run counter to the public interest or the interests of others. An innocent person could be freed if this secret were disclosed. Too bad. The client has autonomy. He can choose not to reveal his role in the murder and allow Logan to languish in prison. Recall William Simon's fundamental principle of professional ethics, that "[t]he lawyer should take those actions that, considering the relevant circumstances of the particular case, seem most likely to promote justice."[45] *This* is what Fried is opposed to. An individual should not be valued under the general concept of justice, but as an individual, with her own interests and rights, because she is a moral agent, too. The friendship analogy may be a bit of a stretch, but it is less central to the theory than the claim about the importance of individual autonomy, which deserves to be protected by the legal system and which is protected by creating a professional role called lawyer, with duties of loyalty to particular clients. "The lawyer acts morally because he helps to preserve and express the autonomy of his client vis-à-vis the legal system," he writes.[46]

Step 3: test the resulting theory against cases

Reading Fried's article is an experience of reflective equilibrium in action. The shift from the friendship metaphor to a more explicit reliance on the value of autonomy comes in the discussion of representing "unworthy" clients. "Pornography may be legal, but it hardly follows that I perform a morally worthy function if I lend money or artistic talent to help the pornographer flourish in the exercise of his right."[47] But, of course, a natural friend of the pornographer would want him to flourish and would lend him money or artistic talent. Fried is concerned here, because he has an

---

[44] Fried, *supra*, at 1073.   [45] Simon, *Ethical Discretion, supra*, at 1090.
[46] Fried, *supra*, at 1074.   [47] Id. at 1074–75.

intuition, based on long-standing professional tradition, that lawyers should not be criticized for representing unpopular clients. Friends, however, can be criticized for hanging with nasty people. Folk morality is full of sayings like, "You are known by the company you keep." Thus, the friendship analogy yields a result that is inconsistent with a considered judgment about a case. What then? Modify the theory. This is where Fried says the friendship metaphor was meant to be suggestive, but the important aspect of it is the underlying value that gives moral worth to both natural friendships and legal "special-purpose" friendships; namely, the individuality, moral agency, autonomy, and rights of the individual. The most important implication of his view is that lawyers should not interfere with citizens having access to the law. "[R]ights are violated if, through ignorance or misinformation about the law, an individual refrains from pursuing a wholly lawful purpose."[48] Providing access to the law is a morally worthy activity because people need to know about their legal rights and duties in order to be fully autonomous. "[T]he individual lawyer does a morally worthy thing whomever he serves."[49]

Fried therefore shifts the theoretical foundation of his theory from the value of personal relationships (friendships) to the autonomy of clients. Recall that Luban rejected the identification of the value of individuals with autonomy. Go back and ask yourself: How would Luban handle the pornographer case? Perhaps you first have to resolve a prior question: How do you think that case ought to come out? Are lawyers subject to justified criticism on the basis of the clients they choose to represent? If your answer is no, then think about which theory does a better job of accounting for that intuition. Or, if you are really not sure, think through the arguments starting with the foundational values and decide which seems to do a better job explaining the connection between morality and professional ethics.

---

[48] Id. at 1075. This makes it sounds like the pornographer has a positive right to legal assistance – that is, that he could insist that a lawyer represent him. In some jurisdictions, including New Zealand and the UK (but only with respect to barristers), the so-called "cab rank" rule requires lawyers to accept the representation of clients as long as there are no conflicts of interest and the lawyer is competent to carry out the representation. In the US, Canada, and elsewhere, a lawyer is at liberty to decline a representation for pretty much any reason. See Chapter 7 on criminal defense and client selection for further discussion of the cab rank rule.

[49] Id. at 1078.

3 The adversary system

The preceding chapter explored ethical arguments at the microlevel, considering the connection between moral values such as dignity and autonomy and the duties they entail as a matter of professional ethics. This chapter shifts to the macrolevel, but retains a similar structure. Lawyers believe they have duties that are justified in the context of the adversary system of adjudication. The questions to be considered in this chapter are, first, what are those duties in general terms? Second, what is the adversary system, and how is it distinctive? And third, how might one go about justifying the adversary system on two types of moral theory – consequentialist and deontological?

3.1 The lawyer's ethical view of the world

In the wrongful conviction case described in Chapter 1, Wilson's lawyers maintained all along that they did not do anything wrong by electing not to disclose Wilson's statement that he, not Logan, had committed the murder for which Logan was serving a lengthy prison term. The lawyers did not believe they were exempt from the demands of ethics. Rather, they believed that they were following a set of ethical principles that was worthy of their respect. Certainly, the law, in the form of the duty of confidentiality within the rules of professional, required them to respect Wilson's decision not to admit publicly that he had killed the security guard. Beyond that, however, the lawyers believed that they did the right thing more generally, that the law *rightly* required them to keep Wilson's secret, and that they should not be subject to criticism in ethical terms for following the law. As one of Wilson's lawyers put it:

> "If I had ratted him out . . . then I could feel guilty, then I could not live with myself," he says. "I'm anguished and always have been over the sad injustice of Alton Logan's conviction. Should I do the right thing by Alton Logan and

43

put my client's neck in the noose or not? It's clear where my responsibility lies and my responsibility lies with my client."[1]

The language of "ratting out" Wilson reveals a *moral* stance toward the *ethical* duty of confidentiality. Despite feeling anguished and believing that Logan was the victim of an injustice, Wilson's lawyer followed the law not merely because it is the law, but because it was also the right thing to do. The subject of this chapter is how a scheme of professional ethical principles – including confidentiality, loyalty, partisanship, and permission to cause certain types of harms (imposition of costs, humiliation, etc.) to others – can be justified in moral terms. It is a fairly general approach to the bridge structure set out in Chapter 1, beginning with some general observations about a lawyer's ethical obligations within an adversarial system of justice and some important basic concepts in moral philosophy, particularly the distinction between consequentialist and deontological justifications for actions (or, as in legal ethics, for a scheme of ethical principles guiding professionals).

The lawyer's statement of his duty to Wilson includes two principles concerning how he should act. The first may be called *partisanship*. That means the lawyer's duties are owed to the client and not to third parties, society as a whole, the public interest, or anyone or anything else. The client is the object of the lawyer's single-minded devotion and effort. It is true that a lawyer cannot violate the law in the representation of a client. Bribing or threatening witnesses in order to secure an acquittal is not ethically permitted because it is not legally permitted. Short of violating the law, however, a lawyer is obligated to use her best efforts to pursue the client's objectives. As American lawyers like to say, the duty is that of "zealous advocacy within the bounds of the law." In addition to partisanship, Wilson's lawyer's language suggests a second principle, which is a kind of filtering or gatekeeping norm. The lawyer says he was anguished and sad over Logan's conviction, but could not do anything about it. This second principle, referred to as the principle of *neutrality*, provides that a lawyer should not take into account reasons, values, emotions, commitments, or relationships that might tend to conflict with the client's interests or diminish the lawyer's vigor in representing the client. The lawyer's sense of regret at Logan's conviction must not be allowed to interfere with his duty to

---

[1] Wilson's lawyer Jamie Kunz, quoted in "After 26 Years, 2 Lawyers Reveal a Killer's Secret," USA Today (April 13, 2008).

Wilson. The principle of neutrality thus excludes from the lawyer's deliberation many considerations that people would ordinarily regard as relevant.

The principles of partisanship and neutrality are so woven into the fabric of the legal profession that lawyers often take them for granted. For this reason, this worldview is often called the Standard Conception of legal ethics.[2] Lawyers do not merely follow the duties prescribed by the Standard Conception; they also believe they are justified in doing so, as against criticism that may be directed at them from the point of view of ordinary, nonprofessional morality. Accordingly, a third principle is sometimes stated as part of the Standard Conception, namely, the principle of *nonaccountability*. This principle does not tell lawyers what to do. Rather, it tells observers how to evaluate, in moral terms, the conduct of lawyers. Lawyers who serve competently, diligently, and faithfully as advocates for their clients' positions and do not take into account any moral qualms they might feel about either the client's goals or the means used to achieve them (as long as they do not violate the law) should not be tainted with any of the moral blame that may appropriately be placed on clients.

The Standard Conception does not only apply to lawyers who represent clients in litigation, either civil or criminal. Lawyers advising clients, negotiating deals, helping clients comply with legal regulations, and performing other types of nonlitigation services are still obligated by the principles of partisanship and neutrality. Both in professional tradition and in legal ethics scholarship, however, a connection has often been drawn between the Standard Conception and the adversary system of adjudication. As you probably know, one of the distinctive features of the common law is that judges are relatively passive. Although there are exceptions in certain types of complex cases, generally, judges decide the issues that are presented to them by the parties. The lawyer for the party who initiates the action – the plaintiff in civil litigation or the prosecution in a criminal case – consults with the client, performs a preliminary investigation, and specifies the issues to be determined by the court. In a civil case, this occurs through the filing of a complaint setting out factual allegations and legal grounds for a remedy. In criminal

---

[2] For the article considered to be the first statement of the Standard Conception, see Murray Schwartz, "The Professionalism and Accountability of Lawyers," *California Law Review* 66: 669–98 (1978). The term for this conception of professional ethics originated, so far as I know, in Gerald J. Postema, "Moral Responsibility and Professional Ethics," *New York University Law Review* 55: 63–89 (1980).

cases, the defendant may have a right to have a grand jury first evaluate the prosecution's charge, or the prosecution may be able to file a document similar to a civil complaint, which again sets out factual contentions and asserts that the facts satisfy the elements of a crime. Lawyers for the defendant then have opportunities to respond to these opening salvos by challenging their legal sufficiency or raising separate defenses. As the proceeding moves along, each party has an opportunity to request relief of various types from the judge by filing motions. Finally, if the dispute goes to a trial, the lawyers control the presentation of evidence through the testimony of witnesses and the introduction of documents and physical evidence.

Obviously, this description glosses over a lot of the details of civil and criminal procedure. The general point, however, is that in important respects the shape and direction of the litigation, as well as the content of the factual record, is determined by the parties and their lawyers acting as partisan representatives of clients, with the judge in a neutral, passive, or, as is sometimes said, "referee" role. This is a defining structural characteristic of legal systems rooted in the English common law. Common law-based, adversarial systems of adjudication are found in the United States (with the partial exception of Louisiana); England, Wales, and Northern Ireland; the Republic of Ireland; all Canadian provinces except for Quebec; Australia and New Zealand; India, Pakistan, and Bangladesh; Malaysia and Singapore; numerous Caribbean nations including Jamaica, Barbados, and Trinidad and Tobago; and several African nations such as Kenya, Nigeria, and Zambia.

Things are very different in legal systems derived from Roman law of antiquity. The systems are often called civil law, to distinguish them from the common law,[3] and they are sometimes referred to as "inquisitorial"

---

[3] Don't be confused, because *within a common law system* lawyers distinguish between civil and criminal law; used in that sense, the word "civil" refers to an action either between two private parties or between the state and a private party in which the available remedies do not include incarceration and where various procedural entitlements such as the presumption of innocence and requirement of proof beyond a reasonable doubt do not apply to the defendant. The theory is that crimes are wrongs to society as a whole, whereas civil wrongs pertain only to the injured party. In the real world, civil and criminal actions may be intertwined. For example, if A beats up B for no reason, B may have a civil action for damages against A (called an action in battery), and the state may also prosecute A for a crime, often called assault and battery. The state may also bring criminal charges and a separate civil action seeking the forfeiture of assets against defendants such as drug dealers and racketeers.

systems to emphasize the active role played by the judge. France and Germany both developed civil law systems to a high degree of sophistication, and these systems continue to serve as the foundation for the legal systems of countries in East Asia (notably Japan and South Korea, with China having a hybrid civil law/socialist legal system, and Hong Kong having a further hybridized system with both Chinese and English common law foundations), Latin America, and Continental Europe. Some nations, including Scotland, Israel, and Norway, have hybrid systems with elements of both the common law and civil law. Civil law systems of adjudication vary in their details, but the unifying feature that distinguishes them from common law systems is that a state official – a judge, examining magistrate, or someone with a similar title – controls the litigation process, from initiating proceedings to investigating facts to deciding which legal claims to assert to regulating the introduction of evidence and to questioning witnesses at trial.[4] Many of the functions performed by lawyers in a common law system, such as drafting documents and advising clients, are performed in civil law systems by members of allied professional groups (e.g., notaries). In some common law systems, such as the United Kingdom and some Australian states, there is a parallel in the distinction between barristers and solicitors, with solicitors doing the out-of-court work of preparing a case for litigation and barristers acting as in-court advocates, but in other common law systems a single occupational group – lawyers – performs both roles, and the same lawyer often represents the client in pretrial and in-court proceedings.

In civil law systems, the adjudicating official is not, even in theory, a neutral referee but plays a central role in shaping the proceedings. As you might expect, the role of lawyers in civil law systems is very different. It is a bit of an exaggeration to say that lawyers are passive in civil law systems because they can affect the direction of proceedings by making written

---

[4] An accessible introduction to civil law systems for common law trained lawyers is John Henry Merryman, *The Civil Law Tradition* (Stanford: Stanford University Press, 2d edn., 1985). A sophisticated theoretical account of the differences between these systems is Mirjan R. Damaška, *The Faces of Justice and State Authority* (New Haven: Yale University Press 1986). A comparative study focusing on the legal profession and judiciary in common law and civil law systems is Geoffrey C. Hazard, Jr. and Angelo Dondi, *Legal Ethics: A Comparative Study* (Stanford: Stanford University Press 2004).

submissions to the judge, suggesting lines of inquiry, and, in some systems, putting questions to witnesses.[5] Nevertheless, the roles of lawyers in common law and civil law systems are sufficiently distinct that many ethical dilemmas facing lawyers in common law systems simply do not arise for lawyers in civil law systems. For example, a civil law lawyer would never have the opportunity to cross-examine a witness known to be telling the truth with the objective of making the witness's testimony appear false. The questioning of the witness in that case would be conducted by the judge, so there would be no ethical dilemma for the lawyer. In common law systems, however, lawyers play a more active role in investigating the facts, asserting legal theories, and requesting rulings from the judge. Many of the ethical issues confronting lawyers in the common law world arise from the division of labor among many different institutional actors. Common law lawyers may be more active than their civilian counterparts, but they often assert that praise or blame in moral terms may be attributed only to the system as a whole, not to individual actors within it.

Philosophers may be concerned with the adversary system in general, inquiring into whether it is justified as a part of a scheme of institutions and norms that serve some social end. To put it another way, we could ask how to integrate the adversarial system into our political ideals and practices as a whole. Given the existence of civil law systems in democratic nations like France, Germany, and Japan, it cannot be the case that democracy necessarily entails an adversarial system of justice. Nevertheless, there may be democratic ideals that are instantiated in the adversarial system and give these practices their justification. For example, adversarial procedures of adjudication may do a better job of protecting individual rights than the procedures of civil law systems, which are directed by state officials. Or, it may be that adversarial procedures are better at ascertaining the truth of the matter – whodunit, as the saying goes. To sort out these different types of ethical defenses of the adversary system, it will be helpful to introduce a distinction from ethical theory between *consequentialist* and *deontological* considerations.

---

[5] See Hazard and Dondi, pp. 66–69, for a cautionary note on the differences among civil law systems and an admonition not to make "misleading comparison[s] of an idealized judge-centered system with a crudely disparaged adversary system."

3.2   Two types of moral theories

3.2.1   Consequentialist theories

Consequentialism is a moral theory holding that the right thing to do in any particular situation is that which will produce the best outcome, the greatest net balance of good over evil.[6] The basic intuitions lying behind consequentialism are that everyone ought to make the world a better place by his or her actions, and that rationality aims at maximizing something, in this case the amount of good in the world. Major issues for consequentialism include (1) the relevant consequences to be considered, for example, whether something is good if it produces pleasure in sentient beings or whether something is good or desirable for other reasons, such as yielding beauty, harmony, rights, fairness, autonomy, truth, and so on; (2) whether the evaluative principle applies to individual actions (direct consequentialism) or something else, such as a rule designed to maximize the good or the dispositions or motives of actors (indirect consequentialism); (3) how the evaluation of an action should take account of the distribution of goods among people, for example, whether a society with millions of people in poverty and a small but spectacularly happy class of wealthy people is worse off than a society with the same number of people, all of whom have an adequate level of resources; (4) whether the theory directs actors to maximize the production of the relevant good or merely to aim at an adequate quantity (satisficing); and (5) whether the evaluative standpoint is impartial (agent-neutral) or whether outcomes are to be judged from the standpoint of the actor (agent-relative). For the purposes of this discussion, we can set aside many of these complexities and focus on the basic theme of *right* action being determined by the production of *good* outcomes.[7]

The best known variety of consequentialism is classical utilitarianism, as developed by Jeremy Bentham, John Stuart Mill, and Henry Sidgwick. Utilitarianism identifies good with satisfaction or pleasure – this is known

---

[6] See generally "Introduction," in Samuel Scheffler, ed., *Consequentialism and Its Critics* (Oxford: Oxford University Press 1988).

[7] For the very helpful point that ethical theories can be differentiated by how they connect the basic concepts of right and good, see John Rawls, *A Theory of Justice* (Cambridge, Mass.: Belknap Press 1971), p. 24.

as *hedonism*. The debate over what counts as pleasure can be seen in two opposing maxims, from Bentham and Mill:

- Bentham: The quantity of pleasure being equal, pushpin is as good as poetry. (Pushpin being a mindless children's game popular at the time. A modern equivalent would be watching reality television or playing Angry Birds.)
- Mill: It is better to be Socrates dissatisfied than a fool satisfied.

The issue here is whether pleasure is simply contentment or whether some objects of desire are intrinsically valuable or whether some things are more valuable than others. Countless thought experiments in philosophy, not to mention depictions in literature and films (think of the Orgasmatron in Woody Allen's *Sleeper* or the sedentary consumers of entertainment in *Wall-E*) are meant to show that value is not reducible to pleasurable sensations alone. The term "utility," as used in economics, attempts to avoid this debate entirely by identifying good with the satisfaction of whatever preferences a person happens to have, remaining agnostic about what sorts of things people ought to desire. In any event, classical utilitarianism is impartial, holding that people have an obligation to promote the good of all, not merely to maximize the satisfaction of their own preferences, a position encapsulated by Mill's motto of seeking the greatest good for the greatest number. It is also aggregative, holding that pleasure is summed across all members of society. Although it is often the case that aggregate pleasure is maximized where people have more or less equal amounts of it, egalitarianism is not a requirement of utilitarianism. "[T]here is no reason in principle why the greater gains of some should not compensate for the lesser losses of others."[8]

3.2.2   Deontological moral theories

Deontology (from the Greek word meaning "duty") is a bit more difficult to define, but the basic idea is that some actions are intrinsically right or wrong regardless of their consequences. Where consequentialism maintains that the right thing to do is determined by what produces good, deontology focuses on rightness and maintains that goodness is doing

[8] Rawls, *supra*, p. 26.

what is right. To put it crudely, but in terms of a common-sense moral principle, deontology holds that the ends do not necessarily justify the means. The deontologist par excellence, Immanuel Kant, stated this idea in one of the three forms of the Categorical Imperative: "Act in such a way that you treat humanity, whether in your own person or in the person of another, always at the same time as an end and never simply as a means."[9] The requirement of treating others as ends in themselves expresses the inherent, inviolable value and dignity of persons. Even if great good could be accomplished by harming a person in some way, a deontological approach to morality would prohibit it. The classic, although to my mind a bit bizarre, illustration of the difference between consequentialist and deontological moral reasoning goes like this: You notice a runaway trolley hurtling down a hill toward a school bus that has stalled on the trolley tracks.[10] If the trolley is not stopped, it will crash into the bus, killing ten children. You are powerless to stop the trolley, but you notice a switch up ahead that can be opened, diverting the trolley to a parallel track. A homeless person is asleep on that track. You are not close enough to yell and wake the homeless person, nor can you alert anyone on the bus. Do you open the switch and divert the trolley away from the school bus, saving the lives of ten children at the expense of the homeless man?

The trolley problem may be used to illustrate many problems in ethics, including the distinction between acts and omissions (are you just as morally responsible for the avoidable deaths of the ten children as you would be for killing the one man by diverting the trolley?) and the so-called doctrine of double effect, which seeks to distinguish an actor's primary intention (saving the children) from foreseeable consequences (killing the homeless man).[11] For our purposes, however, it nicely differentiates consequentialist from deontological reasons. On one type of simple consequentialist analysis, the analysis of what to do is easy: The death of ten children is worse than the death of the homeless man, so the right action – that which

---

[9]   Immanuel Kant, *Grounding for the Metaphysics of Morals* (James W. Ellington, trans.) (Indianapolis: Hackett 1981), at Ak. 429.

[10]   Originally from Philippa Foot, "The Problem of Abortion and the Doctrine of Double Effect," in *Virtues and Vices* (Berkeley: University of California Press 1978).

[11]   See the ingenious variations in Judith Jarvis Thomson, "The Trolley Problem," *Yale Law Journal* 94: 1395–1415 (1985). Thomson's "fat man" and "transplant surgeon" variations clarify that the death of one person is not an unintended consequence of saving the others but is, in fact, aimed at directly by the actor.

maximizes the amount of good and minimizes the amount of bad in the world – is to switch the trolley. Most people have an intuition that, even if the right thing to do is to divert the trolley to the parallel track, the answer is not a no-brainer. The problem has the character of a dilemma, in which there is some wrong, some loss in moral terms, no matter what choice the actor makes. It would be possible to prevent the death of the children, but yet there would be something wrong about switching the trolley to the other track *even though* the numbers are clearly in favor of that option. Your active involvement – your agency – would be involved in causing the death of the man, and that feels wrong somehow even if the result is saving ten innocent lives.

There is something disquieting about a moral theory that says it is clearly, unambiguously right to seek the greatest good for the greatest number, even if it results in harm to some person. One way to accommodate this intuition would be to modify consequentialism, for example by focusing evaluation not on the specific action – to switch the trolley or not – but on a general rule such as, "do not intentionally cause the death of a person." A different response would be to deny that good consequences justify causing harm. The man sleeping on the trolley tracks has rights, and switching the trolley to save the children violates his rights and is therefore not permissible. This idea is sometimes conveyed by the maxim, "*Fiat justitia ruat caelum*" – let justice be done though the heavens fall – and in more modern terms is expressed as the priority of the right over the good. In political ethics, deontological considerations prohibit individuals or the state from interfering with certain important personal interests, such as life, bodily integrity, and property, without a sufficient reason, and being able to do greater good elsewhere in the world is not a sufficient reason.

Deontological principles such as "do not harm others without an adequate reason" may be justified by an appeal to the structure of rationality itself. Kant's influential ethical theory seeks to show that it would be irrational to act on a maxim that the actor could not coherently will to be a universal law.[12] A Kantian maxim is a general principle, specifying a type of action and the circumstances under which it may be performed. The categorical imperative then states that an actor may do something only where it

---

[12] See Andrews Reath, "Kant's Moral Philosophy," in Roger Crisp, ed., *The Oxford Handbook of the History of Ethics* (Oxford: Oxford University Press 2013).

would be possible, in theory, for everyone to adopt the same maxim. This decision procedure rules out certain actions such as lying and breaking promises. If everyone was permitted to deceive when it suited his or her needs, the entire practice of promising or making factual representations would collapse because no one would rely on anyone else's promises or representations about facts. In addition, the actor would be violating the conditions of her own moral agency, because the validity of moral principles depends on their having been self-legislated, as an act of the rational will, and a constitutive principle of rational volition is the universalizability of reasons. Somewhat less abstractly, Kantian ethics recognizes that we belong to a community of free and equal beings in which the pursuit of one's own interest must respect the interests of others.

You can see the influence of deontological reasoning in the explanation given by Wilson's lawyers in the wrongful conviction case. Granted, it would have been possible to accomplish a great good by revealing Wilson's involvement in the crime. An innocent person, Logan, would have been freed from prison. Doing so, however, would have violated Wilson's right to be able to communicate confidentially with his lawyers and was therefore ethically impermissible. Analogizing the wrongful conviction case to the trolley problem, Logan's continuing imprisonment is like the trolley speeding toward the school bus – it is a feature of the world that is simply there, prior to the involvement of any human agent. Wilson's lawyers no more caused Logan's imprisonment than the person standing by the switch in the trolley problem caused the trolley to lose its brakes. Switching the trolley is like disclosing Wilson's secret, in that it causes harm to a specific person. A consequentialist would say the harm is justified, because it leads to a better net balance of good over evil; a deontologist would say some reason other than producing good – consent, for example, or avoiding a greater harm to the same person – is required in order to justify the harm.

3.3   Ethical defenses and critiques of the adversary system

In the lawyer's ethical view of the world, the principles of partisanship and neutrality describe the obligations they owe to clients. Lawyers should provide loyal, competent service to clients; represent them effectively within the bounds of the law; and not be swayed by any moral qualms they have about their clients' character, goals, or the means used to represent them, so long as they are lawful. This is an ethical view because lawyers believe these obligations are grounded in some way in moral values external to the legal profession. The legal profession is not like a criminal gang, which does impose obligations on its members but cannot claim that these obligations are justified in moral terms. Fans of the television show *The Sopranos* or movies such as *Goodfellas* know what happens to a "rat" – a member of the family who cooperates with law enforcement. The young Henry Hill in *Goodfellas* learns an important lesson after his first arrest. His friend Jimmy Conway, played by Robert DeNiro, explains it like this: "Everybody gets pinched but you did it right. You told them nothing and they got nothing. You learned the two greatest things in life: Never rat on your friends and always keep your mouth shut." Becoming a member of an organized crime family requires acceptance of obligations such as never ratting on one's friends. As Henry later says, "Murder was the only way everybody stayed in line. You got out of line, you got whacked. Everybody knew the rules."

One way, admittedly a bit simplistic, to understand the discipline of professional ethics is as an effort to distinguish the justification of the norms governing professions from those of criminal gangs. They do not differ in their rulelike nature or in the potential application of sanctions for their violation but one important difference is standing in the right kind of relationship with the moral commitments of the wider society of which the profession is a part. In Chapters 1 and 2, we considered the "bridge" pattern of justification, showing how moral values and professional obligations can be connected. Many lawyers believe that the adversary system is an institution with sufficient moral weight to serve as a justification for professional obligations such as zealous advocacy and confidentiality. This argument is missing a step, however. The adversary system is just a thing, a system, a fact. To justify conduct that would otherwise be unethical, it has to have features that commend it in ethical terms. Otherwise, the ethical connection is a bridge to nowhere. The remainder of this chapter considers how the adversary system might be justified in consequentialist and deontological terms so that it, in turn, could provide a moral foundation for the professional obligations of lawyers.

3.3.1   Consequentialist defenses

The basic idea in a consequentialist moral theory is that the right thing to do is that which leads to the best outcome. The desirability of outcomes is measured in terms of some good produced, such as pleasure, well-being, or the satisfaction of preferences. A consequentialist justification of the adversary system would rely on some good produced by the legal system. What would that be? The leading contender is the determination of truth.

At least one purpose of a civil lawsuit or a criminal prosecution is to find out the truth about some matter. Did the defendant promise to deliver 10,000 widgets to the plaintiff? Was the traffic signal red at the time of the collision? Did the valet Courvoisier murder Lord Russell? The lawyer's role in an adversarial system, with all of the obligations that pertain to it, may therefore be justified as contributing to the production of truth. One of the commonest criticisms of lawyers, however, is that by their actions they distort the truth or prevent it from emerging at trial. Lawyers cross-examine witnesses known to be telling the truth to make them seem untrustworthy; they assert technical defenses to defeat a meritorious claim; they put on a vigorous defense for clients known to be guilty.[13] It would appear that the professional obligations of lawyers, including keeping client confidences and presenting the client's case as persuasively as possible, serve to prevent the judge and jury (if applicable) from determining what really happened. Defenders of the adversary system and of the Standard Conception of legal ethics have developed two principal lines of defense in response to these sorts of criticisms.

The first is to begin with the observation that people tend to jump to conclusions. As an early and influential American report on lawyers' professional responsibilities in an adversarial system observes, if an adjudicator tries to decide a dispute without the assistance of partisan advocacy,

> at some early point a familiar pattern will seem to emerge from the evidence; an accustomed label is waiting for the case and, without awaiting further proofs, this label is promptly assigned to it ... [W]hat starts as a preliminary

---

[13] See, e.g., Edward F. Barrett, "The Adversary System and the Ethics of Advocacy," *Notre Dame Lawyer* 37: 479–88 (1962). The foil for Barrett's argument is a hypothetical critic who asks: "Isn't it *wrong* to defend a man you *know is guilty?*" "Is it *right* to plead a *technical* defense against a *just* claim?" "Isn't it *plainly dishonest* to cross-examine a witness who *has told the truth?*"

diagnosis designed to direct the inquiry tends, quickly and imperceptibly, to become a fixed conclusion as all that confirms the diagnosis makes a strong imprint on the mind, while all that runs counter to it is received with diverted attention.[14]

Cognitive psychologists would put the same point in terms of unconscious biases and heuristics and of effects such as framing and confirmation bias.[15] In any case, the idea is that the presentation of one-sided versions of the events by partisan advocates keeps the trier of fact in a state of suspended judgment until the presentation of evidence is complete. In the words of the American report on professional responsibility, "[a]n adversary presentation seems the only effective means for combatting this natural human tendency to judge too swiftly in terms of the familiar that which is not yet fully known."[16] The role of partisan advocates has a counterpart in the position of the "devil's advocate" employed by the Roman Catholic Church in canonization proceedings, whose job it is to muster every possible argument against sainthood in order to ensure that the tribunal's decision is as reliable as possible.[17]

There are several problems with this argument. First, it appears that even lawyers don't believe it. Every trial lawyer knows that, to provide effective representation, it is necessary to know the facts of the case. Yet lawyers send out *one* investigator to figure out what happened – they do not hire a second, "devil's advocate" investigator to point out the weaknesses in the other's presentation of the evidence.[18] Having two sets of lawyers searching out relevant evidence seems only to add to the expense and hassle of dispute resolution. Second, correcting for the tendency to prejudge does not justify tactics that aim to distort or suppress the truth. If a judge formed an initial belief that a witness was telling the truth, a lawyer's vigorous cross-examination might convince the judge that the witness was lying or mistaken. This may be permissible according to the norms of adversarial litigation, but it cannot be justified as a contribution to discovery of the

---

[14] Lon L. Fuller and John D. Randall, "Professional Responsibility: Report of the Joint Conference," *American Bar Association Journal*, 44: pp. 1159–62, 1216–18 (1958).

[15] See, e.g., Daniel Kahneman, *Thinking, Fast and Slow* (New York: Farrar, Straus & Giroux 2011).

[16] Fuller and Randall, *supra*, p. 1160.   [17] Bennett, *supra*, pp. 480–81.

[18] David Luban, "The Adversary System Excuse," in David Luban, ed., *The Good Lawyer: Lawyers' Roles and Lawyers' Ethics* (Totowa, N.J.: Rowman & Allanheld 1983), p. 96.

truth. Third, perhaps truth is more likely to emerge from a process in which two equally competent adversaries are matched against each other, but many trials involve a disparity in resources between the parties.[19] It seems perverse that the important goal of truth finding should depend on the relative wealth of the parties.

An alternate line of defense appeals to the incentives of the parties' lawyers. The prospect of victory, an enhanced professional reputation, and perhaps higher fees (either in the future or, under the American system of contingent fees, as a percentage of the client's recovery) motivate lawyers to work harder, investigate the facts thoroughly, and put on the best possible case for their clients. Proponents of the adversary system may imagine judges in civil law systems as bored functionaries, pronouncing judgment after a cursory review of the dossier compiled by clerks. If there is a reluctant witness or hard-to-find document that will prove the client's case, it seems more likely that a partisan advocate identified with her client's cause would be more likely to find that crucial piece of evidence. Partisanship turns what could be drudgery – hunting through files for relevant evidence, interviewing witnesses, and so on – into a game, with the accompanying thrill of competition. The trouble is, not only does this defense make finding the truth like a side effect, but is it plausible to believe that partisan lawyers work harder than state officials charged with finding out the truth from a more impartial perspective? Maybe partisan lawyers would have an incentive to work hard only for clients whose cases seemed like winners or with whom the lawyers otherwise tend to identify.

Any truth-based consequentialist argument for the adversary system has to contend with the observation that civil law systems exist in liberal democratic societies and seem to do just as well at finding out the basic "whodunit" question in criminal cases and fairly assigning liability in various types of tort and contract disputes. It is difficult to test that comparison rigorously, but one would have expected greater convergence in common law and civil law procedures of fact finding if one or the other were manifestly better at ascertaining truth. The best explanation for the persistence of the adversarial system of adjudication is probably pragmatic: This is the system bequeathed to us by history; it works tolerably well, and the

---

[19] Deborah L. Rhode, *In the Interests of Justice: Reforming the Legal Profession* (Oxford: Oxford University Press 2000), pp. 53–54.

available alternatives have their own problems; it lines up well with other political ideals such as individual autonomy and (at least in the US and Australia, although maybe elsewhere as well) a strand of antigovernment sentiment; and it would be enormously disruptive to make large-scale structural changes (which would require, in some countries, constitutional amendments to address institutions such as the jury).[20] Although it is far from perfect, the system is good enough on consequentialist grounds.

3.3.2   Deontological defenses

The ultimate expression of "let justice be done though the heavens fall" in legal ethics comes from a speech in the English House of Commons by Lord Henry Brougham, to which we will have occasion to return frequently throughout this book. Brougham explained that the duty of an advocate in an adversarial system of justice is to the client only, and the lawyer should not consider the interests of others:

> An advocate, in the discharge of his duty, knows but one person in all the world, and that person is his client. To save that client by all means and expedients, and at all hazards and costs to other persons ... is his first and only duty; and in performing this duty he must not regard the alarm, the torments, the destruction which he may bring upon others.[21]

Brougham's words could easily have come from the mouths of the lawyers representing Wilson in the wrongful conviction case. They are ethically

---

[20] See Geoffrey C. Hazard, Jr., *Ethics in the Practice of Law* (New Haven: Yale University Press 1978), pp. 122–29.

[21] Quoted in Tim Dare, *The Counsel of Rogues? A Defence of the Standard Conception of the Lawyer's Role* (Farnham: Ashgate 2009), p. 6. Although Brougham's speech is cited frequently by legal ethics scholars, Dare's discussion of the background to the case is essential reading. To summarize, Caroline and the Prince of Wales entered into an arranged marriage and "seem to have instantly fallen into a deep, mutual and enduring loathing." They lived apart, and Caroline became friends-with-benefits with an Italian cavalry officer. When her husband succeeded to the throne as King George IV, she was offered a payment in exchange for renouncing the title of Queen; when she refused, she was essentially brought up on adultery charges via a bill introduced in the House of Lords that would have compelled her divorce from George. Brougham's defense of Caroline was the raw power of blackmail: He knew that George had secretly contracted a bigamous marriage to a Catholic widow and threatened to reveal this secret if Caroline's opponents did not back down. The government then withdrew the bill.

obligated not to consider "the torments, the destruction" of keeping Logan in prison. Instead, their only job is to protect Wilson's interests, including the interest in keeping secret his involvement in the crime, "by all means and expedients." As to "the hazards and costs" to Logan, they are charged to the system, not to the ethical accounts, as it were, of the lawyers representing Wilson.

"But wait a second!" you might be saying to yourself, "I thought the whole idea of deontological constraints is that inflicting harm on others is impermissible, even if doing so will bring about the greatest good for the greatest number." Logan is like the homeless man in the trolley problem, and it is not permissible to do something that would turn him into collateral damage in the process of saving someone else. Why should deontological reasons not require the lawyer to take account of the suffering of Logan? The best answer to that question builds on the famous observation of John Rawls, that "[u]tilitarianism does not take seriously the distinction between persons."[22] Western liberal philosophy emphasizes the inherent value of each individual. That value is protected by rights possessed by the individual, which can be asserted to prevent certain types of interferences with the individual's interests, even if they would otherwise be made up for by the greater good enjoyed by others. Rights acknowledge the distinctness of individuals. Wilson is not Logan, Logan is not Wilson, and neither is merely a placeholder for a social calculation of the net balance of pleasure over pain. Rights limit what individuals can do to each other and, in the context of a political system, limit what the state may do to individuals, even in the name of the greater good.

Modern democracies and supranational legal instruments purport to guarantee many individual rights. The least controversial, the so-called first-generation rights, protect the traditional privileges of citizenship. For example, the Universal Declaration of Rights, adopted by the United Nations General Assembly in 1948, prohibits slavery, torture, arbitrary interference with privacy, and arbitrary arrest and detention. It declares that everyone has the right to life, liberty, security, freedom of movement, and liberty of thought, conscience, and religion. Anyone charged with a crime has a right to a fair and public hearing by an independent and impartial tribunal. More controversial are rights to welfare or economic

[22] Rawls, *supra*, p. 27.

security, including rights to education, housing, health care, and employment, and rights that pertain to communities, such as those of minority
ethnic or religious groups.[23] One reason that first-generation rights are the
least controversial is that they most closely track the underlying moral
intuition that the distinction between persons matters. There are certain
things that other individuals and the government should not be allowed to
do to individuals. Second- and third-generation rights, by contrast, are less
about taking seriously the distinction between persons and more about
guaranteeing a minimal, adequate set of resources and opportunities to
allow all citizens to flourish. This is an important problem, but one less
directly connected with the inviolability and dignity of individuals.

At any rate, the role of lawyers is traditionally understood in connection
with first-generation rights – negative liberties possessed by individuals and
protected against interference by the state. The principle of partisanship
ensures that the client will have her individuality taken seriously because it
is the lawyer's job to assert the client's position without regard to the
interests of others – "at all hazards and costs to other persons," to use
Brougham's language. In criminal cases, it is easy to understand why the
lawyer representing the accused has a duty, as Lord Reid put it, "fearlessly to
raise every issue, advance every argument, and ask every question, however
distasteful, which he thinks will help his client's case."[24] As we will see in
Chapter 7 on criminal defense, there are consequentialist arguments for the
requirement that lawyers provide a vigorous defense to accused persons.
A free society should rightly be committed to minimizing the likelihood
that an innocent person will be convicted of a crime and deprived of his
liberty, property, or even his life. The state has a great deal of power and
considerable resources to dedicate to law enforcement. In addition, criminal defendants are often stigmatized, not only as accused persons, but
perhaps also as members of social groups (e.g., minorities, poor people,
the mentally ill) already suffering from disadvantages. Societies are sometimes gripped with fear of crime, either in general or of specific types of
highly visible crimes. For all of these reasons, there is a significant risk that
judges or juries may be too quick to conclude that a defendant is guilty as

[23] See Jeremy Waldron, "Rights," in Robert E. Goodin, Philip Pettit, and Thomas Pogge,
eds., *A Companion to Contemporary Political Philosophy* (Chichester: Wiley-Blackwell, 2d
edn., 2012).
[24] *Rondel v. Worsley*, [1967] 3 All E.R. 993, 999 (H.L.).

charged. Procedural entitlements, such as the presumption of innocence and the requirement that the prosecutor prove the state's case beyond a reasonable doubt, seek to ensure against wrongful convictions. Criminal defense lawyers operationalize these procedural entitlements by asserting "every issue … every argument" on behalf of their clients.

You can now see that the arguments considered in Chapter 2 were deontological in nature. David Luban's argument based on human dignity (the value on the "morality" side of the bridge) is meant to show that a criminal defendant, or any litigant, has a right to have his or her voice heard. This right is entailed by an understanding of persons as bearers of dignity, which is related to their status as agents who have their own interests and commitments. Similarly, Charles Fried emphasizes that the ethical concept of personhood presupposes free, choosing, valuing entities whose interests are not those of humanity as a whole. (Again, here are echoes of Rawls's criticism of utilitarianism as not taking seriously the difference between persons.) In Chapter 2, we considered the microlevel justification for professional duties and prerogatives. The lawyer in the poker game case, for example, was permitted to put on the testimony of the three friends to support the inference that the defendant was not guilty of the offense charged. In addition, the arguments of Luban and Fried can be employed at the macrolevel to lend ethical support to an adversarial system of adjudication in which the parties are entitled to be represented by advocates who take their position, advance every argument consistent with it, and are relatively limited in the duties they owe to the tribunal, third parties, and the public interest.

Shifting from the micro- to the macrolevel of evaluation means the object of consideration shifts from individual lawyers and their actions to a complex system of institutions, roles, regulations, and duties. Rather than focusing on questions such as "can the lawyer put on the three friends as witnesses and ask them about the poker game?" we are asking whether the lawyer's role in general is justified. At this point, we can remain agnostic about whether one of these evaluative perspectives has priority over the other. Maybe it is possible to flip-flop back and forth between the point of view of the individual case and the perspective of the system as a whole. For the time being, however, we will move, in Chapter 4, to a consideration of the relationship between law and morality at the most general level, through one of the great debates in legal philosophy, between the theories of law known as positivism and natural law.

4 The nature of law and why it matters

4.1 Law, morality, and legal ethics

Lawyers have obligations, stated in officially promulgated codes of conduct and other authoritative sources of law, to do things such as keep their clients' secrets and be effective advocates for their clients' positions. It is therefore quite tempting to try to justify the conduct of lawyers by referring to the law, for example.: "The law requires lawyers not to disclose confidential information." Think about it for a minute, though. The law may create obligations, but it may not follow that it creates *moral* obligations. Suppose someone says, of the lawyer representing the real killer, Wilson, in the wrongful conviction case from Chapter 1, "You did wrong morally by keeping Wilson's secret." it is not necessarily an adequate answer for the lawyer to say, "I had a legal obligation to do so." There is potentially a gap between legal and moral obligation. Perhaps there is a way across that gap (another bridge!), but it has to be made clear whether, and under what circumstances, a legal obligation makes any difference in the domain of morality.

In an article that was somewhat scandalous when it was first published in the *Harvard Business Review*, Albert Carr, a former advisor to US President Harry Truman, heaped scorn on those who argued that businesspeople ought to be guided by the standards of ordinary morality (which Carr identified as the morality taught in religious traditions). Instead, Carr argued, business ought to be understood as a game, like poker, and the ethical norms of business ought to be only to follow the rules of the game.[1] As long as some action is not illegal, it is ethical as long as it complies with the rules of the game, and the game of business, as it turns out, permits a variety of seeming wrongs, including industrial espionage, deceptive

---

[1] Albert Z. Carr, "Is Business Bluffing Ethical?," *Harvard Business Review* (Jan.–Feb. 1968), p. 143–53.

labeling of food products, firing older workers to reduce pension costs, indifference by auto manufacturers to the safety of their products, and the substitution of inexpensive, possibly dangerous ingredients in health care products.[2]

Two things jump out from the Carr article. One is that he never argues for why the business game has positive ethical value that could outweigh the resulting harms. He appeals a closed normative system without making any effort to connect the system and its rules to wider ethical concerns.[3] His analogy with the way the rules of poker legitimate bluffing, which would otherwise be deceptive, fails because poker offers the positive value of enjoyment, permits bluffing because all participants understand it is part of the rules of the game and have equal opportunities to bluff, and does not impose harms on nonparticipants (what economists would call externalities). The second striking feature of Carr's article is that he does recognize that the moral permission to play by the rules of the game ends where a practice is unlawful. Perhaps this is only a prudential point about the unwillingness of businesspeople to risk criminal prosecution or civil liability, but it also suggests that Carr sees some moral value in the constraints provided by the law. "If the laws governing their businesses change ... [business managers] will make the necessary adjustments. But morally they have in their view done nothing wrong. As long as they comply with the letter of the law, they are within their rights to operate their businesses as they see fit."[4] The law is the only connection Carr concedes between the "special ethics" of business and wider moral concerns.

Lawyers have a powerful intuition that the law must make a difference, morally speaking, to the evaluation of their own conduct. To illustrate, consider a classic case.[5] Lender made a loan of $5,000 to his neighbor, Borrower, to help out his struggling business; Borrower signed a promissory note evidencing the obligation, but subsequently filed bankruptcy, extinguishing the debt. After emerging from bankruptcy, Borrower's business

---

[2] Many of the practices Carr describes would be violations of laws established since the article was written in the late 1960s.

[3] Remember the discussion in Chapter 3 of organized crime norms? Not ratting out your friends is a rule within the "game" or practice of belonging to an organized crime family, but without a connection to more general moral considerations, it cannot be said to be a genuine moral obligation.

[4] Id. at 148.

[5] Based, with a few embellishments, on *Zabella v. Pakel*, 242 F.2d 452 (7th Cir. 1957).

eventually flourished, and he became quite wealthy, while Lender's for-
tunes took a turn for the worse after he lost his job. Lender asked
Borrower to repay the loan, and, when Borrower refused, Lender sued,
alleging that Borrower had made a post-bankruptcy oral promise to repay
the debt. Under contract law, an oral promise that Borrower had made to
repay his debts would be enforceable, if it could be proved that he made one.
However, because of an oversight by Lender's lawyer in the bankruptcy
proceeding, the statute of limitations had expired. That means that
Borrower would be allowed (but not required) to assert that too much
time had elapsed between the original default on the loan and Lender's
demand for payment. Asserting the statute of limitations would result in
dismissal of the case, and Lender would therefore receive nothing. Assume
Borrower could easily repay the $5,000 but has directed his lawyer to avoid
repayment by any means necessary. What would you think, *in moral terms*, of
Borrower and Borrower's lawyer if the lawyer relied on the statute of
limitations to have the case dismissed?

The first reaction many lawyers and law students have to this case is that
it is easy. The law provides a procedural defense, the statute of limitations,
and it applies in situations just like this one. There is nothing abusive or
manipulative about this use of a procedural right; Borrower's lawyer is well
within the bounds of the law to rely on the statute of limitations. What
could the ethical problem possibly be? Notice, however, that this response
is talking past the original question. The question was whether Borrower or
his lawyer were morally justified in using the statute of limitations to avoid
repaying a debt that Borrower clearly owed. The legal entitlement to have
the case dismissed means that Borrower was not legally obligated to repay
the loan, but since promises create moral obligations, Borrower remained
morally obligated to repay the loan. One must avoid making the mistake
Carr made in the article about business ethics and assuming that there is
moral value in doing something simply because it is permitted by the rules
constituting a social practice or institution. It may be a good thing that there
is a social institution like the law, which allows people to plan, form stable
expectations, and arrange their relationships with others in a predictable
way. If that is the case, then contributing to the functioning of this institution may be a moral "plus" for Borrower's lawyer and may even outweigh
the moral "minus" of having helped Borrower avoid repaying his debt.
Borrower may not enjoy this moral permission, since he is not acting within

a social role having as one of its aims to sustain an institution that performs a socially valuable function. Borrower may simply be a jerk.

The relationship between law and morality is one of the great questions considered by the philosophy of law, or jurisprudence. When lawyers rely on the legal permissibility of pleading the statute of limitations as a response to moral criticism for helping Borrower avoid a debt he morally ought to repay to Lender, there may be a jurisprudential issue lurking in the background. Morality, or at least considerations of practical reasonableness, may be built in to the concept of law. This assertion, in various forms, characterizes the camp of legal philosophers known as *natural law* theorists. Alternatively, one may be a legal *positivist*, believing there is no necessary relationship between law and morality at the conceptual level. Positivism does not preclude the belief that there are moral reasons to obey the law or to support the functioning of a legal system, or that the requirements of law may correspond with moral duties; the only restriction is that moral considerations cannot be among the criteria of valid law.

Some legal ethics scholars, most notably William Simon, have suggested that legal positivism is linked with an attitude of indifference to the public interest or the interests of nonclients.[6] As we will see in the next section, the connection between a theory of law (positivism) and the attitudes of professionals toward it was one of the central issues in the Hart-Fuller debate. Simon also worries that the sorts of considerations that judges take into account in deciding cases, and which he believes lawyers should also take into account in deciding how to act, cannot be accounted for on a positivist theory of law.[7] That, as we shall see, is one of the points of contention in the Hart-Dworkin debate. For Simon, jurisprudence and legal ethics are inextricably linked. Other legal ethicists are agonistic on basic theoretical questions concerning the nature of law but are more interested in the question to be considered in Chapter 5, which is that, whatever one thinks about the nature of law, is there a moral obligation to obey the law?

It is important to keep in mind that those questions can be separated, and they should be for the sake of clarity. One can ask about the concept of law as a jurisprudential matter, leaving aside

---

[6] See, e.g., William H. Simon, *The Practice of Justice* (Cambridge, Mass.: Harvard University Press 1998), p. 37.

[7] Id. at 38–39. Simon is not keen to endorse natural law either, so he is attracted to the middle-ground position of Dworkin, considered toward the end of this chapter.

questions, for example, concerning the use to which law should be put, the appropriate limits on legal regulation of individuals' lives, the legitimacy or illegitimacy of various patterns of differentiation among people under the terms of legal norms, the conditions under which a regime of law is a just regime, and so forth.[8]

Some scholars believe that those questions, which belong to the domain of moral and political philosophy, are as important as the "pure" issue of the concept of law. Nevertheless, as you read the following discussion of the jurisprudential traditions of positivism and natural law, be sure to distinguish between issues related to the nature or concept of law – or, if you like, the hallmarks of legal validity – and the moral and political issues concerning the obligation citizens have toward the law, the content the law ought to have, or what practical attitudes citizens ought to take toward the law, such as respect, support, and fidelity, or negative attitudes such as resentment, resistance, or disobedience.

4.2   Positivism: simple and sophisticated

Imagine that you have been given the following intellectual puzzle: Give a theoretical explanation of the concept "law" using only empirical facts – that is, observable facts about the world. You can talk about what Parliament does, how many members Parliament has, how they get elected, who enforces the laws subsequently passed by Parliament, when people are likely to get locked in jail, and so on, but you cannot refer to *normative* notions such as duty, right, or obligation. Your theory has to account for as many features of law, a legal system, and the value of legality as possible. (Maybe you can start by making a list: The law involves locking people in jail, allowing for the making of contracts and wills, and regulating conduct; it is administered by officials and enforced by police officers; it is complex, technical, and takes years of study to master; etc.) The reason for the methodological constraint on normative considerations is that positivism in its modern form developed during a time in which the methods of the natural sciences enjoyed tremendous prestige as the best way of arriving at truth. Every discipline, including philosophy of law, aspired to the rigor of

---

[8] Matthew H. Kramer, *Objectivity and the Rule of Law* (Cambridge: Cambridge University Press 2007), p. 143.

scientific methods, which had succeeded by eliminating from theoretical explanations anything that could not be observed, measured, tested, and verified. This "scientism" influenced many developments in philosophy, such as logical positivism in the theory of knowledge, which bears only a distant family relationship with legal positivism.[9] Evaluative terms, such as calling something a "good" law or contending that one had an obligation to obey the law, were to be avoided unless they could be defined in terms of something observable. As we saw in Chapter 3, utilitarians such as Jeremy Bentham defined good in terms of the quantity of pleasure produced, a respectably scientific way to understand the concept of good. This methodological commitment carried over to the theories of law offered by utilitarians working on the philosophy of law, including Bentham and John Austin.

Austin attempted to explain law in purely empirical terms by relying on a few basic concepts: a command, a rule, and a sovereign.[10] In Austin's theory, a *command* denotes an expression of desire backed by an explicit or implicit threat to do something unpleasant if the desire is not carried out, one made by someone with the wherewithal to inflict the harm. A soldier at a border crossing who says "do not go any farther" has issued a command, in Austin's terms. A *rule* is a command that is general, with respect to classes of persons and classes of acts. In the example he gives, a statute passed by Parliament stating that "no corn may be exported" is a rule, whereas a customs officer stopping a particular shipment of corn from being exported is issuing a command. Finally, the *sovereign* is someone whose commands are habitually obeyed by most of the people, most of the time, and who does not in turn habitually obey someone else. Notice that there are no normative terms anywhere in this set of theoretical building blocks. Austin does not say that the sovereign is someone whose commands ought to be obeyed or who has a right to rule. This is in accordance with the basic methodological commitment of legal positivism to exclude normative considerations from the

---

[9] Etymologically, the word positivism (legal, logical, or otherwise) in philosophy is related to its use in the social sciences to denote a theory that aims to describe the world or explain some phenomenon rather than prescribe what ought to be. Economists often protest, for example, that they intend only to give positive explanations of human behavior but are misunderstood as making normative claims about what people have reason to do.

[10] See John Austin, *The Province of Jurisprudence Determined* (London: J. Murray 1832).

explanation of law. With these concepts, then, Austin can define law as a rule (remember, a general command) issued by a sovereign. In modern terms, Austin gave an account that remained faithful to the methodological requirement of the analytic *separability* of law and morality. He also gave an explanation of law entirely in terms of its social sources – here, the command of a sovereign.

Regarding the statute of limitations example, Austin would point out that, regardless of whether it would be a bad thing, morally speaking, for Borrower to avoid paying what he owes to Lender, it is possible to identify a valid law permitting him to do so. Even this simple example poses a problem for Austin, however, because it is not clear how the statute of limitations, creating a procedural defense that a party may assert, can be analyzed as the command of a sovereign. No political official has said to citizens, "You must bring lawsuits within a specified period of time ... or else bad things will happen to you." The statute of limitations provides a defense to a civil action, which itself is an optional way for an aggrieved person to enforce his or her rights. It is much more natural to think of the law as conferring powers on citizens to act in specified ways rather than seek to explain the law exclusively in terms of negative commands of a sovereign that must be obeyed. The modern theory of legal positivism set out by the English philosopher H. L. A. Hart was developed to respond to difficulties such as this in Austin's account of law.

Hart's critique of Austin's theory in his great book, *The Concept of Law*, is a tour de force.[11] He demolishes Austin's account with the simple but powerful rhetorical strategy of asking what features of law and a legal system he cannot account for using the explanatory terms of command, rule, and sovereign. For example, the law does not consist only of directives and prohibitions – do this, don't do that. It also includes tools that allow people to establish rights and duties among themselves (i.e., the law of contracts), direct the disposition of their property after death (the law of wills and trusts), create business entities that pool invested funds and shelter investors from personal liability for the debt of the business (the law of corporations), apply to the government for various types of licenses and permits, and so on.[12] Although Austin might gamely respond that these doctrines

---

[11] H. L. A. Hart, *The Concept of Law* (Oxford: Oxford University Press, 2d edn., 1994) (with Postscript edited by Penelope A. Bulloch and Joseph Raz).

[12] Hart, *supra*, pp. 27–28.

can be redescribed in command-sanction terms – for example, the law of contracts says, "both parties shall give consideration, or they will each be punished by having the contract deemed invalid" – that seems like an extremely artificial way to describe what is actually going on in a contract. Forming a contract or incorporating a business is not conduct that exists apart from law, to which the law may attach sanctions; rather, it is quite literally made possible only by the law.

Another example of a law that cannot be accounted for on Austin's command-sanction model is the set of norms that governs transitions in sovereignty and the extent of legislative and judicial power. Even in a relatively simple situation like a monarchy there are rules of succession specifying who is entitled to ascend to the throne after the ruling monarch dies.[13] In a more complex structure of government, there are myriad rules detailing the qualifications required of legislators, regulating elections, establishing the criteria an enactment must satisfy in order to be a law, and so on. But how can any of those rules be law if law must emanate as a command from the sovereign? Furthermore, Austin's theory cannot account for legal limits on the power of the sovereign, yet one noteworthy feature of many modern legal systems is the accountability of high-ranking government officials for overstepping the legal boundaries of their power.

A related criticism by Hart is much farther reaching. He shows that Austin's theory cannot explain the idea of someone having a *duty* or an *obligation* to follow the law. Hart analogizes Austin's command-sanction theory to a gunman demanding, "Give me your money or I'll shoot." Clearly, no one would call the gunman's command a law, and Austin would protest that his own theory would deny it that label because the command is not general (a rule) and not issued by a sovereign. Nevertheless, Hart's uses of the gunman analogy reveals something deeper: Austin's theory connects with the practical reasoning of citizens in the wrong way. In a somewhat too-subtle use of language Hart notes that someone may feel *obliged* to hand over his wallet to the gunman, but this is different from having an *obligation*.[14] To have an obligation is to be justifiably subject to criticism for failing to do something and to feel oneself as being required to do something, regardless of what one otherwise wishes to do. No doubt many people obey at least some laws only because they fear detection and

---

[13] Id., pp. 53–54.   [14] Id., p. 82.

punishment for disobedience, but there are others who do what the law requires *because* the law requires it – that is, because they have an obligation to do so.

The fear of sanctions is what philosophers call a *prudential reason*. It relates to one's existing self-interest. The law purports to create reasons for action going beyond prudential reasons – that is, to create obligations.[15] An obligation is a reason to which one is bound (in some sense) to conform. The force of the obligation is not contingent upon whether someone is caught and punished for failing to comply with it and does not arise from the external motivation (such as the gunman's threat) used to enforce conformity with the obligation. To use Hartian terminology, Austin's theory cannot account for the possibility that some people take the *internal point of view* toward rules.[16] Accepting rules from the internal point of view means following rules because they are rules, not for reasons external to the rule, such as the fear of being punished. Because people exist who take the internal point of view with respect to rules, and because Austin's theory lacks the conceptual resources to account for this fact, his theory should be rejected.

Hart has a bit of a tightrope to walk here. He wants to use the possibility of people taking the internal point of view as a criticism of simplistic command-sanction theories like Austin's. At the same time, however, he is committed to the methodology of legal positivism and therefore cannot specify that the internal point of view is a *moral* attitude nor can he attempt to differentiate the law of the state from the command of the gunman by appealing to the legitimacy of state law. Legal positivism is committed to the analytic separability of law and morality. It has to be possible to give criteria for distinguishing law from nonlaw and have (at least in principle) no criterion being that some norm is a requirement of morality. The commitment to explanations in terms of social sources is intended to preserve that separability. Significantly (and this is a source of frequent confusion), taking the internal point of view does not mean that one believes herself to be under a moral obligation to obey the law. It only means that one accepts a rule as creating obligations. Confusion arises because law, like morality,

---

[15] This is sometimes called the problem of legal *normativity*. See, e.g., Leslie Green, "Law and Obligations," in Jules Coleman and Scott Shapiro, eds., *The Oxford Handbook of Jurisprudence & Philosophy of Law* (Oxford: Oxford University Press 2002).

[16] Hart, *supra*, p. 56.

purports to impose duties and obligations.[17] However, "obligation," as Hart uses the term, refers to a general class, including obligations of morality, etiquette, rules of a game, custom, and so on.[18] One may be obligated *qua* the rules of rugby union not to pass the ball forward without being subject to moral criticism for making a forward pass. To have an obligation means to be subject to justifiable criticism in the terms of that domain of obligation. So, a rugby player can be criticized in "rugby terms" (and, more importantly, cause his team to lose possession of the ball) for making a forward pass. Insofar as someone has opted to play rugby, he or she is bound by the rules of the game, but these are merely rules within the game – they have nothing to say about conduct that is not part of playing the game of rugby.

The difference between Hart and Austin is not that the former has admitted moral attitudes into his explanation while the latter has not. The difference, rather, is that Hart relies on different social sources – the idea of rule-governed behavior, the internal point of view, and the general notion of an obligation – as opposed to commands and sanctions to explain what is distinctive about a legal system. The result is a theoretical account of law that is superior to Austin's because it can explain something very central to the very notion of law, namely, that it creates obligations. But Hart's theory still leaves a gap between law and morality because legal obligation, for Hart, is *obligation within law*, just as not making forward passes is an obligation within rugby. The status of some norm as *law* says nothing about whether it is prohibited, permitted, or required, all things considered, where those considerations include moral reasons. Going back to the critique of Albert Carr's article on bluffing and other acts of deception by businesspeople, the fact that bluffing is permitted by the rules of poker and may be permitted by the rules of the "game" of business says nothing about whether it is morally permissible. The rules of the game are one thing; morality is another.

One way to understand legal positivism, therefore, is as a system of rules for the "law game" that may or may not overlap with the requirements of morality. At the foundation of Hart's legal system is the convergent, rule-governed behavior of judges. He insists that one particular rule be accepted

---

[17] See David Lyons, *Ethics and the Rule of Law* (Cambridge: Cambridge University Press 1984), pp. 70–71.

[18] See Frederick Schauer, *The Force of Law* (manuscript, forthcoming 2014), § 3.3.

and practiced from the internal point of view, but only by judges. This is the so-called rule of recognition, which directs judges toward certain considerations that bear on the lawful resolution of disputes before them.[19] As we have noted, the Hartian tightrope is that following the rule of recognition is a special kind of obligation for judges that applies by virtue of their social role (call it O_{LEGAL}, a special kind of legal obligation pertaining to judges), but this obligation does not have any necessary connection with morality (O_{MORAL}, an obligation as a matter of morality). A generally accepted modern definition of positivism, hinging on the idea of the rule of recognition, is that "there exists at least one conceivable legal system in which the rule of recognition does not specify being a principle of morality among the truth conditions for any proposition of law."[20] Judges are obligated (O_{LEGAL}) to practice the rule of recognition from the internal point of view, which means that when deciding cases, they must believe that they will be appropriately subject to criticism if they decide the case on the basis of factors not specified by the rule of recognition or do not take into account factors that are specified as law. For example, a legal system's rule of recognition might include the criterion, "any enactment passed by Parliament and given royal assent is law." If a judge ignores a statute that was recently enacted in Parliament and given royal assent, observers will rightfully criticize the judge for not doing his duty properly.

That does not mean, however, that judges are somehow obligated to take morality into account when deciding cases (O_{MORAL}). The criticism is, rather, in terms of the norms governing the practice of judging. The judge will be considered deficient *as a judge* for ignoring the statute but not necessarily be subject to criticism in moral terms.[21] The rule of recognition may, however,

---

[19] Hart, *supra*, pp. 94–95.

[20] Jules Coleman, "Negative and Positive Positivism," in Marshall Cohen, ed., *Ronald Dworkin and Contemporary Jurisprudence* (Totowa, N.J.: Rowman & Allanheld 1983), p. 31.

[21] In Hart's theory, principles of legal obligation, O_{LEGAL}, depend on conventional social practices, such as praising and criticizing others for their actions. The most important principle within the domain of legal obligation is the requirement that judges follow the rule of recognition. On Hart's account of obligations, this means the judge would be justifiably subject to criticism *as a judge* for ignoring applicable legal norms identified as such by the rule of recognition of the judge's legal system. One controversial aspect of Hart's philosophy is that he conceives of moral obligation, O_{MORAL}, as being conventional in the same way as O_{LEGAL} and other conventional rules, such as norms of etiquette and the rules of games like chess or rugby. See Lyons, *supra*, pp. 72–73.

specify that morality *not* be taken into account in deciding cases. If the rule of recognition in a given legal system does not specify a moral principle as among the truth conditions for a proposition of law, the judge cannot use her moral objection to the statute as a reason to consider it as nonlaw. However, there is no reason that the rule of recognition might not direct judges to consider morality as a criterion of legality. In the United States, for example, judges may have to decide a case arising under the Eighth Amendment to the US Constitution, which prohibits "cruel and unusual punishment." The rule of recognition specifies the Constitution as a source of law, but the Constitution seems to make reference to a moral consideration – namely, whether some punishment is "cruel." A legal positivist of an "incorporationist," "inclusive," or "soft" variety would contend that a theory of law is still positivism and not natural law as long as the rule of recognition is a social rule, in the sense that it is practiced by judges.[22] For example, the rule of recognition may give a judge discretion to refuse to grant relief to a party if the party's position is unjust. The statute of limitations example involves a legal defense, but other defenses are *equitable* and can be asserted only if the party has not engaged in wrongdoing. A rule of recognition that acknowledges equitable defenses may thereby permit the judge to make reference to extralegal moral considerations. Other positivists – "exclusive" or "hard" positivists – conversely insist that whether something is law must be ascertained without reference to moral reasoning.[23] Both inclusive and exclusive positivism are compatible with Hart's theoretical commitment to defining a special type of legal obligation that is analytically separable from moral obligation.

A judge can be criticized in terms of her social role as a judge for not following the rule of recognition, but it bears repeating that this is not the same thing as moral criticism. (That is, O_{LEGAL} does not entail O_{MORAL}.) And it is certainly the case that Hart's view carries no implication for the moral reasons an ordinary citizen may or may not have to obey the law. According to Hart, people can obey the law for "a variety of different reasons and among them may often, though not always, be the knowledge that it will be best for him to do so. He will be aware of the general likely consequences of disobedience: that there are officials who may arrest him and

---

[22] Scott J. Shapiro, *Legality* (Cambridge, Mass.: Harvard University Press 2011), pp. 269–70.
[23] Id. at 271.

others who will try him and send him to prison for breaking the law."[24] As
this passage suggests, citizens may accept primary rules of conduct only
from the external point of view, being concerned with them only as a
heuristic for predicting when they will be sent to jail. It is only judges who
are conceptually required to take up the internal point of view with respect
to the law, and even this is not a moral attitude. Boiled down to its essence,
the central claim of Hart-style legal positivism is that taking up certain
moral attitudes (e.g., approval or disapproval) toward the law cannot conceptually be a criterion of legal validity.

Hart gave an intricate and sophisticated explanation of a special type of
obligation created by the law (O_{LEGAL}), but he had relatively little to say about
moral obligation (O_{MORAL}). For this he was hammered by Lon Fuller in the
famous Hart-Fuller debate, which, among other things, focused on the
relationship between legal positivism and the obligation, or at least tendency, of citizens to obey the law.[25] The debate was conducted against the
backdrop of the still fresh sentiment of horror at the inhumanity of the
regime in Nazi Germany during the 1930s and '40s. Interestingly, though,
Fuller did not argue that legal positivism was deficient as a theory because it
could not explain why citizens have a reason to obey the law. Instead, he
argued that the connection between legal and moral obligation is too tight
on a positivist account of law. His view was that positivism made it too easy
for citizens, lawyers, judges, and other officials to infer a moral obligation to
do what the law requires (or a moral permission to do what the law permits)
from the mere fact of a norm having the status of law.

Hart and Fuller both cited the anguished retrospective analysis of
German legal theorist Gustav Radbruch who ascribed some of the
responsibility for the abuses under the Nazis to the acquiescence by
German judges, lawyers, and citizens in the legality of Nazi laws. Hart
writes:

> Radbruch ... had concluded from the ease with which the Nazi regime had
> exploited subservience to mere law – or expressed, as he thought, in the
> "positivist" slogan "law as law" (*Gesetz als Gesetz*) – and from the failure of the
> German legal profession to protest against the enormities which they were

---

[24] Id., p. 114.

[25] H. L. A. Hart, "Positivism and the Separation of Law and Morals," *Harvard Law Review* 71:
593–629 (1958); Lon L. Fuller, "Positivism and Fidelity to Law – A Reply to Professor
Hart," *Harvard Law Review* 71: 630–72 (1958).

required to perpetrate in the name of law, that "positivism" (meaning here the insistence on the separation of law as it is from law as it ought to be) had powerfully contributed to the horrors.[26]

Hart and Fuller had very different reactions to Radbruch's diagnosis. Hart characterized the passivity of the German legal profession as neglect or ignorance of the fundamental insight of positivism: Legality is one thing, morality another. The fact that something is a law says very little about whether one has an obligation to obey it.[27] Fuller, on the other hand, believed it was preposterous to believe that the status of some norm as a law had no effect on the behavior of officials and citizens. In his view, lawyers and judges should have recognized that the Nazi legal system was so *formally* defective that unjust laws did not deserve the label of "law" at all.[28] This is not because they required or permitted grave violations of human rights but because they failed to satisfy criteria such as publicity, nonretroactivity, and consistency.

In a subsequently published book, Fuller elaborated on what he called the "inner morality of law," by which he meant formal features that the law must have in order to fulfill its function of guiding the actions of citizens.[29] Fuller illustrates the formal features of legality with a parable of a decent but clueless king named (conveniently enough) Rex. Rex tried to govern the kingdom by making laws, but each of his attempts at law making only frustrated and confused his subjects. For example, he appointed himself judge over any disputes that should arise among citizens of the kingdom, but he did not decide cases coming before him consistently, on a principled basis. He then tried to systematize all of the decided cases in a code but kept it as a state secret, leaving his subjects without knowledge of the rules governing their conduct. He finally agreed to publish the code, but it proved to be full of contradictory directives, hopelessly vague standards, or requirements that were impossible to satisfy. And so on, until there was a revolution . . .

---

[26] See Hart, *Positivism*, *supra*, p. 617.

[27] Id. at 618: "[E]verything that [Radbruch] says is really dependent upon an enormous overvaluation of the importance of the bare fact that a rule may be said to be a valid rule of law, as if this, once declared, was conclusive of the final moral question: 'Ought this rule of law to be obeyed.'"

[28] Fuller, *supra*, p. 655.

[29] Lon L. Fuller, *The Morality of Law* (New Haven: Yale University Press, 2d ed., 1964).

While on the surface Hart and Fuller were debating the merits of positivism as a theory of law, the subtext of their debate was over the traditional competitor to positivism, natural law. Unfortunately, natural law is perhaps even more widely misunderstood than positivism. Again, it is important to distinguish between a position on the nature or validity of law (what makes some norm "law" and not something else, such as a requirement of morality, prudence, or the rules of a private association) and a thesis about the obligation to obey or respect the law. When talking about natural law, it is easy to mix up these distinct issues. As the following section shows, there may be quite a bit less of a gap than people sometimes think between positivism and natural law as theories concerning the nature or validity of law. Similarly, when it comes to taking a position on the obligation to respect, support, or obey the law, natural law theorists and positivists may not be that far apart. In other words, the unacknowledged subtext of the Hart-Fuller debate had nothing whatsoever to do with the nature of law but is a normative issue having to do with the way law affects reasons for action or, more broadly, the relationship between citizens and the state. As we will see in Chapter 5, the debate over whether there is an obligation to obey the law, which has been going on at least since Plato's dialogue *Crito*, has not turned on whether it is possible to identify valid law without reference to moral considerations. Nevertheless, natural law theory is often misunderstood as making an implicit claim about the authority of law.

4.3   Natural law: classical and modern

"The existence of law is one thing; its merit or demerit another."[30] So John Austin stated the central claim of legal positivism. In doing so, however, he caricatured the central claim of natural law theory. A careful reader of a natural law theorist in the classical tradition, particularly Thomas Aquinas,[31] or a modern philosopher in the natural law tradition such as John Finnis,[32] will have a hard time finding the thesis that a norm counts as a law only if it has moral merit. Indeed, it is hard to read Aquinas and Finnis as being predominantly concerned with the morality of particular laws.

[30] Austin, *supra*, p. 184.
[31] Thomas Aquinas, *Summa Theologica*, sec. 90, in William P. Baumgarth and Richard J. Regan, eds., *Aquinas on Law, Morality, and Politics* (Indianapolis: Hackett, 2d edn., 2002).
[32] John Finnis, *Natural Law and Natural Rights* (Oxford: Clarendon Press 1980).

Aquinas was addressing fundamentally political problems, such as the nature of the public good, aspects of good government, and the grounds for political obligation. Finnis is primarily setting out a method of philosophical analysis of law, not tests for legal validity. No respectable natural law theorist holds the position described by Austin, that whether or not something counts as a law comes down to a case-by-case examination of the justice of that particular would-be law.

The idea of natural law is potentially confusing right from the start because the word "natural" can take on many different meanings in philosophical usage. It can mean:

- Deriving somehow from facts about *human nature*; for example, that we are rational beings or that we have certain intrinsic capacities or needs.[33]
- A standard discoverable by our *natural faculty* of reason or a norm the content and force of which are related to wider norms of practical rationality.
- Relating somehow to a feature of the *natural world*. (Philosophical naturalism is the position that all knowledge is ultimately grounded in the findings of the empirical sciences.)

In all of these usages, there is more commonality than one might have thought between natural law and positivism because the latter term also has a connotation of being concerned fundamentally with facts about the world. Doing natural law theory does not mean relying on obscure metaphysics or the will of God. Many natural law theorists were or are religious believers, but one could construct an entirely secular natural law theory. Indeed, some perfectionist strands of political liberalism are very close to natural law, particularly in the first sense mentioned above.[34]

---

[33] In a quirky science-fiction-style passage Hart speculates that the nature of the concept of law would have to vary if humans were radically different types of beings. If we were like giant land crabs with invulnerable shells and could extract nutrients from the air like epiphyte plants, we would not be vulnerable to attack by others, nor would we compete for scarce resources. The regulation of a society of giant epiphytic land crabs would be different in kind from the regulation of interactions among mutually vulnerable, dependent creatures such as we are. See Hart, *Positivism*, *supra*, p. 623.

[34] Natural law theorist John Finnis contends that it is self-evident that there are basic forms of human well-being, which are life, knowledge, play, aesthetic experience, friendship, practical reasonableness, and religion. See Finnis, *supra*, pp. 86–90. The secular political philosopher Martha Nussbaum defines a similar list of functions or

Aquinas defines law in the following way: "An ordinance of reason for the common good, made by him who has care of the community, and promulgated."[35] Breaking this definition down into elements, a law is (1) something pertaining to reason, that is, it is meant to affect the practical reasoning of its subjects; (2) directed toward the common good (Aquinas will later discuss corrupt rulers who are concerned only with their own good); (3) by one who is empowered to act on behalf of the community ("the whole people"); and (4) promulgated to its subjects. He then defines several different types of law, which are hierarchically ordered:

1. Eternal law – God's law for the governance of the whole of creation.
2. Natural law – our rational perception of and participation in the eternal law.
3. Human law – "determinations" of the natural law; that is, the natural law specified and applied to particular problems.

The crucial step for Aquinas, critical to understanding the authority of law in human communities, is from (2) to (3). In the process of *determinatio* (I am using his Latin term to clearly identify this as a term of art), rulers who are entrusted with the care of the community do their best to understand how the eternal law ought to be specified as concrete rules for the governance of society.[36] We are fallible beings who are bound to err when trying to apprehend God's law; we see only as through a glass, darkly: "[H]uman reason cannot have a full participation of the dictate of the Divine Reason, but according to its own mode, and imperfectly."[37] Moreover, eternal law is at such a high level of abstraction – pertaining, for instance, to the value of human dignity as related to our nature as creatures created in the image of

capabilities that constitute fully human functioning or flourishing. Those functional capabilities are life, bodily health and integrity, imagination and thought, emotion, practical reason, relationships with other humans and other species, play, and control over one's environment. See Martha C. Nussbaum, *Sex and Social Justice* (Oxford: Oxford University Press, 1999), pp. 41–42. Nussbaum is a perfectionist liberal theorist, meaning she is willing to take a stand on what constitutes the good for humans, but she does not begin with a premise about the existence of God. For that matter, neither does Finnis, although he is a religious believer. What Finnis and Nussbaum have in common is commitment to an *objective* account of the good for humans. Good, for both of them, means good in virtue of something other than what people desire, choose, or for which they reveal preferences by their behavior.

[35] Aquinas, *supra*, Q90.   [36] Id., Q95, 2.   [37] Id. Q91, 3, ro1.

God – that it is of very little use in solving the sorts of concrete problems that face lawmakers. All humans may have dignity, but what should a legal system do when a newspaper reports a false rumor, believing it to be true, that causes damage to the reputation of the subject of the report? Does dignity require giving a remedy to the victim, or are there important countervailing values of press freedom that must be taken into account?

Myriad questions such as these must be resolved by *determinatio* in the elaboration of a society's laws. Different societies may even balance competing considerations differently. On the press freedom and defamation example, consider the differing approaches of the United Kingdom and the United States. To take only one aspect of the differences, in the United Kingdom, truth serves as an affirmative defense to an action for defamation, meaning it must be proven by the defendant; whereas, in the United States, falsity is an element of the plaintiff's case on which the plaintiff bears the burden of proof. Both systems believe they are striking a reasonable balance between the interest of an open society with vigorous public media, on the one hand, and the privacy and dignity of individuals on the other. As Aquinas acknowledges, although there may be only one universal truth at the level of general principles, "as to the proper conclusions of the practical reason, neither is the truth or rectitude the same for all."[38] Thus, the same principles of natural law result in different determinations of human law. This is a claim about what human law is: It is a specification, a *determination*, of principles of practical reasonableness made by those who are empowered to act on behalf of a community. Because the content of that society's law is largely contingent on the needs, traditions, and wider norms of that society, there is not a straightforward reading-off process by which rulers translate God's law into human law. No natural law theorist has ever meant to deny that there is a great deal of human creativity and judgment in the making and administration of law.

Notice that in the discussion of natural law we have not yet spoken of any moral duty to obey the law. The reason is this (there is no way to put this nonconfusingly): Natural law is a claim about the *nature* of law; that is, about what conceptually must be true of some norm in order for it to have the status of law. Questions pertaining to the obligation to obey the law really belong to moral and political theory not to analytic jurisprudence. Other

---

[38] Id. Q94, 4.

than philosophers, however, people generally do not ask analytic or conceptual questions about the nature of law in isolation from normative questions such as what attitudes judges, lawyers, and citizens ought to take up toward the law, whether laws create obligations in general, and whether there is a duty to obey particular unjust laws. Just as the conceptual debate between Hart and Fuller rapidly evolved into a normative debate over the obligation to obey the laws of Nazi Germany, a discussion of natural law theory tends to transition into consideration of the status of unjust laws. With respect to unjust laws, the conceptual question one can ask about the nature of law is, "are unjust laws 'laws' at all?" The normative question is, "does one have an obligation to obey an unjust law?" In the remainder of this section, try to keep those questions distinct in your mind.

Borrowing an example from American history, imagine that a duly constituted national legislature enacts a statute, called the Fugitive Slave Act, requiring all citizens to return runaway slaves to their owners.[39] It was enacted pursuant to all of the formalities generally followed (a majority vote in Congress, signed by the president, etc.), promulgated in the law books, enforced by police officers, and, for the most part, obeyed by citizens, even if sometimes reluctantly. I hope it is clear that the action required by the statute is grossly unjust, even though a number of citizens at the time of its enactment believed it was just. What can we say about the Fugitive Slave Act, with respect to both its status (law, nonlaw, or something else) and the way it affects the reasoning of those subject to it, whether judges, citizens, or lawyers? There are several possibilities:

1. Despite being duly enacted, the statute is not a law at all, by virtue of its extreme injustice. The motto *lex iniusta non est lex* – an unjust law is not law – is often taken to be one of the central claims of natural law.
2. Because it was duly enacted, the statute is valid law. However, it need not be obeyed even though it is law. This is the distinction that, according to Hart, the German judiciary had lost sight of under the Nazi regime.
3. A norm loses its status as a law if it is formally deficient in some way, such as having been passed in secret, having retroactive effect, or

---

[39] The example, and much of the discussion that follows, is from Mark C. Murphy, *Natural Law in Jurisprudence and Politics* (Cambridge: Cambridge University Press 2006). The classic study of the behavior of judges deciding cases under the Fugitive Slave Act is Robert M. Cover, *Justice Accused* (New Haven: Yale University Press 1975).

requiring standards of conduct with which citizens are not capable of complying. A norm requiring something immoral, such as helping the authorities recapture runaway slaves, is likely to have one or more of these formal defects and thus not be law.

4. The statute is law, but it is something less than a fully realized law. Just as a duck that is not a strong swimmer is defective as a duck (while nevertheless remaining a duck), or a broken alarm clock is still an alarm clock, the Fugitive Slave Act is defective as law. The impact of defective laws on the reasoning of citizens is an open question.

Position 1 conflates conceptual and normative questions pertaining to law. It ought to be possible to use the word "law" to refer to the Fugitive Slave Act without thereby committing oneself to a position one way or the other regarding the obligation to obey it. No sensible person has ever denied that there are some laws that are so deeply immoral that no one has an adequate reason to comply with them, but they are still laws, conceptually speaking.[40] One may coherently say something like, "Acting pursuant to a law called the Fugitive Slave Act, the sheriff caught the escaped slave Django and returned him to Mississippi." The law may be grossly unjust, but the criticism is nevertheless of an "unjust law," not an "unjust not-law." Some natural law theorists have resisted the sharp distinction between conceptual and normative jurisprudence. Robert Alexy, for example, contends that, in cases of extreme injustice, a norm forfeits its character as law.[41] On Alexy's view, the Fugitive Slave Act would forfeit its character as law.

Position 2 is, of course, legal positivism, represented by Hart's theory. Whether something is a law is a matter of social fact. We can look at the process of enactment of the Fugitive Slave Act and the rule of recognition as currently practiced by judges in a society and conclude that the statute counts as law. It remains an open question, however, whether *all things considered* judges ought to enforce it. They may have an obligation as judges – Hart's special sense of legal obligation – to follow the rule of recognition,

---

[40] See Murphy, *supra*, pp. 9–10.

[41] See Robert Alexy, *The Argument from Injustice* (Oxford: Oxford University Press, Bonnie Litschewski Paulson and Stanley L. Paulson, trans., 2002). Alexy's discussion centers on the position of Gustav Radbruch, which was the point of contention in the Hart-Fuller debate.

but this does not necessarily entail a moral obligation to do so. The right thing to do, all things considered, may be to decline to enforce the statute.[42] In doing so, a judge may be departing from the judicial role or, in some systems, the judicial role may be understood in a way that permits judges to refuse to enforce grossly unjust laws. Either way, the mere fact of being law does not provide a moral reason for a judge to enforce the Fugitive Slave Act or for a citizen to comply with it.

Position 3 is Lon Fuller's idiosyncratic thesis about the relationship between the form of laws and their capacity to create moral obligations. It is open to the criticism that Fuller's formal principles, such as generality, prospectivity, clarity, and publicity, are criteria of effectiveness at governing, not of morality.[43] Again, however, if one is willing to blur the boundaries between conceptual and normative jurisprudence, Fuller's eight ways to fail at making law can be seen as ways of failing at the goal of governing a community through general rules rather than specific directives. "Governance through general rules, unlike managerial direction, presumes a measure of respect for the moral powers of the governed."[44] Unlike the gunman issuing demands backed by sanctions, a lawmaker issues general rules that acknowledge the subjects of law as responsible agents, capable of understanding and responding to reasons. This is not a conceptual definition of law but a normative argument for the desirability of the rule of law over other forms of government. Even so, it is not clear that Fuller's position would warrant concluding that the Fugitive Slave Act was not law because it had none of the formal defects exhibited by a government's failed attempt to make law.

Position 4 is a modern version of natural law theory that recognizes a continuum in degrees of satisfaction of conditions internal to the concept of law. Just as a person can be missing a few hairs but not be bald, a law can be somewhat defective while still being a law. Stated somewhat technically, we can distinguish between the existence conditions and the

---

[42] "Legal positivism is not a theory about the moral duty of judges. Whether judges have a moral duty to apply the law in any given case is a moral question that can only be answered on moral grounds." Andrei Marmor, *Philosophy of Law* (Princeton, N.J.: Princeton University Press 2011), p. 114.

[43] See Lyons, *supra*, pp. 77–78.

[44] David Luban, "Natural Law as Professional Ethics: A Reading of Fuller," in *Legal Ethics and Human Dignity* (Cambridge: Cambridge University Press 2007), p. 110.

nondefectiveness conditions of law (and so also for ducks and alarm clocks).[45] State laws are determinations of the natural law, and there may be more than one reasonable determination of a principle of natural law, particularly in light of the existence of multiple, sometimes competing principles. Remember the example of freedom of the press. There may be incompatible determinations of the principle of human dignity as it applies to public media. Determination *A* is the American approach, favoring a robust conception of free expression over the protection of individual privacy and reputation. Determination *B* is the British approach that, while remaining committed to a free press, offers more protection to individual reputation and privacy. Because both determinations are reasonable and directed at the common good of the community, neither should be deemed defective laws merely because of a disagreement with them as a matter of justice. The Fugitive Slave Act, however, is a defective law because there is no principle of natural law that can be determined in the form of a requirement to return escaped slaves to their owners.[46]

The positivism versus natural law debate tends to be conducted with reference to grossly unjust legal systems, such as that of Nazi Germany or the United States during the time when slaveholding states dominated the national government. Earlier in the chapter, however, we began with the comparatively humdrum case of the statute of limitations. Do the jurisprudential theories we have been discussing have anything to say about cases like that? Maybe they do, if only they would take more seriously the perspective of a participant in the legal system, such as a judge deciding a case, a lawyer advising a client, or a citizen trying to figure out what the law requires. One of the great virtues of the jurisprudence of Ronald Dworkin is that it gives pride of place to rather ordinary, workaday legal issues and the lawyers and judges who have to deal with them. In doing so, he not only admits morality into his theory, but also makes it central to the definition of the concept of law. For Dworkin, law is fundamentally that which interprets and justifies the political acts of a community.

---

[45] Murphy, *supra*, p. 25. Some of Fuller's eight ways to fail at being law can identify respects in which a law is defective, if they illustrate respects in which the law fails to serve as reasons for action for those subject to it. Id. at 34.

[46] See Cover, *supra*, pp. 8–19, for a summary of centuries of condemnations of slavery in terms of natural law.

4.4   Locating Dworkin

Ronald Dworkin's jurisprudence overlaps in many ways with the traditions of positivism and natural law. Dworkin established himself early in his career as a trenchant critic of Hart, but it is unclear whether the position he put forward as an alternative should be considered a variety of natural law. In an early and important paper, Dworkin argued that Hart's theory of law, which emphasizes the social "pedigree" of law, cannot account for the way judges actually decide cases.[47] According to Dworkin, Hart's rule of recognition permits judges to identify some norm as law only on the basis of its manner of enactment or development – for example, a statute enacted by a legislature or the *ratio* of a judicial decision. But judges consider more than the pedigree of a norm; they also take account of "a sense of appropriateness developed in the profession" that identifies certain *moral* principles as bearing on the proper resolution of legal disputes.[48] In his famous example of *Riggs v. Palmer*,[49] the named heir in a will murdered the testator, his grandfather. The court conceded that the will, and therefore the bequest to the murdering heir, were valid under the applicable statute, which set out certain formal requirements for wills. But the court went on to deny the murderer the bequest, reasoning that all laws are constrained by certain fundamental maxims such as, "[n]o one shall be permitted to … take advantage of his own wrong, or to found any claim upon his own iniquity, or to acquire property by his own crime." Although it may be possible for a Hartian positivist to modify the rule of recognition to identify these maxims as being part of the law, doing so does not meet the force of Dworkin's criticism because he contends that it is the *content* of the maxim, not its social source, that makes it relevant to judges and other participants in the legal system. Deciding the murdering-heir case is not like the predicament of judges asked to apply the Fugitive Slave Act. There is nothing unjust about a statute prescribing the requirements for valid wills. Nevertheless, according to Dworkin, judging is a moral act even in a run-of-the-mill case, and a judge should be concerned to reach the decision that accords with principles of justice, not merely social sources of law.

---

[47] Ronald Dworkin, "The Model of Rules I," in *Taking Rights Seriously* (Cambridge, Mass.: Harvard University Press 1977).
[48] Id., p. 40.   [49] 22 N.E. 188 (N.Y. 1889).

Dworkin later developed the argument that the judges in the murdering-heir case were not merely identifying the social sources of law, but were also *interpreting* the law in light of background principles of justice. Discussing the case in *Law's Empire*, Dworkin said that the court in *Riggs v. Palmer* implicitly adopted a theory of statutory meaning, which was that "judges should construct a statute so as to make it conform as closely as possible to principles of justice assumed elsewhere in the law."[50] (Notice that this is a normative theory of judging from which a conceptual theory of law is derived.) Judges, according to Dworkin, should understand their role as contributing to the integrity of a political community. A community characterized by integrity is one in which members treat one another as governed by a coherent set of moral principles – a "common scheme of justice" – to which all are committed by their citizenship in the community.[51] The community is governed by shared principles, "not just by rules hammered out in political compromise." This means that judges have an obligation to look beyond the "particular decisions their political institutions have reached" (identified by their social sources or pedigree) and consider the underlying "scheme of principles those decisions presuppose and endorse."[52] A judge, then, should decide on the outcome and give reasons to support it based on "the principles of justice, fairness, and procedural due process that provide the best constructive interpretation of the community's legal practice."[53] The judge's decision should both fit with past decisions and justify them as part of a coherent system of rights and duties aiming to show the community in its best possible light from the standpoint of political morality.[54] In the murdering-heir case, a judge (or a lawyer seeking to predict a judge's decision) would be unable to determine the content of the law without considering moral reasons such as the wrongfulness of allowing the murderer to receive a bequest under the will.

It is impossible to fully cover here the back-and-forth between Dworkin and positivists of various stripes who have responded to his critiques with modifications of Hart's position.[55] For our purposes, the important thing to notice is Dworkin's rejection of the separability of law and morality, at least

---

[50] Ronald Dworkin, *Law's Empire* (Cambridge, Mass.: Harvard University Press 1986), p. 19.

[51] Id., p. 190. [52] Id., p. 211. [53] Id., p. 225. [54] Id., p. 249.

[55] For an excellent summary, see Scott J. Shapiro, "The 'Hart-Dworkin' Debate: A Short Guide for the Perplexed," in Arthur Ripstein, ed., *Ronald Dworkin* (Cambridge: Cambridge University Press 2007).

from the perspective of a participant in the legal system. A judge deciding a case or a lawyer advising a client must be prepared to offer a constructive interpretation of the community's legal practice, one that includes not only past political decisions – statutes, administrative agency regulations, judicial decisions, and so on – but also the scheme of principles that undergirds and justifies these political decisions. Deciding the murdering-heir case was about doing justice in the moral sense, not just following a rule that distinguished law from nonlaw on the basis of social sources. To see why this matters for the ethics of participants in the legal system, particularly lawyers and judges, we come full circle to the problem at the beginning of the chapter, the statute of limitations case.

Imagine that someone criticized the lawyer representing Borrower, demanding to know how she could help her client "cheat" on a debt he owed. The lawyer responds that Borrower only has legal obligations, as described in the contract with Lender; to which the critic replies that contractual obligations overlap with the moral obligation created by Borrower's promise.[56] The lawyer then takes a different tack and argues that it is not cheating to plead the statute of limitations because the legal system refuses to enforce stale obligations on the theory that, with the passage of time, evidence may be lost and the recollection of witnesses may grow hazy. "But wait," says the critic, "Borrower admits that he owes the money – this is not a case in which a mistaken decision will be reached on unreliable evidence." The lawyer thinks for a moment and offers a second justification for the statute, that people should not have to worry about debts incurred long ago. The critic acknowledges that this argument may have force where an event in the truly remote past has been forgotten by all the participants, but, in this case, it seems like a thin pretext for Borrower to avoid doing what he has known all along was his duty.

A Dworkin-inspired observation is that when people talk about the law, they inevitably refer to the policies behind legal rules. It would be an inadequate response for the lawyer to assert the legal validity of the statute of limitations as a justification for doing something that seems immoral to the critic. Remember the discussion earlier of the article on business bluffing? The author seemed to think it was sufficient to point out that certain forms of deception in business were permissible according to the rules of

---

[56] See Charles Fried, *Contract as Promise* (Cambridge, Mass.: Harvard University Press 1981).

the game. This argument utterly fails to address the possibility that the entire game may be corrupt. A critic of business ethics who points out rampant deception by participants in some market will not be mollified by reassurances that it is all permissible under the rules of the game, unless the critic is given reasons to think that the rules of the game make a difference, morally speaking. Dworkin's theory of law explains why law makes a difference, morally speaking. (Whether a similar theoretical move could be made in business ethics is an interesting question.) According to Dworkin, legal interpretation is necessarily moral in nature, seeking to show the community in its best light from the standpoint of political morality. This means that a lawyer deciding whether it is morally permissible to plead the statute of limitations in opposition to Lender's claim against Borrower would have to decide whether doing so is justified by moral principles such as justice, fairness, or procedural due process.[57]

The legal-moral arguments offered by the lawyer in the little dialogue here are generally taken to be sound, even by scholars who are otherwise fairly skeptical of the Standard Conception of legal ethics.[58] Notice how they blend the identification of a norm of positive law (the statute of limitations), which would presumably be specified by Hart's rule of recognition, with an argument justifying the statute of limitations within the community's scheme of principles. Fairness and procedural due process are both values implicated by the statute of limitations, which is intended to protect against the introduction of unreliable evidence and the litigation of stale claims. It is true that the statute has the effect of defeating a claim for a debt incurred by Borrower and not paid back, but the legal system frequently denies relief to parties with a substantively well-founded claim in order to vindicate another interest, such as efficiency or fairness.[59] A Dworkinian move in legal ethics would thus be to defend the lawyer's decision to plead the statute of limitations as a constructive interpretation of the community's legal system in light of its background moral and political commitments.

---

[57] Dworkin, *Law's Empire*, *supra*, p. 243.   [58] See, e.g., Simon, *supra*, pp. 32–33.

[59] The rules of civil procedure applicable to federal court proceedings in the United States state that they are intended to facilitate the "just, speedy, and inexpensive determination of every action." Pretty obviously, those three goals can be in conflict in many cases.

Where does that leave non-Dworkinians? As the discussion in this chapter has shown, other theories concerning the nature of law leave an open question concerning the practical attitudes that citizens, lawyers, and judges ought to take toward the law. One may be a legal positivist, believing that it is possible to understand the concept of law based on social facts alone, and she may further believe either that (1) there are reasons that people should respect the law and lend support to legal institutions, or (2) there are not such reasons. The same may be true for those who subscribe to some versions of the natural law thesis. The next step in this discussion is therefore to consider what philosophers have had to say about the notions of legal obligation and the authority of law.

5   Legal obligation and authority

This chapter moves from conceptual questions about the nature of law to moral questions about the relationship between citizens and government. The notions of obligation and authority are central to the way we understand the role of law in society. If someone standing on a street corner told you to wear a helmet while riding your bicycle, you would probably reply, "says who?", or something less polite. But if your town council got together and enacted an ordinance requiring bicycle riders to wear helmets within the town limits, you would probably conclude that you now have a reason to wear a helmet, even if you did not think you did before the new law was passed. One way to put this point is that law purports or claims to have *authority* over its subjects, even if sometimes it turns out not to have authority.[1] A legal system claims to issue commands that its subjects regard as binding. The law says bicycle riders have to wear helmets ... so they have to wear helmets. One must do what the law says *because* it is the law.

Authority can be understood as the right to command obedience. H. L. A. Hart criticized John Austin's theory of law for resembling the threat of a gunman: "Hand over your wallet or I'll shoot." The gunman may have power to command the victim to hand over his wallet, but he lacks authority (i.e., the *right* to command action).[2] Remember Hart's distinction between being obliged (the gunman's threat) and having an obligation? An obligation is correlated with a right. If a person or institution, A, does not have a right to rule over another, B, then B does not have an obligation to obey A's command.

---

[1] "[E]very legal system claims that it possesses legitimate authority. If the claim to authority is part of the nature of law, then whatever else the law is it must be capable of possessing authority." Joseph Raz, "Authority, Law, and Morality," in *Ethics in the Public Domain* (Oxford: Oxford University Press 1994), p. 215.

[2] Scott J. Shapiro, "Authority," in Jules Coleman and Scott Shapiro, eds., *The Oxford Handbook of Jurisprudence and Philosophy of Law* (Oxford: Oxford University Press 2002), p. 385.

If *A* has rightful authority over *B*, then *B* has an obligation to obey *A*. The town council may be a legitimate authority within its jurisdiction, in which case bicycle riders would have an obligation to wear helmets.

The word "obligation" is ambiguous.[3] It may refer to something that one has a sufficient reason to do, which may conflict with other obligations, or it may refer to something that one ought to do, "all things considered." The former sense of obligation can be called a *prima facie obligation*.[4] The latter can be called a *conclusive obligation*. A prima facie obligation requires a person to do something unless there is a more compelling reason to do something else. Suppose P., an emergency physician, has promised her daughter to pick her up after softball practice and, having been late in the past, P. made a particularly solemn promise to be on time. The promise creates a prima facie obligation, and, in the absence of a weightier reason for a different action, it also creates a conclusive obligation. But now imagine that on the way to softball practice P. notices someone in serious distress by the side of the road, evidently having a heart attack. With her medical training, she would be able to stop and possibly save the life of the heart attack victim. Many philosophers would contend that P. has an obligation to stop and render assistance and would further contend that this obligation outweighs the obligation created by the promise to P.'s daughter. All things considered, P. ought to help the heart attack victim. Perhaps she owes her daughter a particularly profuse apology for being late once again to softball practice, but in view of the comparative weights of the obligations, P. did the right thing, all things considered. As lawyers would say, prima facie obligations create a presumption in favor of doing something, but the presumption may be overridden or rebutted by stronger reasons to do something else.

Many scholars have contended that there is not even a prima facie obligation, let alone a conclusive obligation, to obey the law.[5] Indeed, there is a prominent tradition in political philosophy denying that citizens have an obligation to obey the law, or at least narrowly confining any

---

[3] See the helpful discussions in A. John Simmons, *Moral Principles and Political Obligations* (Princeton, N.J.: Princeton University Press 1979), pp. 9–12; Margaret Gilbert, *A Theory of Political Obligation* (Oxford: Oxford University Press 2006), pp. 26–42.

[4] That term is from W. D. Ross, *The Right and the Good* (Oxford: Oxford University Press 1930).

[5] See, e.g., Joseph Raz, "The Obligation to Obey the Law," in *The Authority of Law* (Oxford: Oxford University Press 1979).

such duty.[6] The reason for this skepticism about authority is that people are *autonomous*. This means that metaphysically – that is, simply because of the kinds of creatures we are – human beings have the capacity to choose how we should act. We act not whimsically or merely by instinct in response to stimuli, but for reasons, upon which we can reflect and deliberate. We are responsible for our choices only because we can understand and act upon reasons. It is a commonplace of both moral theory and the criminal law (expressed by the common law M'Naghten Rules) that someone who is insane and therefore incapable of appreciating and being moved by reasons cannot be held morally or legally responsible. Someone who can understand and deliberate on reasons, however, has an obligation to take responsibility for his or her actions. Acting at the directive of an authority appears to be inconsistent with taking responsibility for one's actions. "Because the law says so" is a different kind of reason from "because it is the right thing to do." Subjecting oneself to the will of another, including a king or legislator, is the very antithesis of acting autonomously. Autonomy is the refusal to be ruled. An autonomous person may do what someone else tells her to do, but it can never be *because* she was told to do so.[7]

The discussion of autonomy shows that the problem of authority is really focused on cases in which there is no preexisting obligation to do what the law requires. The law prohibits murder and theft, but there are already moral obligations not to kill or steal. The interesting cases are those like the bicycle helmet case, where there are no preexisting moral obligations, or cases in which the law claims to impose duties that conflict with other obligations. In those cases, the law essentially says, "You ought to do this *because* the law says so." Recall the Fugitive Slave Act example from the previous chapter. A well-meaning citizen in the northern United States might believe that there is a moral obligation to assist escaped slaves in making their way to freedom in Canada. The law, however, purports to establish a duty to assist in the capture of the fugitive slave. Must that law be

---

[6] See, e.g., Simmons, *supra*; Robert Paul Wolff, *In Defense of Anarchy* (New York: Harper & Row 1970); M. B. E. Smith, "Is There a Prima Facie Obligation to Obey the Law?," *Yale Law Journal* 82: 950–76 (1973). For a more sympathetic view of political obligation see Kent Greenawalt, *Conflicts of Law and Morality* (Oxford: Oxford University Press 1989).

[7] Robert Paul Wolff, "The Conflict Between Authority and Autonomy," in Joseph Raz, ed., *Authority* (New York: New York University Press 1990), pp. 26–27.

obeyed? Does the fact that the law requires returning fugitive slaves make it the case that someone ought to do so?

The question can be generalized from specific laws to the right of a government to rule over its subjects. In that form, it is often called the question of the *legitimacy* of government.[8] A legitimate government is thought to generate political obligations to comply with the law of one's country. A political obligation is one that pertains to one's citizenship (i.e., membership in a particular political community), generally of a nation-state.[9] In that way, political obligation is different from moral obligation, which applies to all persons insofar as we are autonomous, rational beings. A theory of law may or may not explicitly link the authority of law to the legitimacy of government. A legal system may be generally just, but a citizen may nevertheless have a right to disobey a particular law. Thus, one should be careful to distinguish political questions pertaining to the right of a government to rule over its subjects from a determination of what duties a citizen has, all things considered.

Whether the issue pertains to specific laws, such as the Fugitive Slave Act, or governments in general, and whether the resulting obligation is held to be conclusive or merely prima facie, there are several traditional arguments intended to show that citizens do have an obligation to obey the law. These are the subject of the next section.

5.1 Gratitude

Socrates was sentenced to death for the crime of corrupting the youth of Athens. On the eve of his execution, his friends visited him in prison and

---

[8] See Richard E. Flathman, "Legitimacy," in Robert E. Goodin, Philip Pettit, and Thomas Pogge, eds., *A Companion to Contemporary Political Philosophy* (Malden, Mass.: Wiley-Blackwell, 2d edn., 2012).

[9] The particularity of political obligation is one of its puzzling features. When I moved from the United States to New Zealand for six months, I had some obligations vis-à-vis the laws and institutions of New Zealand, such as obeying the law and paying taxes, but I did not have others, such as voting in elections and serving in the military (in the extremely unlikely event that the government of New Zealand would institute a draft). This is true notwithstanding that I reasonably believe it to be the case that the political institutions of New Zealand are at least as just as those of the United States. Citizenship in the United States is morally relevant to some of my obligations, but not others. Thus, political obligation cannot depend on features such as whether a country's political institutions are just. See Simmons, *supra*, pp. 32–35.

urged him to try to escape, pointing out the injustice of his conviction and sentence and the tremendous loss his death would represent, both to his friends and to the city. But Socrates responds that he should not respond to a wrongful conviction by doing wrong to the laws of Athens, which had given him life, educated him, and given good things to him and his family. He had an opportunity to leave the city upon becoming an adult but, having chosen to remain and receive the benefits of its laws, he was obligated to obey them. The attitude he ought to take toward the laws is gratitude, not defiance.[10] As the personified laws argue to Socrates, disobeying is wrong because, among other things, the laws are like parents to the citizens of the city.[11] As a child owes an obligation to support his or her parents in various ways, a citizen likewise owes an obligation to support the government. One aspect of that support would be obeying the laws enacted by the government.

Hardly anyone today would analogize the laws, or the government, to his or her parents, but it is still the case that governments provide substantial benefits to their citizens. Like the obligation of gratitude one owes to one's parents, it may be the case that the citizens of a beneficent government owe something in return for providing safety, education, a clean environment, and other benefits.[12] The obligation is one of reciprocation. But there are several well-known problems with the argument from gratitude.[13] One is that A has an obligation to be grateful to B only when B has acted to benefit A, but in an actual society many laws enacted by B are not for the benefit of A, but for other people, including perhaps a powerful faction upon whom B depends to remain in power. In the example of the Fugitive Slave Act, the law was enacted to benefit slave owners in the southern United States – a crucial interest group for southern office holders to be sure, but not for the northern citizens who were purportedly obligated to return escaped slaves to their owners. It would be bizarre to assert that northerners who opposed slavery should express gratitude to the government by assisting in the capture of escaped slaves.

---

[10] Plato, "Crito," Hugh Tredennick, trans., in Edith Hamilton and Huntington Cairns, eds., *Plato: The Complete Dialogues* (Princeton, N.J.: Princeton University Press 1961).

[11] Id., 51e.

[12] For a modern version of the argument from gratitude see A. D. M. Walker, "Political Obligation and the Argument from Gratitude," *Philosophy and Public Affairs* 17: 191–211 (1988).

[13] See Smith, *supra*, p. 953; Simmons, *supra*, ch. VII.

Another objection is that, even assuming A has an obligation to be grateful to B, it does not follow that the proper way for A to manifest this gratitude is to do whatever B says. The obligation to obey the law is a rather stringent one, and A may discharge whatever duty of gratitude she has by performing acts short of obeying the law. For example, A may engage in routine, ritualized performances such as saluting the flag or singing God Save the Queen, or she may do something requiring a greater sacrifice, such as paying her fair share of taxes. In other words, it is unclear how to specify the content of the obligation that counts as reciprocation. Finally, although a person may owe an obligation of reciprocation to another person, the moral content of this type of obligation, which typically arises in the context of interpersonal relationships, may not translate into a context in which the benefits are provided by institutions, such as legislatures, administrative agencies, and enforcement officials.[14] For these reasons, even if citizens have a reason to feel grateful to their government for providing certain benefits, gratitude does not underwrite a duty of obedience to the law.

5.2   Consent or social contract theories

Perhaps no idea is more prominent in Western political thought than the claim that the legitimate authority of the state is derived from the consent of those living under it. The influential view of John Locke, from his *Second Treatise on Government*, is that political authority can flow only from the consent of the governed. (American readers will recognize that phrase from the Declaration of Independence.) Locke insisted that all people are naturally born free, not subject to the will of any other person.[15] The only law to which people are naturally subject is the law of reason.[16] In fact, freedom depends on reason – we are free only to the extent that we are rational and can understand how we should act. We are subject to the limitations of morality, but we are not bound by any other constraint on our freedom, and, in particular, we are not under the arbitrary will of anyone else. At the same time, we are also naturally social beings and desire to live and work together with others. We may be naturally free, but the enjoyment of that freedom is insecure.[17] Others may threaten us with

---

[14] Simmons, *supra*, p. 187.

[15] John Locke, *Second Treatise of Civil Government* (1690), ch. IV, sec. 22.

[16] Id., ch. VI, sec. 57.   [17] Id., ch. IX, sec. 123.

physical harm or the loss of our property. Thus, we leave the state of nature and voluntarily enter into civil society by giving up part of our "uncontrolled enjoyment of all the rights and privileges of the law of nature"[18] in exchange for the benefits of civil society. These benefits include the law – established and settled in advance and administered by impartial judges with the power to enforce rightful judgments.[19]

Locke's argument nicely reconciles the authority of law with the autonomy of citizens through the medium of consent. Free, autonomous persons can obligate themselves by performing an act indicating their willingness to be bound. The ethical significance of promising and the legal institution of contracts can both be understood in this way. People who know what is in their own best interests ought to be free to obligate themselves through consensual acts like promising. Moreover, a promise may be made conditional, so that the surrender of liberty to a sovereign is not absolute and irrevocable but depends on the sovereign's performance of its end of the bargain, such as ruling justly.

The problem with social contract as a theory of political obligation is that – well, where is the contract? David Hume argued that virtually every actual government was founded "either on usurpation or conquest, or both, without any pretence of a fair consent or voluntary subjection of the people."[20] Moreover, how would one account for the authority of law over disenfranchised citizens, such as the women, slaves, and foreigners in Athens who were bound by Athenian law despite having no voice in its government?[21] A social contract theorist might respond that the bit about leaving the state of nature and voluntarily giving up our natural rights is a fiction. Other than immigrants who become citizens by taking an oath of allegiance to their new country, most citizens have never expressly agreed to become subject to the authority of the institutions of a country but were simply born there. Rather than appealing to the actual consent of citizens, which Hume rightly points out was never given, a theorist may therefore rely on hypothetical or tacit consent. Perhaps by remaining voluntarily in the country of one's birth and receiving the benefits of its laws, a citizen tacitly consents to be bound by those laws.

---

[18] Id., ch. VII, sec. 87.   [19] Id., ch. IX, secs. 124–26.

[20] David Hume, "On the Original Contract," reprinted in Ernest Barker, ed., *Social Contract* (Oxford: Oxford University Press 1947), p. 151.

[21] Id., p. 153.

Tacit consent theories have their own well-known difficulties. In general, tacit consent is that which is given by remaining silent when presented with an option. It still must be genuine consent, intentionally given – the only modification made to social contract theory is that consent may be inferred from silence under appropriate background conditions, as well as manifested by putting it into words.[22] To constitute consent, a person's silence must be given under circumstances in which it is clear that consent is called for, that silence will constitute consent, and that means of dissent are available, capable of being performed at relatively little cost, and will be considered, and that lack of consent will not be an occasion for retaliation against the dissenter.[23] The acts that are generally taken to signify consent to be bound by state laws do not satisfy these conditions. In fact, as critics since Hume's time have pointed out, governments often secure the appearance of consent by some combination of force, fraud, and relying on relatively unthinking obedience to whomever happens to be in power. People may not perceive that their allegiance depends on their consent, and so they may simply obey the law out of habit or a misplaced sense of reverence for the government. Failure to exercise an exit option does not constitute tacit consent because many citizens may lack the material resources, foreign-language ability, in-demand job skills, and other prerequisites to emigrate from the country of their birth, or they simply may prefer putting up with a lousy government to leaving their friends and family to settle in a new country.

Locke attempted to infer tacit consent from a wide variety of ways in which people actively or passively participate in a society:

> [E]very man that hath any possession or enjoyment of any part of the dominions of any government doth thereby give his tacit consent, and is as far forth obliged to obedience to the laws of that government, during such enjoyment, as any one under it, whether this his possession be of land to him and his heirs for ever, or a lodging only for a week; or whether it be barely traveling freely on the highway; and, in effect, it reaches as far as the very being of anyone within the territories of that government.[24]

Locke's account does not require that someone remain silent under circumstances in which others reasonably can infer that the silence was intended

---

[22] Arthur Isak Applbaum, *Ethics for Adversaries* (Princeton, N.J.: Princeton University Press 1999), pp. 116–20.
[23] Simmons, *supra*, p. 80–81.   [24] Locke, *supra*, ch. 8, sec. 119.

to communicate consent. Rather, any receipt of the benefits of government is taken to constitute consent. This is stretching the notion of consent to its breaking point. Binding consent cannot be given unintentionally, and many of the acts cited by Locke, such as owning property and traveling on the highway, are not intended to signify consent. Many of the acts involve the receipt of quite trivial benefits from which stringent obligations are said to follow. Breathing clean air within the territory of a state is undoubtedly a benefit, but is one thereby obligated to perform military service if commanded by the government? Moreover, one may own property within the territory of a tyrannical government and, on Locke's account of tacit consent, one would thereby have consented to be ruled by the tyrant.[25] But Locke clearly maintained that the power of a government constituted by the consent of its subjects can never extend beyond protecting the "peace, safety, and public good of the people."[26] People retain natural rights that cannot be infringed by governments, such as the right to protection of their property and freedom of religion. Thus, neither express nor tacit consent may legitimate a government that infringes the natural rights of its people.

Perhaps it is the case that legitimacy derives from the quality of a cooperative arrangement entered into by free and equal people, not from the mere fact of consent. Along these lines, a more modern version of consent theory relies on the *hypothetical* consent of citizens. Hypothetical social contract theory, best exemplified by John Rawls's 1971 book, *A Theory of Justice*,[27] seeks to determine what reasonable, free, and equal persons would agree to in an imaginary original bargaining position. Modern hypothetical social contract accounts generally begin with conceptions of rationality or reasonableness and rely on principles of rational choice to derive constitutional principles for the regulation of the institutions of government and a civil society. Rawls's well-known thought experiment involving the original position and veil of ignorance generates principles of justice but leaves open the question of obligation. Government institutions may be

---

[25] Simmons, *supra*, pp. 84–85 (discussing Hanna Pitkin, "Obligation and Consent - I," *American Political Science Review* 59: 990–99 [1965]).

[26] Locke, *supra*, ch. IX, sec. 131.

[27] John Rawls, *A Theory of Justice* (Cambridge, Mass.: Harvard University Press 1971) (revised edition published 1999). For an accessible summary of Rawls's thought, see Samuel Freeman, "John Rawls - An Introduction," in Samuel Freeman, ed., *The Cambridge Companion to Rawls* (Cambridge: Cambridge University Press 2003).

just, but does that alone create an obligation to obey the law? Interestingly, it was Rawls himself, in an earlier influential paper, who proposed one way of answering that question in the affirmative.

5.3 Fairness

Rawls and H. L. A. Hart both proposed that a moral obligation to obey the law may be grounded in considerations of fairness to one's fellow citizens.[28] The principle of fairness does not require that anyone give express or implied consent to be obligated. Rather, the fair play principle demands that we do our share to sustain a reasonably just scheme of social cooperation from which we willingly benefit and not free-ride on the efforts of others. Illustrations of the obligation deriving from the fair play principle generally involve small-scale cooperative enterprises. Suppose, for example, the residents of a small town through which a busy highway passes are troubled by the litter left by travelers. Most of the residents meet publicly and agree to share the work of cleaning up litter, with each resident choosing a weekend day to perform the work. Jones was out of town and did not attend the meeting; thus, he did not consent to the work-sharing arrangement. Nevertheless, if he benefits from the newly beautified condition of the town, it would be unfair to his neighbors if Jones refused to do his share. Jones therefore has an obligation to take a day to clean up litter.

The argument from fairness avoids relying on actual or tacit consent. Jones did not attend the meeting and agree to the work-sharing arrangement, nor did he remain silent under circumstances in which silence would be understood as a manifestation of consent. But there are still conditions that must be satisfied before Jones will be obligated to pick up litter. First, he must have voluntarily accepted the benefits of the cooperative scheme. Second, it must be the case that the benefits enjoyed by Jones and his neighbors would be lost if everyone failed to do his or her share of the work. Third, it must be possible to free-ride on the efforts of others; that is, the benefits of the scheme are still available to Jones even if he sits around watching television on the day appointed for his participation. The upshot of the third condition is that cooperation is unstable. If

---

[28] See H. L. A. Hart, "Are There Any Natural Rights?," *Philosophical Review* 64: 175–91 (1955); John Rawls, "Legal Obligation and the Duty of Fair Play," in Samuel Freeman, ed., *John Rawls: Collected Papers* (Cambridge, Mass.: Harvard University Press 1999).

Jones knows that most of the others will do their part, he will still be able to benefit from the cooperation of others even if he does not do his share of the work. It is this possibility that creates the obligation to cooperate. It would be unfair to the other residents if Jones voluntarily accepts the benefits of the cooperative scheme without doing his part. The duty to do his share follows from the sacrifice his fellow residents made for the benefit of all, including Jones.

You will not be surprised to learn that numerous questions have been raised about the fair play principle as a source of obligation. For one thing, what counts as the voluntary receipt of benefits? While it might be a good thing to have litter-free streets, Jones does not really have any choice in the matter. The neighbors came up with the arrangement and, in effect, presented it to Jones as a fait accompli. There is a difference between benefitting and accepting benefits.[29] Relying on Jones's continued residence in the neighborhood as evidence of his voluntary acceptance of benefits runs into the same difficulty we saw previously with respect to tacit consent theory. In the absence of a practical, relatively costless exit option, continued residence in a territory does not constitute consent to the receipt of benefits. That may be a feature, not a bug, of fairness-based accounts of obligation. The principle of fair play is meant to serve as a ground of obligation even in the absence of consent (actual or tacit). It nevertheless seems that members of a community may in some cases be compelled to pay for something they would not have considered a benefit if they had been given the opportunity to be heard on the matter.

> [S]uppose my neighbors have mowed a shortcut through a common meadow. I was more advantaged by the open meadow – I do not like the foot traffic, I did not want to disturb the flowers or rabbits. Now that there is a shortcut, I use it, rather than walk around the long way, because what I valued about the undisturbed meadow has already been ruined .... Do I violate the fair-play principle by refusing to pay my share [for the upkeep of the path]? I think not. The venture was not organized for *my* advantage, and my preferences and interests are frustrated by its existence.[30]

The intuition behind this example is that "others should not be able to *force* any scheme they like upon us, with the attendant obligations."[31] But forced or not, the scheme did produce a shortcut through the meadow, which the

---

[29] Simmons, *supra*, p. 107.   [30] Applbaum, *supra*, p. 128.   [31] Simmons, *supra*, p. 121.

dissenter voluntarily used. Is it thereby a benefit, and the user a free-rider for not paying for its upkeep?

One way to revise the principle of fair play to protect the interests of dissenters and innocent bystanders is to limit the obligation to support the scheme of those who actively participated in it. The relevant distinction is therefore not benefitting versus accepting benefits, but benefitting from a cooperative scheme versus participating in one. The principle of fair play may bind only those beneficiaries who are also participants in some significant way. "[M]erely being a member of some group, other members of which institute a scheme, is not enough to make one a participant."[32] Under this amendment to the fair play principle, if most of the residents of a town concoct a scheme to gather litter from the highway, Jones is not bound by the principle of fair play, even though he is a resident of the town. But the amendment leaves out the important insight that free-riding, by voluntarily accepting benefits while not contributing to their production, is unfair to those whose sacrifice made the benefits possible. Jones would be a bit of a jerk if he enjoyed his beautiful town without doing his part to clean up litter off the streets. Thus, one might further amend the fair play principle by seeking to identify a middle-ground notion of *accepting* benefits, one that lies somewhere between merely receiving benefits (too weak) and actively participating in the scheme to produce benefits (too strong). The person who walked on the newly mown path through the meadow has arguably voluntarily accepted the benefit of the path, even though he would have preferred to leave the meadow in its natural state.

Whatever you think of the principle of fair play as applied to small-scale cooperative schemes, it runs into real difficulties when a theorist attempts to translate it into a ground of political obligation in a large-scale society.[33] If we are resistant to binding people to support a scheme that has been thrust on them without their voluntary acceptance of benefits, it will be difficult to generalize a political obligation to those who were merely born into a particular society and had no real choice regarding the acceptance of benefits. I breathe clean air thanks to my national and local governments, but I have no real choice in the matter. I may even have beliefs and attitudes like those of Socrates in the *Crito* – gratitude to the government and its laws for making available the benefit of clean air – but many of my fellow

---

[32] Id., p. 123.   [33] Id., pp. 138–39; Smith, pp. 957–58.

citizens do not. They regard the burdens of government to be excessive (in terms of cost and restrictions on liberty) relative to the benefits provided. They may believe, rightly or wrongly, that there are market-based mechanisms that would do a better job of protecting the environment than government regulation, or they may believe (again, rightly or wrongly) that some of the restrictions on emissions imposed by the government are not justified by a rigorous analysis of their economic costs and benefits. These dissenters do not voluntarily accept the benefits of government but have the products of this large-scale cooperative scheme thrust upon them. If we call them free-riders, we are really saying that the principle of fair play extends to anyone who *receives* a benefit traceable to the activities of government, regardless of their attitude toward receipt of the benefit. A principle that expansive proves too much.

5.4 Associative obligations

The fair play principle may not capture exactly what is wrong with disregarding democratically enacted laws, but there does seem to be something about membership in a community that creates an obligation toward other members and to the community itself. A more modern theory of legal obligation takes membership in a community as fundamental. When we talked about theories of the nature of law in Chapter 4, we considered Ronald Dworkin's view that a judge interpreting the law was required to discern a coherent set of principles about the rights and duties of citizens in a particular political community in light of that community's fundamental moral commitments.[34] The word "community" is very important for Dworkin, and elsewhere he uses the self-consciously old-fashioned word "fraternity" to locate an ideal of mutual respect and concern among community members.[35] It may be the case that people have simply found themselves thrown together in close proximity. They may even consent to give up part of their natural liberties in exchange for protection by a powerful ruler, as imagined by Hobbes or Locke.[36] Dworkin asks whether this

---

[34] Ronald Dworkin, *Law's Empire* (Cambridge, Mass.: Harvard University Press 1986), p. 255.

[35] Id., p. 206.

[36] The political theory of Thomas Hobbes begins with the observation that, in the state of nature, each person is the judge of the rightness of his or her own actions. Everyone

collection of individuals might ask a deeper question, namely, what follows from the self-evident truth that "each person is as worthy as any other [and] each must be treated with equal concern according to some coherent conception of what that means"?[37] We could assume that people behave selfishly and simply try to maximize the satisfaction of their preferences. That is certainly the view of Hobbes, but this sort of community would manifest a failure of mutual concern among its members. Dworkin calls such a thin association a "rulebook community" and argues that it is inferior to a fraternal or genuinely associative community. Only laws adopted and interpreted with reference to a coherent scheme of moral rights and duties properly express the inherent dignity and equality of all citizens. Only those laws can claim moral legitimacy.

Associative obligations are "antivoluntarist," meaning an intentional act such as manifesting consent or voluntarily receiving benefits is not required in order to be bound by the law. In this way, they harken back to Socrates' analogy, in the *Crito*, between his obligation to his family and to the Laws of Athens. We are born into a family and owe obligations to other family members; we are born into a political community and likewise owe obligations to our fellow citizens, one of which is to obey the laws of the community. More than the mere accident of birth into a particular community, the force of associative obligation is thought to derive from participation in a shared history, which is manifested in the laws of a community. As a result, associative obligations are also particular. For better or worse, the Fugitive Slave Act is an aspect of my history as a citizen of the United States, just as the Treaty of Waitangi is a unique aspect of the political history of

---

agrees that he or she has the right of self-defense against attack by others, but the extent of that right and the occasions of resort to it are subject to disagreement, and this disagreement leads to instability and violence. The only thing people can agree on is that, because everyone desires the security of his or her own body and property, and because it would be absurd to believe that self-preservation is more likely in a state of war than in a state of peace, it is necessary for everyone to give up his or her natural right of self-defense (and the corresponding right to judge whether an act of self-defense is right or wrong) and accept the judgment of a common authority – the sovereign. Conflict in the state of nature arises from disagreements among people over what constitutes a danger and the extent of one's right to self-defense. Therefore peace may be established by preferring the judgments of a common authority to each individual's own judgments. See the helpful discussion in Richard Tuck, "Hobbes," in *Great Political Thinkers* (Oxford: Oxford University Press 1992).

[37] Dworkin, *supra*, pp. 213–14.

New Zealand. The legacy of slavery in the United States and the binational constitution of New Zealand as a Maori/Pakeha partnership cannot help but influence the way citizens, lawyers, and judges approach legal issues touching on the rights of a minority group within the society. As an American citizen (and lawyer), it makes a difference that, as a historical fact, my community has adopted a particular scheme of rights and duties.[38] That history is, in a sense, thrust upon me just as Socrates found himself born into his family and into the city of Athens.

The force of an associative obligation need not derive only from shared history. A community is also constituted by jointly manifested attitudes of commitment to a common project.[39] Joint commitment is not the same thing as the social contract. It is, rather, a shared sense of "us-ness," of thinking and speaking in the first person plural as a participant in a common undertaking, a belief that we're all in this together. If a problem arises that implicates the rights and duties owed by community members to each other, it is *their* problem, jointly. If two people disagree over the use of a common resource, or one person does something that another believes to be harmful to her interests, the solution to the controversy should proceed from the point of view of the community of which everyone is a member – a community that recognizes that, whatever the content of the solution, it ought to be arrived at by a process that is as respectful as possible of the equal entitlement to respect and concern of all affected persons.[40] Scott Shapiro has helpfully invoked the logic of planning to explain the value of the rule of law.[41] Communities face problems that need to be addressed from a common point of view. Members of the community desire norms to guide, organize, and monitor the behavior of individuals and groups within the community.[42] The law permits the community to settle matters that were in dispute and establish a set of norms for the guidance of community members. The simple logic of planning dictates that, henceforth, members of the community should not deliberate on their own about what is to be

---

[38] Id. at 211.

[39] See, e.g., Margaret Gilbert, "Group Membership and Political Obligation," *The Monist* 76: 119–31 (1993).

[40] I made an argument along these lines in W. Bradley Wendel, *Lawyers and Fidelity to Law* (Princeton, N.J.: Princeton University Press 2010).

[41] Scott J. Shapiro, *Legality* (Cambridge, Mass.: Harvard University Press 2011).

[42] Id., pp. 200–03.

done but should consult the plan for guidance.[43] The law of the community therefore is morally valuable to the extent that it solves a problem common to all members of the community – namely, the headache and cost of relying on other, less efficient modes of ordering.[44]

Critics of associative theories of obligation would point out that the problem we begin with is the tension between autonomy and authority. It is an abdication of our moral agency, a failure of responsibility, acting (as Sartre would say) in bad faith, to allow ourselves to be ruled by another. That is just as true if the "other" is a vague collective called "the community" as it would be if the ruler is an absolute monarch. Social contract and fairness theories at least have the virtue of locating the force of political obligation in a voluntary decision by an individual to consent to giving up liberty or to accept the benefits of a cooperative arrangement. Associative obligations seem to require a great deal from unwilling participants who happen to wind up in a particular group purely as an accident of history and geography. Moreover, it may be the case that obligations arise within families or small groups, where the ties between people are direct and personal, but these types of relationships are atypical in a large-scale political community.[45] Most of our interactions are at arm's-length, so to speak, not with people to whom we feel any real personal ties of commitment. What we owe them are thin duties, such as refraining from injuring or taking advantage of them in particular ways, not thick duties such as equal care and concern. Finally, to adapt a criticism that has been leveled against the obligation from gratitude, it may be the case that part of one's identity is membership in a political community (being an American, a New Zealander, etc.), but it does not follow that the most appropriate way to acknowledge that membership is to follow the laws of whatever government happens to be in power at the time without regard to independent normative considerations such as the justice of those laws.

The fascinating thing about the issue of obligation is that, notwithstanding some very persuasive criticisms of the arguments for political obligation made by thinkers including Hume, Robert Paul Wolff, John Simmons, and Joseph Raz, many people continue to believe it makes a difference that something is lawfully required. There is actually a New York State law

---

[43] Id., p. 275.   [44] Id., p. 213.

[45] A. John Simmons, "Associative Political Obligations," *Ethics* 106: 247–73 (1996), pp. 256–57.

requiring that all bicycles be equipped with a horn or bell, and I feel a vague sense of guilt that my bicycle is not so equipped. In my view, it is a stupid law because I can get the attention of pedestrians (surely the point of the law) much more effectively by shouting than by ringing a little bell, but nevertheless I believe that I am doing something wrong by not having the bell because it is the law. Granted, this is a fairly trivial variety of wrong-doing – it does not keep me awake at night, nor motivate me to buy a bell. Still, it is hard to shake the feeling that I have an obligation to do what the law requires, despite being well acquainted with the criticisms of Wolff, Simmons, Raz, and others.

The discussion of reflective equilibrium in Chapter 2 suggests that if we generally have an intuition that there is an obligation to obey the law, but theoretical considerations suggest the opposite conclusion, there are two options. One is to reject our intuitions as inadequately supported, perhaps also seeking to educate citizens that they do not have an obligation to obey the law. The second option is to continue to refine our theories in the hopes of bringing them into better alignment with our intuitions. One possible theoretical refinement is to explore the possibility that multiple, partially overlapping grounds of obligation may be at work or that the true ground of obligation is some kind of hybrid of consent, gratitude, fairness, and asso-ciative theories.[46] Theories do not have to be all-or-nothing. All of the argu-ments given in the preceding section have something in their favor. Socrates alluded to many of them in the *Crito*, and they continue to be discussed 2,500 years later. You may be convinced that there is no obliga-tion, not even a weak prima facie one, to obey the law. That's okay. Hang on to that feeling and think about what effect there would be, if any, on the role of lawyers and judges if people did not have an obligation to obey the law. The following chapter, however, will shift the burden of proof. Assume for the sake of argument that there is an obligation to obey the laws of a reasonably just legal system. When would that obligation run out? Most people will answer, "when the law is unjust." Chapter 6 considers the problem of unjust laws and legal systems and the responses of civil disobe-dience and conscientious objection.

---

[46] See the suggestion in Richard Dagger, "Political Obligation," *Stanford Encyclopedia of Philosophy*.

6 Unjust laws and legal systems

Consider the predicament of Captain Vere in Herman Melville's novella *Billy Budd*. Billy, the protagonist, is a good but simple sailor who is wrongfully accused by the malevolent petty officer Claggart of conspiring to mutiny. Suffering from a speech impediment and thus unable to speak in his own defense, Billy strikes Claggart and kills him. Vere believes he has no choice but to convene a court martial to consider the capital charge against Billy of striking a superior officer during wartime. Many readers of Billy Budd are not aware that the character of Captain Vere was modeled on Melville's father-in-law, Chief Justice Lemuel Shaw of the Supreme Judicial Court of Massachusetts, who was renowned for his opposition to slavery yet was the author of several judgments enforcing the Fugitive Slave Act.[1] Melville clearly means his readers to see Vere as a wise, humane, decent officer. At the same time, he has Vere represent the harshness and rigidity of the law in contrast with considerations of justice. Billy was innocent, framed by Claggart, and Vere knew of his innocence, but Vere nevertheless persuades the other officers to order Billy's execution by reminding them that leniency might encourage mutiny in the Royal Navy during wartime.

Like the fictional Captain Vere, the real Justice Shaw was a righteous man, yet he saw no alternative to following the law and sending fugitive slaves back to their owners. In Justice Shaw's eyes, the Fugitive Slave Act, however unjust, was a regrettable necessity in a nation sharply divided over the question of slavery; it was a political compromise that averted the far worse outcome of civil war (which, of course, came in the end anyway). Agree or disagree with Justice Shaw's reasoning, most historians see him as a decent person faced with a genuine conflict of obligations, not an Eichmann-type official mindlessly serving as a cog in a monstrous

[1] See Robert M. Cover, *Justice Accused* (New Haven: Yale University Press 1975).

machine.[2] Like Captain Vere, Justice Shaw believed he had an obligation to follow the law, despite the clear injustice of the cases before him.

Your attitude toward the Standard Conception of legal ethics, in which lawyers can displace moral accountability to the legal system rather than accepting personal moral responsibility for their actions, is likely to depend on whether you believe the law is a valuable social institution or whether it is merely another means through which the powerful entrench their domination over the powerless.[3] To put the point very generally, lawyers believe they can do justice *through* law, by playing their part in system that, by and large, achieves some good in society. If you are inclined to believe that the existing political and legal institutions in society are more productive of hardship, oppression, inequality, and injustice than the protection of human dignity, autonomy, and equality, you are likely to be less receptive to the arguments offered in defense of the Standard Conception. You may see that lawyers, like Captain Vere and Justice Shaw, have choices – they need not simply follow the law uncritically, but should seek a deeper connection between their professional activities and justice. Alternatively, you may see more room for creativity and discretion in professional roles. Perhaps Captain Vere could have done something to underscore that mutiny would not be tolerated, but which took into account his recognition that Billy was innocent. If professional roles, such as ship captain, judge, or lawyer, allow for creativity and the exercise of judgment, then the role of lawyer may not be as simple as the principles of partisanship, neutrality, and nonaccountability suggest. Although I am quite sympathetic to political liberalism and the rule of law, it is hard to ignore the pervasiveness of legal

---

[2] Although this interpretation is controversial, the philosopher Hannah Arendt's account of the trial of Adolf Eichmann has come to stand for the idea of the "banality of evil" – that is, the possibility that terrible crimes against humanity may be perpetrated by a system made up of individuals who, on a personal level, may be motivated not by hatred but by petty concerns such as the desire for advancement. See Hannah Arendt, *Eichmann in Jerusalem* (New York: Viking 1963). Justice Shaw differs from Arendt's portrayal of Eichmann in that Shaw deliberated carefully about his responsibilities while Eichmann was merely sucking up to his bosses. It is important to keep in mind that Arendt never intended to deny Eichmann's responsibility; her point was instead that having subjectively harmless intentions does not negate responsibility when one participates in a system of mass murder. See Susan Neiman, *Evil in Modern Thought* (Princeton, N.J.: Princeton University Press 2002), pp. 270–77.

[3] For an example of this critique, see Allan C. Hutchinson, "Calgary and Everything After: A Postmodern Re-Vision of Lawyering," *Alberta Law Review* 33: 768–86 (1995).

injustice. Thus, this chapter attempts to add a bit of nuance to the picture
sketched in the preceding two chapters of the virtues of the rule of law and
to suggest the implications for legal ethics.

6.1   A typology of injustice

Injustice can occur at many levels. A legal system can be comprehensively
unjust if it is merely an instrument of a totalitarian government used to
retain power, suppress dissent, and keep the population under control. To
take an extreme example, consider the government of North Korea, which

> allows no organized political opposition, free media, functioning civil
> society, or religious freedom. Arbitrary arrest, detention, lack of due
> process, and torture and ill-treatment of detainees remain serious and
> endemic problems. North Korea also practices collective punishment for
> various anti-state offenses, for which it enslaves hundreds of thousands of
> citizens in prison camps, including children. The government periodically
> publicly executes citizens for stealing state property, hoarding food, and
> other "anti-socialist" crimes.[4]

Alternatively, a legal system's injustice may be local, not comprehensive.
For example, a government may permit political opposition and expres-
sions of dissent and may have generally well-functioning courts, such that it
is just from the majority's point of view while denying important political
or social rights to minority groups. Legal systems in South Africa during the
apartheid regime and the southern region of the United States in the first
half of the twentieth century featured legal systems that functioned pretty
well from the standpoint of a member of the white majority. They were
massively unjust from the point of view of minority citizens, but, in a sense,
this injustice was local. Martin Luther King, Jr. famously wrote that "injustice anywhere is a threat to justice everywhere,"[5] but if two citizens from
the dominant social group in South Africa or the United States had a dispute
about performance under a contract, the resolution of *that* dispute by the
courts would likely have satisfied any conceivable standard of justice. Local

---

[4] Human Rights Watch, *World Report 2012: North Korea*: http://www.hrw.org/world-report-
2012/world-report-2012-north-korea

[5] Martin Luther King, Jr., "Letter from Birmingham Jail" (April 16, 1963). Hugo
Adam Bedau, ed., *Civil Disobedience in Focus* (London: Routledge 1991), pp. 68–84.

injustice that is severe or pervasive enough can render a legal system comprehensively unjust, but there is at least a distinction in principle between these two senses of injustice.

The injustice of a legal system may be manifested in formal ways or the system may be substantively unjust. Totalitarian systems often feature *formal* defects in legality, such as the use of secret laws, retroactive laws, and corrupt judges who are willing to disregard statutes and precedent where necessary to further the ends of the regime.[6] But a system of government may fail at being law even if well intentioned. As discussed in Chapter 4, in *The Morality of Law*, Lon Fuller tells a story about an imaginary ruler, the well-meaning but bumbling King Rex.[7] Try as he might, Rex never seemed to get his style of government right as *law*. He decided cases one at a time without concern for whether there were principles that explained why one case was treated differently from another. He drafted a legal code, but kept it locked away in a box in his bedroom. When he finally released a public version of his code, it was so badly drafted and obscure that even professional lawyers could not make heads or tails of it. And so on. Whether or not Fuller's thesis should properly be called a version of natural law, it is generally accepted that his eight canons are indicia of legality. Laws should exhibit (1) generality (taking the form of rules rather than case-by-case directives), (2) publicity, (3) prospectivity, (4) clarity, (5) logical consistency, (6) feasibility – that is, they must be capable of being obeyed, (7) consistency through time, and (8) congruence between the rules as announced and their actual administration. King Rex in Fuller's parable was not an evil dictator; he was merely inept. Nevertheless, by failing to respect the canons of legality, he ended up making things in his country worse by attempting to make law.

A Fuller-inspired critique of a real legal system might focus on something like the military commission system set up by the United States government at Guantánamo Bay, Cuba, to try suspected terrorists.[8] The key word here is

---

[6] The legal system of Nazi Germany is a historical example of these kinds of abuses. See Ingo Muller, *Hitler's Justice: The Courts of the Third Reich* (Cambridge, Mass.: Harvard University Press 1992); Lon L. Fuller, "Positivism and Fidelity to Law: A Reply to Professor Hart," *Harvard Law Review* 71: 630–72 (1958), pp. 650–52.

[7] See Lon L. Fuller, *The Morality of Law* (New Haven: Yale University Press, rev'd edn., 1964).

[8] See, e.g., Clive Stafford Smith, *Eight O'clock Ferry to the Windward Side: Seeking Justice in Guantánamo Bay* (New York: Nation Books 2007); Joseph Margulies, *Guantánamo and the Abuse of Presidential Power* (New York: Simon & Schuster 2006); Alexandra D. Lahav,

"suspected," as it seems likely that only a tiny fraction of the detainees in Guantánamo have anything to do with radical Islamist terrorism. "Many of [the detainees] assert they are cases of mistaken identity: some were captured by Afghani bounty hunters who didn't care if they had the right man, while others were names spewed forth by captives who were tortured."[9] A just, decent legal system would incorporate procedures for determining, among other issues, whether the wrong person had been imprisoned. The US government initially argued, however, that detainees were entitled to no due process at all; the say-so of government officials was a sufficient basis to keep them imprisoned for a potentially indefinite period. The US Supreme Court rejected that position and held that a detainee was entitled to a meaningful opportunity to contest the factual basis for his detention.[10] The government responded by creating Combatant Status Review Tribunals but sought to prevent detainees from having lawyers to represent them in those Tribunals. When lawyers were eventually permitted to represent detainees, they faced systematic attempts to "drive a wedge" between them and their clients, including the requirement that they submit letters and notes to review by government officials to determine whether they contained classified information. Fuller would surely appreciate the irony that the criteria for determining whether material is classified are, themselves, classified.[11] Some lawyers were also requested to sign a waiver of the right to object to procedures to be adopted in the future by the Tribunal despite having no idea what the content of those procedures might be.[12] Rules and procedures were changed frequently and without notice, which had the effect of making lawyers seem powerless in the eyes of their clients and sowing mistrust.[13] In short, the injustice of Guantánamo is largely procedural. It is Fuller's nightmare of secret, retroactive, ad hoc decisions that fail to deserve the title of law.

In addition to exhibiting formal or procedural injustices (for these purposes those terms can be taken to mean the same thing), a legal system may be *substantively* unjust if it permits or requires moral wrongdoing. The

"Portraits of Resistance: Lawyer Responses to Unjust Proceedings," *UCLA Law Review* 57: 725–87 (2010).

[9] David Luban, "Lawfare and Legal Ethics in Guantánamo," *Stanford Law Review* 60: 1981–2026 (2008), p. 1987.

[10] *Hamdi v. Rumsfeld*, 542 U.S. 507 (2004).   [11] Luban, *supra*, p. 1990.

[12] Lahav, *supra*, p. 726–27.   [13] Luban, *supra*, pp. 1997–98.

legislation passed during the Nazi period in Germany complied with all of the formal criteria of legality – it was nonretroactive, public, followed consistently, capable of being obeyed, and so on – but it was frequently substantively unjust. For example, the Nuremburg Laws, which, among other things, prohibited Jews from working as physicians, lawyers, or journalists, were unjust even though passed by the German *Reichstag* pursuant to its usual procedures and enforced with complete consistency. This kind of substantive injustice can be comprehensive or local. Nazi Germany is now a watchword for an evil regime, but there are many citizens of otherwise tolerably decent democratic political systems who believe their countries' laws are substantively unjust to the extent that they permit or prohibit abortion (or permit or limit the availability of certain procedures, or impose certain conditions); grant legal recognition or refuse to grant legal recognition to same-sex unions; permit or prohibit prayer in public schools; engage in or prohibit government decision making that attempts to rectify wrongs to historically marginalized groups; affirmatively mistreat prisoners or fail to provide adequate assistance for people with mental illnesses; or use tax, fiscal, or regulatory means to either increase economic inequality or engage in progressive redistribution of income to reduce economic inequality. In the sincere, good faith judgment of some citizens, laws that permit, prohibit, or require these things are unjust without regard to having been enacted by fairly constituted legislatures, through regular procedures, and enforced impartially and without bias.

A great deal of legal injustice within a tolerably just society may not be dramatic but may take the form of routine harassment and insults to human dignity. "In daily interchange women and men of color must prove their respectability," writes a theorist of injustice. "At first they are not treated by strangers with respectful distance or deference," whereas white men enjoy a prima facie entitlement to be treated with respect.[14] This kind of subtle disrespect can be compounded when one is dealing with the bureaucratic institutions of the legal system, which tend to dehumanize everyone by treating them as merely a problem to be dealt with rather than as human beings who deserve to be treated with respect.

---

[14] Iris Marion Young, *Justice and the Politics of Difference* (Princeton: Princeton University Press 1990), p. 59.

6.2   Critical legal studies and the law–politics distinction

Legal philosophers tend to talk about the concept of law in terms of the formal features that a law must necessarily have in order to be a law and not something else, such as a principle of morality or a custom. Legal positivists, in particular, are keen to deny any necessary connection between law and morality. As a result, one can get the impression that positivists deny that the law can take sides, as it were, in contested moral and political issues. Critics of unjust laws sometimes ascribe to the law a claim to be a neutral, value-free domain of reasoning, as distinct from politics, in which individuals and institutions can take a position on contested social issues. Critics then show that procedures neutral on their face can have the effect of entrenching certain substantive rights and duties that work to the detriment of relatively powerless groups in society. For example, the legal historian Morton Horwitz has argued that the doctrines of tort law that developed during the Industrial Revolution had the effect of favoring the interests of employers over those of workers to the extent of providing an economic subsidy to emerging industries.[15] Significantly, the transformation of substantive law to favor the interests of powerful corporations was accompanied by the emergence of what Horwitz calls *legal classicism*, the tenets of which are a belief in the separation of law and politics and the possibility of deducing legal categories (such as tort vs. contract, duty and negligence in tort law, etc.) from purely logical considerations. The rule of law could be made to appear neutral and apolitical, which had the effect of muting criticism of mercantile capitalism and the widening inequality that accompanied industrialization.

Critical legal studies (or CLS) is an umbrella term for a number of related intellectual movements in the legal academy in roughly the 1970s and '80s that were united in their efforts to unmask the law's pretensions to neutrality – to show that what appears to be neutral, apolitical, natural, or rational is in fact the outcome of a political struggle over the scope and content of law.[16] There were many different strands of CLS. One emphasized the logical

---

[15] Morton Horwitz, *The Transformation of American Law, 1780–1860* (Cambridge, Mass.: Harvard University Press 1977).

[16] See generally Mark Kelman, *A Guide to Critical Legal Studies* (Cambridge, Mass.: Harvard University Press 1987); Guyora Binder, "Critical Legal Studies," in Dennis Patterson, ed., *A Companion to Philosophy of Law and Legal Theory* (Malden, Mass.: Blackwell 1996).

indeterminacy of law, the contingency of outcomes, and therefore the discretion enjoyed by judges and other actors within the legal system to implement their own ideological ends.[17] This strand has affinities for postmodern and deconstructive scholarship in other disciplines, such as literary criticism. A different strand, more aligned with Marxist and other left political theory, focused on the way in which law and power reinforce each other, the role law plays in the subordination of marginal groups within society, and (more abstractly) the way power constructs a distinctive way of understanding the world, which purports to be neutral but is in fact highly ideological.[18] Feminist legal theory and critical race theory overlapped with CLS in some ways – for instance, in emphasizing the disparate impact of purportedly neutral laws on social groups in and out of power – but there were significant points of contention as well.[19] Some scholars of color have emphasized the role of positive law in securing the moral rights of minorities. Patricia Williams, for example, has argued that the legal discourse of rights provides a means for African Americans to describe their needs or interests (which have historically been ignored by the white majority) as matters of entitlement:[20]

> For the historically disempowered, the conferring of rights is symbolic of all the denied aspects of their humanity: rights imply a respect that places one in the referential range of self and others, that elevates one's status from human body to social being.[21]

Rights may be indeterminate in application, but they do provide a way of representing the humanity of powerless persons to a majority-dominated state.

Although it is dangerous to generalize about CLS, one theme that bears emphasis is the critique of the purported neutrality of law. Law has a political and ethical agenda; it takes a position. But it does so while

---

[17] See, e.g., Duncan Kennedy, *A Critique of Adjudication {fin de siècle}* (Cambridge, Mass.: Harvard University Press 1997).

[18] See, e.g., Roberto Mangabeira Unger, *Knowledge and Politics* (New York: Free Press 1987).

[19] See, e.g., Kimberle Crenshaw, "A Black Feminist Critique of Antidiscrimination Law and Politics," in David Kairys, ed., *The Politics of Law: A Progressive Critique* (New York: Pantheon Books, rev'd edn., 1990).

[20] Patricia J. Williams, "The Pain of Word Bondage," in *The Alchemy of Race and Rights* (Cambridge, Mass.: Harvard University Press 1991).

[21] Id., p. 153.

presenting a public face of impartiality. As we noted at the beginning of Chapter 4, if a stranger on the street corner told you to wear a helmet while riding a bicycle, you might have replied, "who the heck are you?" If you were informed that The Law, in all its majesty, told you to wear a helmet, however, your reaction might be different. "Oh, The Law says to do it – all right, then." That is exactly the attitude that critical legal scholars sought to expose and critique. Why should the identity of something as a law make a difference if it is pointless or unjust to do the thing the law requires? Or, if it makes sense to do what the law requires, then why is it relevant that the law requires it? Maybe wearing a bicycle helmet is a good idea, apart from what anyone has to say about it.[22] This line of thinking should sound familiar, because it was at the core of the Hart-Fuller debate discussed in Chapter 4. Hart and Fuller disagreed about the significance of calling directives of the Nazi regime "law." In effect, Hart can be understood as saying that all of the interesting questions pertaining to the behavior of citizens and officials with respect to the law in the Nazi period are political and moral questions about the legitimacy of the state and the obligation to obey the law. They are not conceptual questions about the nature of law. Fuller, in response, would contend that these two types of questions cannot be disentangled. If something purports to be a law, then it implicitly claims to rightfully command obedience.

Whatever your views about the conceptual questions explored in the Hart-Fuller debate, it would require almost willful blindness to deny the

[22] The scholar who has done the most to illuminate the concept of authority is Joseph Raz. He distinguishes theoretical and practical authorities, with the former having an epistemic function – that is, they inform people of the reasons that apply to them anyway. For example, if an automobile safety research institute determines that a particular brand of car is unsafe, I might choose not to buy that car on the authority of the institute. The institute does not change the reasons that would otherwise apply to me; it merely informs me of something I would not otherwise have known. In this way, it is a theoretical authority, as would be the person in the text who told someone else that wearing a bicycle helmet is a good idea. See Joseph Raz, *The Morality of Freedom* (Oxford: Oxford University Press 1986), p. 52. A practical authority, by contrast, has normative power. The directive of a practical authority creates a new reason for action that replaces preexisting reasons. See Joseph Raz, *The Authority of Law* (Oxford: Oxford University Press 1979), pp. 16–17. The normal justification for authority is that the subject of authority is likely to do better at complying with reasons that apply to him by accepting the directives of the authority as binding. Joseph Raz, "Authority, Law, and Morality," in *Ethics in the Public Domain* (Oxford: Oxford University Press 1994), p. 214.

existence of some unjust laws, even within a more or less just legal system. For the sake of discussion, let us assume that a nation such as Canada, New Zealand, or the United Kingdom is, for the most part, a tolerably just democratic society. Even so, there may be specific laws that require citizens to do some things that they consider to be morally wrong or prevent them from doing some things they consider to be morally required. Of course, if every citizen were free to do whatever he or she believed to be the best thing, morally speaking, the law would lose its capacity to resolve the inevitable disagreements about morality that arise in a pluralistic society. The claim of law to create obligations cannot be absolute but neither can the demands of conscience. In some cases, a citizen's views about what ought to be done must yield to a determination, through a tolerably fair political process, of what should be done. However, a just society will also acknowledge the importance of giving morally motivated citizens an alternative to obeying the law in some cases. Civil disobedience and conscientious objection are two related strategies for dealing with the inevitable conflicts between law and morality.

6.3   Civil disobedience and conscientious objection

On the one hand . . .

> Most philosophers who have written on the subject have argued that, at least in democratic societies, there is always a strong moral reason to obey the law.[23]

On the other . . .

> As strongly as we may believe in the wrongness of disobedience, most of us recognize as well that at least sometimes it is legal *obedience* that would be wrong.[24]

You may believe there is an obligation to obey the law and a quite strong one at that. Still, hardly anyone would contend this is an absolute obligation that must be obeyed no matter what. At some point. a particular law or an entire legal system may be so unjust that no valid moral argument could be offered for the conclusion that one ought to do what the law says. If a would-

---

[23] Smith, *supra*, p. 972.

[24] A. John Simmons, *Political Philosophy* (Oxford: Oxford University Press 2008), p. 40.

be law of North Korea imposes the death penalty for stealing food, no one would be morally permitted to report another citizen to the police for doing so or otherwise assist in the arrest, prosecution, and execution of someone for that alleged crime. Of course, people living under totalitarian governments often obey out of fear or because they have been so conditioned by propaganda and repression that they fail to perceive the wrongness of their actions. As a matter of moral justification, however, the fact that something is dressed up as a law does not create an obligation to do what the would-be law says, and, indeed, it may be morally wrongful to obey the law. The injustice of the law may be procedural or formal, as Fuller would argue, or it may be substantive because no one deserves to be killed for stealing food, but in any event the injustice is so clear and grave that there could be no moral case made for obedience.

In the Hart-Fuller debate, there was not really any question that egregiously unjust Nazi laws did not deserve the allegiance of citizens. The debate was, rather, over how best to give a theoretical account of the lack of legitimate authority of these directives – should they be called nonlaws, as Fuller argued, or laws that need not be obeyed? Although there are other historical examples of comparably unjust legal regimes, such as South Africa under apartheid, most readers will have the good fortune to be subject to the authority of legal systems that are at least moderately just, in which it can be said that the society is "well-ordered for the most part but in which some serious violations of justice nevertheless do occur."[25] The difficult ethical questions for citizens, lawyers, and judges in these mostly just legal systems pertain to local, not comprehensive injustice. In those cases, the person subject to the law would believe that she is justified in not obeying that particular law because to do so would be unethical, even though the law was enacted through reasonably fair procedures by institutions of a basically just government. This is different from simply disobeying and hoping not to get caught and punished or acting out of ignorance of the requirements of law. The cases that interest us involve morally motivated conduct.[26]

Consider the case of a citizen of a basically just society who is required by law to perform military service in an armed conflict that the citizen believes is illegal, unjust, and involves violations of human rights and is also a

---

[25] Rawls, *Theory of Justice*, *supra*, p. 363.

[26] Joseph Raz, "A Right to Dissent? Civil Disobedience," in *The Authority of Law* (Oxford: Oxford University Press 1979).

violation of that citizen's religious beliefs, which forbid participation in acts of war. A claim to justified disobedience of the law requiring military service might take one of two forms:

Civil disobedience is "a public, nonviolent, conscientious yet political act contrary to law usually done with the aim of bringing about a change in the law or policies of the government."[27] There are several significant points to note about this definition. First, civil disobedience does not appeal to the personal beliefs of the actor. Instead, it appeals to the community's shared conception of justice. The citizen in our example would not be relying on his or her own pacifist religious beliefs in justification but would instead make an appeal to the commitment shared by a majority within the political community to principles of international law and human rights. Civil disobedience is open, not covert, and it is nonviolent. It is also performed in a way that manifests respect for the political community and its legal institutions. The civilly disobedient citizen not only engages in an open act, but does so with a willingness to accept the legal consequences of the action. Civil disobedience is therefore "disobedience to law within the limits of fidelity to law."[28]

Paradigmatic examples of civil disobedience include sit-ins by African Americans at segregated lunch counters in defiance of laws requiring separate seating for black and white patrons and the March to the Sea led by Mahatma Gandhi to make salt in violation of British law. American civil rights leader Martin Luther King, Jr. was inspired by Gandhi to articulate a nonviolent means of resistance to legal injustice, one that emphasized that both the oppressor and the oppressed are members of the same political community in which justice must be fully realized.[29] Rawls has argued that civil disobedience serves a stabilizing function within a pluralistic democracy by calling public attention to serious departures from the political community's sense of justice.[30] In the case of both the lunch counter sit-ins and the March to the Sea, pervasive legal violations of human rights were eventually rectified by changes to the law made in response to civil disobedience. It is a strategy for changing the law, not simply extricating a morally

---

[27] Rawls, *supra*, p. 364.   [28] Id., p. 366.

[29] Robert K. Vischer, *Martin Luther King Jr. and the Morality of Legal Practice* (Cambridge: Cambridge University Press 2013), pp. 210–13.

[30] Id., p. 383.

motivated citizen from a difficult dilemma involving the choice between respecting the law and honoring her moral beliefs and commitments.

Conscientious objection is not an act that appeals to the sense of justice of the majority of the political community. Instead, it is based on the personal beliefs of the affected citizen, beliefs that may be at odds with those of the majority, who holds that following the requirements of law would involve a grave moral violation.[31] Only those laws that require what citizens reasonably believe are particularly grave moral violations may be justifiably disobeyed on grounds of conscience. Many philosophers believe that a clear case of justified conscientious objection is a religiously motivated refusal to serve in the armed forces. Assuming the law requiring military service was enacted by a fair democratic process, the religious beliefs of the majority of citizens would evidently not be at odds with serving in the armed forces. Nevertheless, there may be members of minority religious groups committed to pacifism who refuse to comply with the state's law out of a sense of obligation to a higher law. Unlike civil disobedience, which is a public, political act aimed at changing the law, conscientious objection is a private act, engaged in by someone who believes it would be morally wrong to do what the law requires in a particular case.[32] In effect, the claim of the conscientious objector is that the law may legitimately demand many things, but, at some point, the demands of the law must yield to an individual's obligation as an autonomous agent to take responsibility for her actions. A decent legal system will very likely provide some space within which conscientious objection is permissible. Many national laws, for example, exempt from military service the members of pacifist religious sects. A just society may be made stronger, not weaker, by tolerating morally motivated objections by loyal, thoughtful citizens.

Analytically, it is possible to separate questions that may be asked from the point of view of the citizen and that of the state: From the citizen's perspective, when do the demands of conscience override the reasons to obey the law? From the state's perspective, should citizens who engage in morally motivated action, either civil disobedience or conscientious objection, be punished? The first question is relatively straightforward to analyze, if not to answer. The concerned citizen considers the reasons she may have to obey the law – whether gratitude for benefits received, fairness to

---

[31] Greenawalt, *supra*, p. 313.   [32] Rawls, *supra*, p. 369.

others, a sense of belonging to a community, or the like – and compares them with the reasons for taking a contrary action. (The desire to avoid punishment or inconvenience may be a factor, but it is not a moral reason.) Just as a soldier has an obligation to obey the orders of a superior officer, which can be overridden if the order is to commit a grave violation of human rights, a citizen's obligation to obey the law may be overridden in appropriate cases.[33] This type of morally motivated disobedience is not the same thing as anarchism. The disobedient citizen acknowledges a general obligation to respect the law and her fellow citizens. The requirement that civil disobedience be open, and that conscientious objection be rarely resorted to, manifests respect for the majority of citizens who support the law. A citizen who objects to military service has to accept the possibility of being punished for refusing to serve, but nevertheless refuses based on a superior moral obligation.

The second question, from the perspective of the state or a public official, is more complicated. For one thing, many government officials have discretion regarding enforcement of the law. Captain Vere in *Billy Budd* might have decided not to try Billy for mutiny or to commute his death sentence. Prosecuting attorneys may decide for a variety of reasons not to seek punishment against someone who violated the criminal law, including the desire to allocate scarce enforcement resources to more serious offenses, a belief that the offender is not a danger to the community, or even a judgment that strictly enforcing the law would be unjustified from a moral point of view (see Chapter 8). An interesting illustration of prosecutorial discretion is provided by a recent decision of the Attorney General of the United States not to enforce federal laws against the possession of marijuana in states that have permitted the recreational or medical use of marijuana as a matter of state law.[34] Federal criminal law still applies to the sale and possession of marijuana, but for policy reasons including respect for the decisions of citizens in these states, federal prosecutors exercised their discretion not to enforce these laws. The existence of discretion does not imply that government officials are free to do whatever they want. They must have good reasons to enforce a particular law or not. Reasons to enforce the law

---

[33] David Lyons, *Ethics and the Rule of Law* (Cambridge: Cambridge University Press 1984), pp. 84–85.

[34] Ashley Southall and Jack Healy, "U.S. Won't Sue to Reverse States' Legalization of Marijuana," *N.Y. Times* (Aug. 29, 2013).

include respecting the wishes of the majority of citizens who support the law, preserving public order and preventing lawlessness, and maintaining the law as a means to resolve disagreement about moral matters. Captain Vere's decision to hang Billy was motivated by the tangible possibility of encouraging mutiny among crews in the Royal Navy. In the marijuana case, the Attorney General had to balance reasons to enforce federal drug laws against the claims by supporters of marijuana legalization that these laws are unjust and a waste of scarce enforcement resources. The process involved moral, political, and practical reasoning about how best to accomplish the goals of a government law enforcement agency. In a democratic political system, as opposed to on a ship in wartime, these enforcement decisions are subject to political controls. If citizens who favor strict federal drug laws are sufficiently motivated and organized, they may make the Attorney General's decision into an issue in an upcoming election.

6.4 Lawyers and injustice

Lawyers occupy an intriguing middle ground between ordinary citizens and public officials such as judges and prosecutors. A citizen can, for the most part, treat the law as a given. Suppose a statute criminalizes the failure to perform compulsory military service. A morally motivated citizen may have to decide whether to accept the penalties prescribed by the statute and refuse to register for the draft or follow the law and act against the dictates of conscience. In either case, that law simply is – it is a data point, something to take into account when deciding how to act, but more or less fixed with respect to content and application. Many public officials, by contrast, have discretion with respect to interpreting and enforcing the law. An appointed or elected prosecuting attorney may decide not to punish citizens who burn their draft cards as an act of civil disobedience. A judge may determine that the best interpretation of the draft registration law, in light of broader constitutional principles, would not justify punishing citizens who refuse to register for military service.[35] Lawyers are not literally state officials, but they do play a vital role in interpreting and applying the law to the activities of citizens. In sociological terms, the legal profession performs a mediating

---

[35] A position taken by Dworkin. See Ronald Dworkin, "Civil Disobedience," in *Taking Rights Seriously* (Cambridge, Mass.: Harvard University Press 1977), pp. 207–11.

role between citizens and the state. Thus, questions pertaining to the authority of arguably unjust laws arise in a particularly subtle way for lawyers. The following example is not as dramatic as the dilemma facing Captain Vere in *Billy Budd* or Justice Shaw in the Fugitive Slave Act cases, but it nicely illustrates the problem of the weight a lawyer ought to give the law when deciding how to act, and it also shows the way in which lawyers function in a mediating role between individuals and the government.

A legal aid lawyer provides assistance to people with limited income in their dealings with the government. She is frequently called on to assist clients in obtaining various forms of government benefits, such as food and housing aid. One day, she interviews a client who wishes to apply for government income assistance after becoming disabled in an accident. The client is living rent-free with his cousin, but even so can barely make ends meet. The lawyer knows that, under the applicable regulations, the receipt of rent-free housing from a family member counts as in-kind income and should be reported on the client's application for benefits. If the client discloses his free housing, his monthly benefits will be reduced by $150. Being a clever person, the lawyer realizes she could advise the client to make a nominal payment – say, $5 per month – to his cousin and no longer be required to report the receipt of rent-free housing. If the client lost the $150 per month, he would be unable to finish an educational program that represents his only real chance to escape poverty and become financially self-supporting. Should the lawyer give him the advice to make the nominal payment to his cousin?

This hypothetical has been discussed by Deborah Rhode and William Simon, both of whom believe it would be unjust for the client's benefits to be reduced.[36] As Deborah Rhode argues, "[m]any impoverished clients have compelling claims for assistance that the law fails to acknowledge," including the claim to an income adequate to meet basic subsistence needs.[37] It is also clear under the applicable regulations, however, that the ruse of paying $5 a month to the cousin would amount to a fraud, and therefore the lawyer's advice to make the $5 payment would be tantamount to advising

---

[36] William H. Simon, "Ethical Discretion in Lawyering," Harvard Law Review 101: 1083–1145 (1988), pp. 1105–06; Deborah L. Rhode, *In the Interests of Justice* (Oxford: Oxford University Press 2000), pp. 76–79.

[37] Rhode, *supra*, p. 76.

the client to evade the law.[38] Granting the truth of this observation, would it be *morally* justified to advise the client to make the nominal payment, notwithstanding the legal conclusion that it would be a fraud? There are several positions one might take.

6.4.1   Law deserves respect because it resolves moral conflict

The lawyer should not substitute her moral judgment for the requirements of law. A lawyer who follows the law here is not exhibiting sheeplike obedience to authority but is responding appropriately to the law as an institution that resolves contested moral issues in the name of the community as a whole. In this case, funds with which to pay disability benefits may be scarce and therefore must be allocated according to criteria of need. In an ideal world, the government would have sufficient funds to guarantee all citizens a minimally adequate income to meet basic subsistence needs, but, in times of scarcity, difficult allocation decisions must be made. Disagreement may be expected over the criteria used to make these allocation decisions, so the law is required in order to settle this conflict and establish a stable, workable scheme for distributing income assistance to persons in need. The lawyer's advice to make the payment would be a form of cheating, in moral as well as legal terms, because the law embodies a difficult but necessary tradeoff among competing claims on scarce resources.[39] Thus, although the lawyer may sincerely believe that it would be unjust for her client's benefits to be reduced, her advice should be that the client must report the in-kind income. If the lawyer is troubled by the injustice in this case, she can petition the agency for an exception, work to reform the law, or criticize it in a public forum, but she may not simply disregard it.

---

[38] The regulations referred to in Simon's article, which require a reduction in income support to reflect in-kind income, were based on a state regulation that no longer exists. However, the current US federal regulations governing Supplemental Security Income (that is, disability) benefits similarly require a one-third reduction in the benefit amount if an applicant is receiving in-kind support and maintenance (IKSM), including housing. See 20 C.F.R. § 416.1130. An applicant is deemed to be receiving IKSM if he or she pays less than the pro rata amount of food and shelter expenses. Under these regulations, a neutral decision maker such as an administrative law judge would conclude that the applicant is still receiving IKSM even if she made the $5 payment to her cousin because $5 is considerably less than a pro rata share of the household's expenses.

[39] See Chapter 9 on civil litigation for a similar argument.

6.4.2   Law is one thing, morality another

Focusing on whether the law is valid as law obscures the relationship between the law and morality. The law can be a means through which injustice is entrenched. In particular, the law may serve to legitimate inequality. By acquiescing in the reduction of her client's benefits, the lawyer may be perceived as endorsing the conclusion that her client does not deserve more as a matter of distributive justice. Remember Hart's position in the Hart-Fuller debate. He argued that the tendency of the German legal profession not to question the morality of obeying Nazi laws

> is really dependent upon an enormous overvaluation of the importance of the bare fact that a rule may be said to be a valid rule of law, as if this, once declared, was conclusive of the final moral question: "Ought this rule of law to be obeyed?"[40]

Thus, the bare fact that the law requires reporting in-kind income is not conclusive as to the moral question, "ought the lawyer to advise the client not to make the nominal payment?" A lawyer who advises the client to commit fraud may be subject to professional discipline for doing so,[41] but if the lawyer believes herself to be morally obligated to help the client obtain an adequate level of income support, she may choose to violate the law and accept the possibility of punishment. In the language of CLS, the lawyer may attempt to "politicize" the law by exposing the way it reinforces social inequalities and injustices that underlie the legal system.[42] To do so, however, the lawyer must position herself as an "insider" within the legal system; otherwise, her critique will be dismissed as anarchism. A dissident lawyer must walk a fine line, manifesting respect for the law while holding up legal injustice to public scrutiny and criticism. She is therefore analogous to the civilly disobedient citizen who violates the law openly and with the objective of changing the law.

[40] H. L. A. Hart, "Positivism and the Separation of Law and Morals," *Harvard Law Review* 71: 593–629 (1958), p. 618.
[41] In the American law governing lawyers, state courts have adopted a version of American Bar Association Model Rule 1.2(d), which forbids a lawyer to "counsel a client to engage, or assist a client, in conduct that the lawyer knows is criminal or fraudulent."
[42] Neta Ziv, "Lawyers Talking Rights and Clients Breaking Rules: Between Legal Positivism and Distributive Justice in Israeli Poverty Lawyering," *Clinical Law Review* 11: 209–39 (2004), p. 228; Hutchinson, *supra.*

6.4.3   Law cannot be interpreted apart from morality

We should not assume so quickly that the law in fact requires reporting in-kind income or prohibits the work-around of making the nominal payment. This is Simon's approach to the problem, which is very much inspired by the jurisprudence of Ronald Dworkin.[43] Simon directs lawyers to consider the substantive merits of the law, not merely the law's formal expression. The regulations may appear to require reporting in-kind income, but, properly interpreted, they do not. There may be a more fundamental right, perhaps as a matter of constitutional law, to a minimally adequate level of income support. The text of the regulation must be interpreted in light of broader constitutional principles. For Dworkin, the task of a judge applying the law should be understood as giving the best constructive interpretation of the community's legal practice, which necessarily requires engagement with principles of political morality such as justice, fairness, and due process.[44] In the murdering-heir case, the beneficiary of the will was not entitled to his bequest, even though the will complied with all the formal requirements of the Statute of Wills, because of the principle that no person should profit from his own wrongdoing. Simon asks why, if judges can reason in this way, lawyers should not be required to do so as well. If a lawyer plausibly could conclude that the best constructive interpretation of the community's legal principles would not require reporting in-kind income, then the lawyer would not be committing a fraud by advising the client to make the $5 payment.

Each of these positions has weaknesses. Option 1 requires the lawyer to be an active participant in what she sincerely believes to be injustice. The horrors of Nazi Germany were possible only through the acquiescence of numberless citizens, lawyers, and government officials who were all too willing to overlook the injustice of laws. Option 2 does not provide much relief for a lawyer. A lawyer faced with a massive injustice, such as the laws of Nazi Germany or the Fugitive Slave Act, may decide from the standpoint of morality that there is no alternative to violating the law and accepting

---

[43] Simon, *supra*, pp. 1106–07.

[44] Ronald Dworkin, *Law's Empire* (Cambridge, Mass.: Harvard University Press 1986), p. 225.

punishment, but that seems like an extreme response to a more structural type of injustice that is grounded in the social problems of poverty and inequality. Option 3 seems to reintroduce the moral disagreement that the law is designed to settle. Deborah Rhode argues that "[a]n impoverished mother struggling to escape welfare stands on a different footing than a wealthy executive attempting to escape taxes."[45] That may be so, but the regulations pertaining to disability benefits are aimed at the different moral problem of how to allocate scarce resources among a number of potentially deserving claimants.

Notice that each of these options concede something to the idea of role-differentiated morality, discussed in Chapter 2. Chapter 1 proposed under-standing the problem using a geographic metaphor of two lands connected by a bridge. The bridge connects moral values with the special obligations and permissions of professional ethics. The options for dealing with injus-tice pay attention to both sides of the bridge. As a matter of professional ethics, lawyers are not free to disregard the law whenever it is disadvanta-geous to their clients, nor to advise their clients to ignore the law. As a matter of morality, the lawyer cannot help but feel a sense of injustice that her client's benefits will be reduced to a level that will make it impossible for him to complete an essential job training program. The challenge for a theory of legal ethics is to respect both of these normative domains. It makes at least some difference that the actor in this case is a lawyer – someone whose social role necessarily involves a commitment to the value of legality. One might reason as follows: If the client had figured out the little ruse of making a $5 payment on his own, never asked for legal advice, and simply failed to report the rent-free housing as in-kind income, that might be wrong, but it would be worse if a lawyer had advised him to do so. I am not necessarily endorsing that argument, but the point is, whatever one thinks about the obligation of citizens to respect the law, lawyers arguably have a more demanding obligation. At the same time, lawyers should not be law-following machines. They remain moral agents even when acting in a professional role. The injustice of the client's predicament is relevant somehow, even if only to create a sense of regret that the law was inflexible regarding in-kind income. The aim of this book is not to convince you that any particular resolution is correct but only to persuade you that

---

[45] Rhode, *supra*, p. 79.

the tension between morality and professional obligations is a deep, structural feature of legal ethics.

One further possibility should be considered, and it will serve as a segue into the next section of the book. That possibility is that the social role of "lawyer" should not be understood as a monolith but should itself be differentiated into subroles with distinctive duties. The lawyer in the government benefits case is serving as an advisor, telling the client what the law requires and how to comply with it. The lawyer's actions are essentially forward-looking; they affect what the client will do in the future. Significantly, the lawyer's advice will not be reviewed, at least in ordinary cases, by any official state decision maker. The lawyer will tell the client what to do, the client will go off and do it, and that will be the end of the matter. The lawyer is therefore a kind of private lawgiver to the client. As a contrasting case, one can imagine a lawyer called on to defend a client in a prosecution for fraud on the disability benefits system. In that case, the lawyer's actions would be backward-looking. The clients actions would be a given – nothing the lawyer could do would affect them, being wholly in the past – and the lawyer's only job would be to urge a court not to punish the client for his actions. Unlike the advising case, the lawyer's interpretation of the law is offered to an official state decision maker, the court, which can accept or reject it. The client may wish to challenge the application of the regulations that require the reporting of in-kind income. The official proceeding against the client gives him an avenue to contest the justice of the case in a public manner, as opposed to simply evading the law covertly.

For all these reasons, one might contend that a lawyer representing a client in a litigated matter – that is, a case pending before a court or other tribunal – should have greater latitude to rely on interpretations of the law that are less well supported by precedent as compared with the situation of a lawyer acting as a counselor or transactional planner. One might further contend that it makes a difference whether the client is charged with a criminal offense, in which case he may be facing the power of the state and looking at the possibility of a significant deprivation of liberty, or whether the lawsuit is a civil action between two private parties. These arguments on the professional ethics side of the bridge, but they are still connected with considerations on the morality side. A reasonably complex legal system may require, or at least permit, that the social role of lawyer be differentiated functionally, according to factors such as whether the lawyer's role is forward- or backward-looking, the identity of the parties (private or state, individual or corporate), and the matters at stake for the parties (property, liberty, or even life). The ethical obligations of lawyers may vary according to whether the lawyer is a public prosecutor, a criminal defense attorney, a lawyer representing parties in civil litigation, an advisor or transactional planner, a lawyer for the government or a large corporation, or a judge or other neutral decision maker. This contextualization of the lawyer's ethical role, which is a feature of actual legal systems in both the civil and common law worlds, will be considered in Chapter 7.

Part II

The many roles of lawyers

7 Criminal defense and the problem of client selection

7.1 How can you represent that person?

Kenneth Murray, a criminal defense attorney in a small town north of Toronto, Ontario, was retained by Paul Bernardo to defend him against charges of kidnapping, rape, and murder.[1] Bernardo had been arrested in connection with several rapes that had occurred elsewhere in Ontario, and the police suspected him of involvement in the murder of two teenaged girls who had disappeared and whose bodies had been found with signs of sexual abuse. The police searched Bernardo's house and found no incriminating evidence. Subsequently, Bernardo told his lawyer, Murray, that there were cameras placed in the bedroom of his house and that he and his wife had not only tortured, raped, and murdered the two girls, but also had videotaped the acts. (Bernardo's wife was represented by separate lawyers.[2] Bernardo wanted his lawyer to see the tapes in order to establish his defense that it was his wife, not Bernardo, who had killed the girls.) Murray went to Bernardo's house and, following Bernardo's instructions, found the videotapes hidden in a light fixture. Murray brought the tapes back to his office and viewed them. They indeed showed several hours of horrific acts by Bernardo and his wife, including the wife administering a dose of toxic gas to her own sister, which subsequently resulted in her sister's death.

---

[1] The account of this case is based upon Austin Cooper, Q.C., "The Ken Murray Case: Defence Counsel's Dilemma," *Criminal Law Quarterly* 47: 41 (2009); and Christopher D. Clemmer, "Obstructing the Bernardo Investigation: Kenneth Murray and the Defence Counsel's Conflicting Obligations to Clients and the Court," *Osgoode Hall Review of Law and Policy* 1: 137–97 (2008). Mr. Cooper served as defense counsel for Ken Murray in the obstruction of justice prosecution.

[2] Can you think of why separate representation of Bernardo and his wife is necessary? Think about the interests of each defendant and how they might differ, and then ask whether one lawyer could simultaneously represent both defendants.

131

Criminal defense lawyers often assert that they do not know whether their clients are guilty. The police say one thing, the client says another, and it is for the trier of fact – the judge or jury – to sort things out and determine what happened. It is not the lawyer's job to evaluate the guilt or innocence of her client. In fact, in light of some of the lawyer's duties to the court (which we consider later in this chapter), it may be best for the lawyer not to know whether the client is guilty. Nevertheless, the Bernardo case shows that it may be possible for the lawyer not merely to have a pretty strong suspicion, but actually to know that the client did the act for which he is being prosecuted. Paul Bernardo admitted his involvement to his lawyer, and all possible doubt was removed when the lawyer watched the video-tapes, at least as to Bernardo's involvement in numerous aggravated rapes. The videotapes also provided compelling circumstantial evidence that Bernardo had also killed the two girls. And this is, needless to say, not a case over which reasonable people may disagree about the appropriateness of punishment – as in, for example, a prosecution for obscenity or posses-sion of small quantities of drugs. Nevertheless, Murray, the lawyer, contin-ued to represent Bernardo.

As a matter of professional ethics in Canada, Murray was not required to represent Bernardo.[3] Some legal systems sharing the heritage of the English common law, including those of England and Wales, Australia, New Zealand, India, and Malaysia, recognize the so-called *cab rank rule* as a pro-fessional obligation.[4] The idea is that a barrister may not pick and choose among potential clients but must take clients in the order they present themselves in the barrister's office, as one would take the first taxicab from a waiting queue. There are exceptions in cases of a conflict of interest or

---

[3] Alice Woolley, *Understanding Lawyers' Ethics in Canada* (Markham, Ont.: LexisNexis 2011), p. 46–52.

[4] See, e.g., Code of Conduct of the Bar of England and Wales, Rule 601; *R v. Ulcay & Toygun* [2007] EWCA Crim. 2379 (Court of Appeal), ¶ 39; New Zealand Rules of Conduct and Client Care for Lawyers § 4; New South Wales Barristers' Rules § 21; Bar Council of India, Rules on Professional Standards, Rules on an Advocate's Duty Toward the Client, Rule 1; Malaysian Bar, Legal Profession (Practice and Etiquette) Rules 1978, Rule 2. See also Stan Ross, *Ethics in Law: Lawyers' Responsibility and Accountability in Australia* (Sydney: Butterworths 1995), pp. 143–54; Duncan Webb, *Ethics: Professional Responsibility and the Lawyer* (Wellington: Butterworths 2000), pp. 153–61. The rule in England does not apply to solicitors, but in Malaysia, New Zealand, and some Australian states both in-court and office representation are covered by the rule.

where the barrister would not be competent to accept the representation, and, in reality, barristers, through their clerks, can often circumvent the cab rank rule.[5] Nevertheless, the cab rank rule stands for the important ethical ideal that a lawyer should not reject clients because the lawyer finds the crimes with which they have been accused repugnant, but should instead provide the highest quality of professional representation regardless of any moral qualms the lawyer may have. This is the principle of neutrality, the second part of the standard conception of legal ethics (Chapter 3). It follows that lawyers who respect the cab rank rule should be insulated from criticism based on the clients they represent. This is the principle of non-accountability, the third aspect of the Standard Conception. Neutrality and nonaccountability work together to ensure that all accused persons can obtain representation. As Lord Reid stated in a well-known modern defense of the cab rank rule:

> If counsel is bound to act for such a person, no reasonable man could think the less of any counsel because of his association with such a client, but, if counsel could pick and choose, his reputation might suffer if he chose to act for such a client, and the client might have great difficulty in obtaining proper legal assistance.[6]

If lawyers were free to decline to represent someone accused of terrible crimes, that person might go unrepresented, and the rights conferred upon him by law would be rendered meaningless. The answer to the question, "how could you represent such a person?" is therefore, "I must, and the

---

[5] See John A. Flood, *Barristers' Clerks: The Law's Middlemen* (Manchester: Manchester University Press 1983). I am using the American term, acceptance of "representation," where an English or Australian barrister would talk about accepting a brief or instructions from a solicitor. Solicitors tend to use the terminology of acceptance of a *retainer*.

[6] *Rondel v. Worsley* [1969] A.C. 191. In the classic defense of the cab rank rule, Thomas Erskine, who represented Thomas Paine in his trial for treason for the publication of *The Rights of Man*, said:

> From the moment that any advocate can be permitted to say that he will or will not stand between the Crown and the subject arraigned in the court where he daily sits to practice, from that moment the liberties of England are at an end. If the advocate refuses to defend, from what he may think of the charge or the defence, he assumes the character of the judge; nay, he assumes it before the hour of judgement.

R. v. Paine (1792), 22 State Trials 357, 412 (quoted in Tim Dare, *The Counsel of Rogues? A Defence of the Standard Conception of the Lawyer's Role* [Farnham, Surrey: Ashgate 2009], p. 10).

reason is that the rule of law depends on clients having access to legal representation."

Even in countries like the United States and Canada without a formal cab rank rule, the ideal of neutrality is frequently asserted when lawyers are criticized for representing particular clients. So, for example, when a Defense Department official in the administration of President George W. Bush criticized prominent law firms for representing suspected terrorists, many lawyers rushed to defend the law firms. Conservative law professor Charles Fried (yes, the same scholar whose "Lawyer as Friend" article we considered in Chapter 2) wrote in support of the firms representing the detainees:

> It is the pride of a nation built on the rule of law that it affords to every man a zealous advocate to defend his rights in court, and of a liberal profession in such a nation that not only is the representation of the dishonorable honorable (and any lawyer is free to represent any person he chooses), but that it is the duty of the profession to make sure that every man has that representation.[7]

Fried concedes that "any lawyer is free to represent any person he [or she] chooses," but he still appeals to the ideal of neutrality underlying the cab rank rule because more general values associated with the rule of law require that lawyers be provided to defend even dishonorable clients without being criticized for somehow supporting their clients' causes.

Canadian lawyers often discuss the Bernardo case with reference to a specific issue of professional ethics, namely, what duty a lawyer has when receiving possession of physical evidence of a crime.[8] But the case clearly also raises a *moral* issue concerning the representation of people charged with committing almost unimaginable crimes. Just thinking about Paul Bernardo is enough to give most people the creeps, so imagine serving as Bernardo's lawyer – spending time talking to him, investigating the crimes, and working long hours to prepare a defense that might result in him being set free. What

---

[7] Charles Fried, Op-Ed, "Mr. Stimson and the American Way," *Wall Street Journal* (January 16, 2007). I mention Fried's political orientation – he had served as Solicitor General under President Ronald Reagan – merely to point out that support for the cab rank rule and for the ideal of professional neutrality cuts across conventional left/right ideological boundaries.

[8] See Alice Woolley et al., *Lawyers' Ethics and Professional Regulation* (Markham, Ont.: LexisNexis 2008), pp. 383–94.

kind of person would do that and why? You have probably thought about this question in connection with some terrible crime in your own country and wondered about the ethics of criminal defense. Not surprisingly, this question is vitally important to criminal defense lawyers, many of whom have written eloquent apologias for representing awful people.[9] The arguments given in defense of defending generally emphasize similar considerations, many with a long tradition extending far back into the history of English common law. As you read through them, consider these defenses not as a matter of legal history but as a matter of morality. To what extent do they appeal to considerations on the morality side of the bridge? Do you think the moral arguments justify the duty (or at least permission) as a matter of professional ethics to defend people charged with heinous crimes? The moral issues in criminal defense go beyond the initial decision of whether or not to represent a client and extend to the means used in the defense. The public sometimes condemns lawyers for using what appear to be deceptive means in persuading the jury that the state has not proven its case. Consider the following arguments as an attempt to justify not only the decision *whom* to represent, but also *by what means.*

7.1.1 Everyone deserves to be treated with dignity by the criminal justice system, even people accused of terrible crimes

Individuals in a liberal democracy have rights, including the right to be treated with dignity and respect by the state. Part of what it means to be a right, to use Ronald Dworkin's famous expression, is to "trump" other

---

[9] See, e.g., Abbe Smith and Monroe Freedman, *How Can You Represent Those People?* (New York: Palgrave MacMillan 2013); Alan M. Dershowitz, *Reasonable Doubts: The Criminal Justice System and the O. J. Simpson Case* (New York: Touchstone 1997); James S. Kunen, "How Can You Defend Those People?": The Making of a Criminal Lawyer (New York: Random House 1983); Seymour Wishman, *Confessions of a Criminal Lawyer* (New York: Times Books 1981); Abbe Smith, "Defending Defending: The Case for Unmitigated Zeal on Behalf of People Who Do Terrible Things," *Hofstra Law Review* 28: 925–61 (2000); Charles J. Ogletree, Jr., "Beyond Justifications: Seeking Motivations to Sustain Public Defenders," *Harvard Law Review* 106: 1239–94 (1993); Michael E. Tigar, "Defending," *Texas Law Review* 74: 101–110 (1995); Barbara Babcock, "Defending the Guilty," *Cleveland State Law Review* 32: 175–87 (1983); John B. Mitchell, "The Ethics of the Criminal Defense Attorney – New Answers to Old Questions," *Stanford Law Review* 32: 293–337 (1980). Babcock and Tigar both updated and republished their essays in Smith and Freedman, *supra.*

considerations, just as in certain card games low cards from the trump suit will win the trick over high cards from another suit.[10] Dworkin's point is that rights may trump another "background justification for political decisions that states a goal for the community as a whole."[11] In other words, from the point of view of social welfare, it may be a good thing that guilty people are punished and incapacitated from committing additional offenses. From the point of view of rights, however, an individual's right to be treated with dignity trumps this background justification, appealing as it does to considerations of collective or social welfare. The justification for individual rights is not that they contribute to shared social goals such as preventing crime and punishing the guilty. Rather, the justification depends only on the inherent worth and dignity of each individual person. Remember from Chapter 2 that David Luban has argued that everyone deserves not to be humiliated and that humiliation consists of treating people as though they have no point of view worth taking seriously.[12] If humiliating people denies them their dignity, then representing people, giving them a voice with which to express themselves in a way that powerful actors are forced to take seriously, is a way of honoring their dignity. More concretely, lawyers protect individual rights that are linked with dignity, such as the right to be free from unlawful searches and seizures of property and the right against being forced to testify against oneself. People do not forfeit those rights merely because they have been accused of committing terrible crimes. Even someone like Paul Bernardo deserves to be treated with dignity during the process of determining his guilt or innocence.

7.1.2   Determining the truth is the role of the jury or judge; it is not for defense counsel to judge whether the client is guilty or a bad person

The adversary system of adjudication requires the parties themselves to present evidence and argument to the court. Unlike civil law systems, in

---

[10] See Ronald Dworkin, "Rights as Trumps," in Jeremy Waldron, ed., *Theories of Rights* (Oxford: Oxford University Press 1994).

[11] Id., p. 153.

[12] See David Luban, "Lawyers as Upholders of Human Dignity (When They're Not Busy Assaulting It)," in *Legal Ethics and Human Dignity* (Cambridge: Cambridge University Press 2007), pp. 71–72.

which the judge plays an active role in the investigation, judges in a common law, adversarial system are relatively passive. The functioning of the system depends, to a significant extent, on lawyers to provide "inputs" in the form of the testimony of witnesses, documents and physical evidence, and arguments concerning the application of the law to the evidence produced. Thus, one of the defense lawyer's most important duties, as a matter of professional ethics, is to avoid forming any opinion about the guilt or innocence of one's client.[13] Sometimes people who are alleged to have done terrible things turn out to be innocent. A man named John Demjanjuk was arrested in 1977 and charged with being a guard at the Treblinka concentration camp known as "Ivan the Terrible," responsible for the murders of thousands of people. He was convicted and sent to Israel, where he was sentenced to death. His lawyer, Michael Tigar, took considerable abuse in the press, even from other lawyers, for representing Demjanjuk, until he proved that the American government had lied and suppressed evidence showing that someone else was "Ivan the Terrible." As Tigar argued, if a lawyer had not been willing to withstand criticism and accept the moral cost of representing an accused Nazi war criminal, an innocent man would have been hanged after spending seven years in solitary confinement.

Apart from the decision of whether or not to represent a particular client (in jurisdictions without a strict cab rank rule), lawyers can do many things that have an effect on the process of searching for the truth. It is clear, however, that defense lawyers are not supposed to aim directly at ascertaining truth. Rather, they present evidence inconsistent with the state's theory of their client's guilt and seek to undermine the state's case by such tactics as cross-examining witnesses to show bias, uncertainty, or contradiction. This is a simple but powerful point: The goal of the process (finding truth) does not have to be the goal of individual participants in the process. The truth-finding function of the adversary system does exert some influence on the duties of lawyers who are prohibited from knowingly introducing false testimony (a subject we consider in the next section). But the systemic goal of ascertaining truth does not require lawyers to withhold representation from clients known to be, or strongly suspected of being, guilty.

[13] Woolley, *supra*, p. 374.

Former criminal defense lawyer and law professor Barbara Babcock calls this the "legalistic or positivist's reason" for representing criminal defendants.[14] What is the connection with legal positivism? Recall the discussion in Chapter 4 suggesting that legal positivism can be understood as a theory of the rules of a game, like poker, chess, or rugby, but that it is importantly *only* a theory of rules of a game. Law is one thing, morality is another. A criminal defense lawyer who is a legal positivist may therefore believe herself to be no more subject to moral criticism than someone who bluffs while playing poker.[15] The client's actual guilt, and the moral condemnation that would follow from it, is not the lawyer's concern. The response to this argument should be fairly obvious: Unlike a true game, such as poker, the "game" of the criminal justice system affects people who are not players, such as the victims of crime and people who feel insecure due to the threat of crime. These nonplayers do not consent to be subject to the rules of the game, so it is unclear why they should have to suffer the consequences of a result that is permitted by the rules of the game, such as the acquittal of a guilty person who goes free possibly to commit more crimes. Note, however, that legal positivism does not deny the possibility that a system of rules may have a moral purpose; it only denies that it must be the case that, in order to count as "law," a system of rules must have a moral purpose. One can therefore be a legal positivist and believe, as most lawyers do, that the criminal justice system is aimed at a number of morally worthwhile ends, such as ascertaining the truth about whether someone committed a crime, restraining the power of police officers and prosecutors, and ensuring that accused persons are treated with dignity.

7.1.3   Anyway, who knows what the truth is?

This defense of representing guilty clients is a variation of the previous one, which assigns the responsibility for ascertaining truth to another decision maker. This version, however, makes a direct appeal to the idea of epistemological skepticism. Lawyers say things like this:

---

[14] Babcock, *supra*, pp. 177–78.

[15] "The law proceeds on what is made to appear according to the rules of the game, not on what 'really' is." Geoffrey C. Hazard, Jr., "Quis Custodiet Ipsos Custodes?," *Yale Law Journal* 95: 1523–35 (1986) (book review), p. 1529.

The truth is at the bottom of a bottomless pit.[16]

Truth exists somewhere between what you can prove and can't – that we know.[17]

Less dramatically, lawyers point out that all people tend to make snap judgments that later are proved wrong, and so lawyers learn to suspend judgment in the early stages of investigation and litigation until they know what the facts are.[18] Something may appear to be one way based on incomplete evidence but turn out to be another when all the evidence is in. Cognitive psychology tells us that once we assume something to be true, we will unconsciously tend to notice evidence that confirms this belief and ignore disconfirming evidence, a tendency known as *confirmation bias*.[19] Holding one's judgment in abeyance may help mitigate confirmation bias and allow lawyers to do a better job of developing a strong case for their clients. One of the cardinal rules of advocacy is to think about one's case from the perspective of the adversary or the court in order to develop an effective response to what is likely to be the adversary's position. Lawyers also remind us that witnesses may have faulty memories, biases, and, in some cases, a motivation to lie. A witness's account is only one version of events and may deserve to be regarded with some doubt until other evidence is considered. The government's witnesses may be lying, and something even worse, such as official persecution or a cover-up, may be afoot.

> Consider the Haymarket trial, in which innocent men were railroaded, and only those who escaped the noose could be pardoned years later. Sacco and Vanzetti were swept up in the xenophobic hysteria fomented by the federal government, most visibly in the person of Attorney General A. Mitchell Palmer. More recently, a Cleveland auto worker spent years in a death cell convicted of being Ivan the Terrible of Treblinka; not only was

[16] Civil defense lawyer Jerome Facher, quoted in Jonathan Harr, *A Civil Action* (New York: Random House 1995), p. 340.

[17] Lawrence Joseph, *Lawyerland: What Lawyers Talk About when They Talk about Law* (New York: Farrar, Straus & Giroux 1997), p. 127.

[18] Hazard, Geoffrey C., Jr. and Dana A. Remus, "Advocacy Revalued," *University of Pennsylvania Law Review* 159: 751–81 (2011).

[19] See, e.g., Thomas Gilovich and Dale W. Griffin, "Judgment and Decision Making," in Thomas Gilovich, Dacher Keltner, and Richard E. Nisbett, eds., in *Social Psychology* (New York: Norton, 2d edn., 2011), pp. 246–58.

he innocent of that charge, but our own government had defrauded the federal courts to get him extradited to Israel for trial.[20]

Given the risk of uncertainty, the cost of erroneous judgments, and the myriad reasons to doubt the veracity of the evidence presented by the state, defense lawyers prefer not to think in terms of truth or falsity but instead of what they can prove at trial with the available evidence.

Adopting a moderately disinterested, even skeptical attitude toward one's client's guilt or innocence is probably a good thing from the point of view of providing effective representation to clients, but it does not avoid the moral problem when the lawyer knows the client is guilty. Make no mistake about it – sometimes lawyers are able to say with certainty, or at least to the level of "beyond a reasonable doubt," that their clients are guilty. One reason for beginning this chapter with the case of Paul Bernardo is that his lawyer was able to view videotaped evidence of his client's guilt. Clients sometimes tell their lawyers that they committed the crime and will lie if given the chance (although to avoid the impact of legal rules governing the presentation of false evidence, defense lawyers would prefer not to hear this from clients).[21] There are also cases in which clients may deny guilt but tell such an incredible story that no reasonable person could reach a conclusion other than that the client is lying. The argument that sometimes, in many cases, or even in most cases the truth is unknowable is not responsive to the problem in a case in which the lawyer is certain of the truth of the matter. For those cases, the lawyer must resort to another one of the arguments considered here.

7.1.4 Finding out the truth – whether the defendant committed the crime charged – is one goal of the process, but it is not the only goal

Other goals served by the criminal justice system include treating people swept up within it with at least a modicum of human dignity (argument 1)

---

[20] Michael E. Tigar, "Defending," *Texas Law Review* 74: 101–110 (1995), p. 104.

[21] For example, the client in *State v. McDowell*, 681 N.W.2d 500 (Wis. 2004), said "I'll say what I need to say to help myself out and if I have something untruthful to say I'll say that. I need to help myself out."

and, as is commonly asserted, checking the power of the state. Indeed, the adversary system in criminal cases is deliberately designed to make it difficult to conclude with a finding of guilt. The accused begins with a presumption of innocence and may be convicted only if a jury believes in guilt beyond a reasonable doubt.[22] Lawyers are fond of quoting Blackstone, who said it is better for ten guilty people to go free than for one innocent person to be convicted.[23] That principle clearly puts a thumb on the scale in the direction of requiring scrupulous compliance by the state with procedures designed to protect innocent people from wrongful convictions. As a result, criminal pretrial and trial procedures are designed to promote goals other than ascertaining the guilt or innocence of the accused. For example, evidence of guilt may be excluded from the proceeding if it was obtained by the police in violation of the defendant's rights, as in a warrantless search. Even if the evidence is highly probative of guilt – say, for example, it consists of a kilo of cocaine and a list of customers – it may not be considered by the jury if the police simply barged into the defendant's house without a warrant and found the items. The defense lawyer will file a motion to suppress the evidence, and it will not be introduced at trial by the prosecutor. Key functions of the criminal defense lawyer are to "police the police," to serve as a watchdog against abuses of government power, and to perform this monitoring role through the representation of individual clients.[24]

If procedures are designed to further goals such as guarding against abuses of state power and protecting the rights of the accused, and if one believes that rights are "trumps" – that is, they are justified on the ground of protecting the individual from abuse in the name of society as a whole – then it follows that a lawyer is morally justified in representing a client

---

[22] American criminal procedure includes the evidentiary standard of proving guilt "beyond a reasonable doubt," but the law of other common law countries also features the presumption of innocence as a protection for individual rights. See, e.g., Section 11(d) of the Canadian Charter of Rights and Freedoms and Section 25(c) of the New Zealand Bill of Rights Act 1990.

[23] See William Blackstone, *Commentaries on the Laws of England* *358. For the connection between Blackstone's maxim and the "beyond a reasonable doubt" evidentiary standard, see Kevin M. Clermont, *Standards of Decision in Law* (Durham, N.C.: Carolina Academic Press 2013), pp. 29–30.

[24] See Johnnie L. Cochran, Jr., "How Can You Defend Those People?," *Loyola of Los Angeles Law Review* 30: 39–43 (1996), p. 42.

despite the lawyer's knowledge of the client's guilt. Awful as he is, Paul Bernardo has rights, and the fact that he undeniably committed a horrible crime does not cause those rights to be forfeited until he has been convicted using fair procedures. A decent society would not allow Bernardo to be convicted based on a confession he made after being tortured. Similarly, there is a social interest in making sure that law enforcement personnel respect the privacy rights of all citizens. For this reason, a lawyer would be justified in arguing that the police acted wrongly in seizing the videotape evidence if they acted without a warrant. Although this might result in the acquittal of a murderer, it is essential that the police, the prosecutor, and other government actors understand that their violations of the rights of citizens have such consequences in order to deter abuses of official state power. The criminal trial is not only about whether Bernardo committed the crime, but also about whether the police officers and prosecutors played by the rules that are intended for the protection of individual rights.

Even before being convicted of a crime, criminal defendants may experience significant deprivations of fundamental liberties. People suspected of crimes are subject to arrest and personal searches, their property may be searched and seized pursuant to a warrant or a recognized exception permitting it, and accusation of a crime carries a significant social stigma that may be difficult or impossible to rebut. Conviction of a crime is accompanied by the possibility of a loss of property through a fine or forfeiture of "tainted" assets, imprisonment, and, in some countries, even death. Moreover, criminal convictions often have significant collateral consequences, such as the loss of the right to vote, possess firearms, or practice certain professions. An academic historian who served on a jury in a murder case describes being sequestered in a hotel room, pondering the day's events, and keeping a journal of his reactions. Near the end of the trial, he wrote out an insight that crystalized for him the explanation for the seeming oddities of the procedure he was witnessing: "We have seen the power of the state," it read simply. The jurors did not appreciate state power in a merely abstract way, but experienced in its concrete manifestations every day:

> [T]he state could take control of your person, it could refuse to let you go home, it could send men with guns to watch you take a piss, it could deny you access to a lawyer, it could embarrass you in public and force you to reply

meekly, it could, ultimately, send you to jail – all this, apparently, without even accusing you of a crime.[25]

The historian is not exactly correct – the state at least does have to accuse the defendant of a crime – but his point is nevertheless well taken that the state has the means of coercive force at its disposal to deprive citizens of the rights normally taken for granted (such as being able to use the bathroom without being watched by men with guns). That power needs to be counterbalanced somehow, which is the essence of the criminal defense lawyer's role.

7.1.5   Many crimes are committed by people who themselves are victims of gross social injustices, such as poverty and racism; they deserve compassion and support for this reason

The full power of the criminal justice system is often deployed against members of communities who are already powerless – people of color, poor people, immigrants, the unemployed, and young people. As American public defender and law professor Abbe Smith observes:

> [P]unishment is regarded as the answer to almost all of our social problems. We cannot seem to build prisons fast enough, and we are on the road to the virtual banishment of young African-American men from society.[26]

Many criminal defenders are drawn to this work as a way of fighting for the underdog and working for social justice. Alternatively, they are motivated not by the good of the community of which the defendant is a part but by the satisfaction of providing an individual with a modicum of concern and the possibility of mitigating the harshness of the law as it affects that person's life.[27]

---

[25] D. Graham Burnett, *A Trial by Jury* (New York: Knopf 2001), pp. 160–61.

[26] Smith, *supra*, p. 952 (citing statistics showing that, in some cities, more than half of young African-American men between the ages of 18 and 35 are in prison or otherwise under the supervision of the criminal justice system). See also David Cole, *No Equal Justice: Race and Class in the American Criminal Justice System* (New York: New Press 1999).

[27] See Babcock, *supra*, p. 178 (calling this the "social worker's reason" for working as a public defender).

Many criminal defense lawyers come to feel empathy for their clients, despite the allegations that they committed serious crimes. Lawyers perceive their clients as frightened, overwhelmed, facing a dehumanizing and terrifying system, and in need of someone to relate to them as a human being.[28] This kind of empathy is importantly different from Charles Fried's idea of the lawyer as a special-purpose friend (Chapter 2). Fried does want to generalize a professional ethical duty of loyalty from the intense, individualized bonds of affection between friends.[29] But he stretches the metaphor to its breaking point by arguing that one ought to prefer the interests of an identifiable individual over the welfare of society when one is representing a stranger or an institution. For many criminal defenders, however, friendship is not a metaphor but a lived aspect of the experience of representing clients who truly are alone in the world and in need of someone to see them as humans, not as monsters or social jetsam to be rigorously eliminated by the machinery of the justice system. Some lawyers have religious grounds for extending care and concern to people accused of crimes. Monroe Freedman, for example, invokes the Jewish ideal of *rachmanut*, or compassion, for suffering people,[30] and a Christian lawyer might consider the representation of guilty clients as an act of ministry, recognizing that, theologically speaking, we are all guilty.[31] Defense lawyers frequently must contend with barriers created by their clients' understandable mistrust of lawyers as part of the system that condemns them, but, in many cases, lawyers can come to understand and represent their clients as flesh-and-blood human beings, not mere abstractions.

Each of these arguments relies on a narrowing of the defense lawyer's moral universe. It is not hard to see why defending people accused of heinous crimes seems to be an activity that stands entirely apart from morality. Criminal defense lawyers not only hang around with people like accused murderers and concentration camp guards, but they also devote countless hours of their lives and dedicate all their skill and training to helping them

[28] See, e.g., Ogletree, *supra*, p. 1271–74.

[29] Charles Fried, "The Lawyer as Friend: The Moral Foundations of the Lawyer-Client Relation," *Yale Law Journal* 85: 1060–89 (1976), p. 1070.

[30] Monroe H. Freedman, "Why It's Essential to Represent 'Those People'," in Smith and Freedman, *supra*, pp. 76–77.

[31] Thomas L. Shaffer, *On Being a Christian and a Lawyer* (Provo, Utah: Brigham Young University Press 1981), pp. 75–76.

escape punishment. The arguments in this section mean to show that the lawyer's role is not, in fact, isolated from morality. Rather, the morality of the defense lawyer's role is special, in the sense of being peculiar, or concerned with some values rather than others. Paradigmatically, the most important value is loyalty to the client, but defense lawyers also express allegiance to rule of law values, such as insisting that the state exercise power only subject to regular, impartially administered procedures. Some moral considerations, but not others, are permitted across the bridge between the domains of morality and professional ethics. What those considerations are, and how much they justify, remain hotly contested issues.

Michael Tigar defended his decision to represent the accused "Ivan the Terrible" with an eloquent moral argument:

> We must remember the Holocaust, and we should pursue and punish its perpetrators. We dishonor that memory and besmirch the pursuit if we fail to accord those accused of Holocaust crimes the same measure of legality and due process that we would give to anyone accused of wrongdoing. Precisely because a charge of culpable participation in the Holocaust is so damning, the method of judgment whether such a charge is true should be above reproach.[32]

Tigar offered this defense in a debate with Monroe Freedman, who insisted that lawyers are morally accountable for their choice of clients. Freedman noted that Tigar had once sided with student activists who had picketed a large Washington, DC, law firm that had chosen to represent General Motors in an air pollution case.[33] Tigar had urged the law firm's lawyers to ask themselves this moral question:

> Which side are you on? The decision is whether or not you will commit your skills, your talents, your resources to the vindication of the interests of the vast majority of Americans or the vindication of the interests of . . . the minority of Americans who own the instruments of pollution and repression.[34]

---

[32] Michael E. Tigar, "Setting the Record Straight on the Defense of John Demjanjuk," *Legal Times* (Sept. 6, 1993), reprinted in Monroe Freedman and Abbe Smith, *Understanding Lawyers' Ethics* (New Providence, N.J.: LexisNexis, 4th edn., 2010), Appendix A, p. 371.

[33] See Monroe H. Freedman, "The Lawyer's Moral Obligation of Justification," *Texas Law Review* 74: 111–118 (1995).

[34] Id. at 113 (quoting Debate at George Washington University Law School [1970]; transcript on file with the Texas Law Review).

Are the moral standards different for justifying the representation of accused criminal defendants and parties in civil litigation? Does it matter whether the client is a powerless individual or a huge multinational corporation? Is it ever legitimate to ask a lawyer the moral question "which side are you on?" or does the Principle of Nonaccountability relieve the lawyer of ever having to justify her choice of clients? Does it follow from the proposition that every client is entitled to a lawyer that a particular client is entitled to *you* as a lawyer? In other words, if you know the client will be represented, may you permissibly decline the representation? Can we consistently praise lawyers who work for civil rights causes, such as the lawyers who argued desegregation cases throughout the American South in the 1940s and '50s, while withholding judgment from other lawyers who represent clients who act contrary to the interests of justice, such as tobacco companies or polluters? If it is permissible for a lawyer to turn down a client who cannot afford to pay her fee, how can the lawyer consistently avoid moral blame for choosing to represent an odious client? Think about those ethical questions in connection with the following case.

A prestigious law firm in New York (or London, Toronto, or Sydney) has been approached by a Swiss bank facing a class action lawsuit filed by survivors of the Holocaust.[35] The lawsuit alleges that the bank had accepted gold that had been stolen by the Nazis from Jews in territory conquered by German armies, including gold that had been extracted from the teeth of victims after they had been killed in concentration camps, converted the gold into Swiss francs, and, in turn, lent money to help finance Hitler's vast military machine. Assume two variations on this problem:

---

[35] This example is drawn from the controversy over the representation of Credit Suisse by the New York law firm Cravath, Swaine & Moore and the Washington, DC, law firm Wilmer, Cutler & Pickering. I blended the facts of the two cases together for the purposes of making a more difficult discussion case. See, e.g., Blaine Harden and Saundra Torry, "N.Y. Law Firm to Advise Swiss Bank Accused of Laundering Nazi Loot," *Washington Post* (Feb. 28, 1997), p. A3; *In re Holocaust Victims Assets Litigation*, 319 F.Supp.2d 301, 303 (E.D.N.Y. 2004) (federal judge excoriating Swiss banks for "continually distort[ing] and obscure[ing] the truth"); see also Christine Parker and Adrian Evans, "Case Study 2.1: The Nazi Gold," in *Inside Lawyers' Ethics* (Cambridge: Cambridge University Press 2007), pp. 37–39. For an in-depth discussion see Michael J. Bazyler, "Gray Zones of Holocaust Restitution: American Justice and Holocaust Morality," in Jonathan Petropoulos and John K. Roth eds., *Gray Zones: Ambiguity and Compromise in the Holocaust and Its Aftermath* (New York: Berghan Books 2005), p. 339.

(A) Partners in the law firm (including Jewish partners) have consulted widely with lawyers in other firms active in Jewish affairs and were told that representing the bank would be acceptable only if the goal was to ensure that the bank was acting responsibly in resolving the case in a way that satisfied Holocaust survivors. The firm told the bank it would accept the representation only if the bank's goal was to make full disclosure about the past, identify a fair solution "as measured by world opinion," and in all respects be "cleaner than a hound's tooth."[36]

(B) Lawyers in the firm realized from the outset that the class action suit implicates complex issues of jurisdiction, choice of law, and statutes of limitation. There are numerous plausible legal grounds to argue that the lawsuit should be dismissed by the court. The bank is interested in minimizing the financial cost of paying claims to victims and their families and is particularly concerned about the possibility that fraudulent claims will be brought against it. Moreover, the bank is keen to "set the record straight," which in its view means denying or minimizing its complicity in Nazi atrocities.[37] The firm agreed to represent the bank and to provide "zealous advocacy" to defend the rights of the bank in court.

Should the law firm accept the representation of the bank? Does it make a difference whether the bank's objective is to make full and complete disclosure (Version A) or to vigorously contest the charges of complicity and minimize its financial exposure (Version B)? Is the bank subject to moral criticism – that is, does the Principle of Nonaccountability hold – in either case? There is no cab rank rule in the United States, so the law firm has discretion, as a matter of the law governing lawyers, to accept or reject the representation for any reason at all.

7.2   Lying, storytelling, and arguing for reasonable doubt

Criminal defense lawyers are frequently accused of lying, or at least of putting on a defense that is deceptive, when they defend a client known to have committed the offense. Defense lawyers generally respond that it is

---

[36] This is the version of the Cravath firm's conduct described in John J. Goldman, "Venerable Firm in Spotlight for Holocaust Assets Case Role," *Los Angeles Times* (Apr. 3, 1997).

[37] This version of the facts seems to be a fair inference from the conduct described in the opinion of US District Judge Edward Korman. See *In re Holocaust Victims Assets Litigation*, 319 F.Supp.2d 301 (E.D.N.Y. 2004).

not their job to evaluate the truth or falsity of the charges – that is the task for the jury, and the government has the burden of proving its case beyond a reasonable doubt. This response is fine as far as it goes, but it still leaves some people uneasy about the tactics used by advocates at trial. Lawyers traditionally understand themselves as "officers of the court," which means, among other things, that they are prohibited from putting on the testimony of witnesses they know to be lying.[38] Thus, it is unclear how the requirement that the state prove guilt beyond a reasonable doubt serves to license a story that is at odds with the truth, at least as the lawyer understands it.[39] The answer is that establishing the truth or falsity of some account of reality is fundamentally a matter of persuading people by telling stories and that there is no way for an attorney to defend the client's right to be presumed innocent without having the latitude to tell a story that is inconsistent with the client's guilt. Consider this example offered by a criminal defense attorney.[40] Usefully, this case does not involve an odious crime, but a rather humdrum offense. It nevertheless presents the important moral question of how far a lawyer is justified in stretching the truth while representing a client.

A person is stopped on suspicion of shoplifting after leaving a store with an inexpensive item, worth a few dollars at most. As the manager is talking to her, someone inside the store calls out "there's a fire!" and the manager has to go back inside. When he comes back out, the alleged shoplifter is still there, standing on the sidewalk. She agrees to be searched. and the manager discovers that she has $10 in her pocket. In the actual case, the client admitted to her lawyer that she intended to steal the item. Thus, any story ending with "therefore, my client could not have intended to steal the goods" is false with respect to the factual truth of the matter. Nevertheless, at trial, the defense lawyer uses these bits of data to argue

---

[38] See, e.g., American Bar Association, Model Rules of Professional Conduct, Rule 3.3(a); Code of Conduct of the Bar of England and Wales, Rule 302.

[39] Sissela Bok defines lying as communicating a message with the intention that others believe something the speaker does not believe. See Sissela Bok, *Lying: Moral Choice in Public and Private Life* (New York: Pantheon Books 1978), p. 13. By relying on the speaker's belief, this definition sidesteps the question of whether the speaker *knows* the message is untrue.

[40] John B. Mitchell, "Reasonable Doubts Are Where You Find Them," *Georgetown Journal of Legal Ethics* 1: 339–61 (1987). The example is similar in structure to the poker game alibi and the stolen television cases discussed in Chapter 2.

that the defendant could not possibly have intended to steal the item. If she did have this intent, surely she would have used the opportunity provided by the report of the fire to flee the scene. The fact that she stuck around to talk to the manager suggests she must have an innocent explanation – for example, that she had put the property in her pocket absent-mindedly. This explanation is supported by the fact that the client had sufficient money to pay for the goods. On behalf of the client at trial, the lawyer argues that the whole thing was an innocent mistake.

Is this story deceptive? Maybe. Suppose, for the sake of discussion, that the client admitted to her lawyer that she intended to steal the item. Under applicable rules of conduct, the lawyer would not be allowed to make a closing argument to the jury that includes the statement, "My client did not intend to steal the goods." That would be a direct lie. When it comes to telling a story that is inconsistent with the client's statement that she intended to steal the item, however, most criminal defense lawyers would argue that it is *permissible* deception, justified as the only way to give practical effect to the defendant's right to have guilt proven beyond a reasonable doubt, with the burden of proof resting squarely on the prosecution. To vindicate the defendant's right, her advocate must be able not only to argue that the prosecution's story is untrue, but also to tell a story of her own, inconsistent with the defendant's guilt. Juries are persuaded by stories, not by bland denials of the facts as recounted by the prosecution. A defense lawyer cannot be limited simply to nitpicking the prosecution's case because isolated bits of evidence do not carry meaning and therefore cannot persuade. Persuasion is a meaning-making process, and meaning is conveyed by assembling events into a coherent story that has direction or a purpose.

In this example, the defense lawyer would practically be talking gibberish if she simply stated to the jury, "The state did not prove its case beyond a reasonable doubt." It would not be much better to assert the facts blandly without arguing for an interpretation of the facts that is inconsistent with the defendant's guilt, such as: "My client had $10 in her pocket; she didn't run when the manager went back inside." This would be a truthful statement of the evidence, but it would not mean much unless the implications of the evidence were laid out for the jury. The only intelligible way to present that kind of defense would be to connect the dots, as it were, by telling a story: "Now, if my client intended to steal the item, wouldn't she have taken off as soon as the manager went inside to deal with the fire? The fact that she waited for him to return suggests that it was just an innocent mistake. That has to be the right explanation, considering she had enough money in her pocket to pay for the property, too." The implication of that story is false – the client admitted intending to steal the property – but the defense lawyer must be permitted to tell the client's story as a way of asserting the client's right to, as lawyers say, put the state to its proof. As a matter of human psychology, people understand events and persuade each other by telling stories.[41] Denying the lawyer permission to tell a story inconsistent with guilt would undercut the *client's* right to have her guilt established at trial beyond a reasonable doubt.

To make a somewhat deeper point, which may strike some readers as sophistry, a lawyer might deny that the story told on behalf of the client is false because truth and falsity in legal narratives is not simply a matter of bland factual reporting – did the client steal the goods or not? Rather, a story told at trial is part of a broader narrative in which the meaning of the law is elaborated, including such matters as whether it is legitimate to punish this person for this offense. The law's claim to our allegiance depends on its being a way of understanding that "rings true" for its subjects. Narratives not only constitute the reality for the individuals whose stories are told at trial, but they also constitute the very idea of justice. Understood in this way, the conclusion of the defense lawyer's story is not "my client didn't steal the item" but "my client does not deserve punishment." Factual data are parts of the narrative. but so are explicit or implicit claims about desert, blame, responsibility, excuse, and other normative notions. A story is believed or not if it makes the right kind of sense of both the facts and the values implicated by an event. "[N]arrative is a mode of discourse that takes directly into account the normative elements on which law is based – the existence of a legitimate, canonical state of things that has been compli-cated by some human action in some particular context or setting."[42] Specifically with regard to a criminal trial, the discourse of the participants is the rhetoric of blaming, which is aimed at identifying and restoring the

---

[41] See Anthony Amsterdam and Jerome Bruner, *Minding the Law* (Cambridge, Mass.: Harvard University Press 2000), p. 111–42; Nancy Pennington and Reid Hastie, "A Cognitive Theory of Juror Decision Making: The Story Model," *Cardozo Law Review* 13: 519–57 (1991).

[42] Amsterdam and Bruner, *supra*, p. 141.

right relationships among members of a community.[43] The community therefore creates and sustains itself through judgments of blame made on the basis of stories meant to justify punishment or mercy.

The most difficult moral dilemmas in criminal defense arise when the story the lawyer tells on behalf of the client may have the effect of deepening and intensifying the harm to the victim. In the shoplifting story, the victim is a store that expects to lose some amount of inventory to theft. This does not excuse the defendant's conduct, but it is tempting to write off the victim as a nameless, faceless corporation, less deserving of moral concern than the individual human client represented by the defense lawyer. (A lawyer seeking to persuade her audience will know of ways to subtly convey this message if she believes it will contribute to a narrative inconsistent with her client's blameworthiness.) But many crime victims are individuals, and sometimes the victims perceive the criminal trial process as a second victimization. The defendant in a criminal trial may tell a story that is inconsistent with his or her blameworthiness but is at the same time deeply wounding to another participant. In that case, the lawyer really would be living out the ethical principle identified by Lord Brougham in his defense of Queen Caroline (Chapter 3): "To save that client by all means and expedients, and at all hazards and costs to other persons . . . is [the lawyer's] first and only duty; and in performing this duty he must not regard the alarm, the torments, the destruction which he may bring upon others." Few cases illustrate the infliction of torments and destruction upon another as vividly as the representation of a criminal defendant in a rape prosecution where the defendant seeks to establish innocence on the grounds of consent.[44] Consider this example:

---

[43] See James Boyd White, "Making Sense of What We Do: The Criminal Law as a System of Meaning," in *Heracles' Bow: Essays on the Rhetoric and Poetics of the Law* (Madison: University of Wisconsin Press 1985), pp. 207–09.

[44] This example is borrowed from Monroe Freedman, one of the staunchest defenders of the adversary system. See Monroe H. Freedman, *Lawyers' Ethics in an Adversary System* (Indianapolis: Bobbs-Merrill 1975), pp. 43–45. The problem continues to feature in the book by Professor Freedman and his co-author Abbe Smith. See *Understanding Lawyers' Ethics* (New Providence, N.J.: LexisNexis, 4th edn., 2010) § 7.12, pp. 207–08. Professor Smith has written separately, and with great sensitivity, about the defense of the police officer accused of having violently assaulted Haitian immigrant Abner Louima in a police station house. The lawyer's defense included insinuations that Louima's injuries could have resulted from consensual homosexual activities. See Smith, *supra*,

The defendant works at a gas (petrol) station on the outskirts of a medium-sized university town, which is the site of the alleged assault. The alleged victim is a 22-year-old woman who is a graduate student at the university's divinity school. The defendant at first was reluctant to talk about the event but eventually told the lawyer that he had sex with the young woman, but it was consensual. He said he had seen her on several prior occasions on which they had talked and flirted. On the night in question, he described how she had come on to him, they began talking in her car, one thing led to another, and they had sex. They were interrupted by the arrival of another car at the station, and, when the defendant got out to help the customer, the young woman drove away. The young woman told police and the grand jury that she was returning late at night from a conference at which she had presented a paper when she noticed that her car was almost on empty. She stopped at the station and asked the attendant for help, at which point he forced his way into her car, made threats, and had sex with her against her will, stopping only when another car drove into the station.

In the course of investigation, the lawyer discovered that the alleged victim had been romantically involved with at least two other local men before becoming engaged to her current fiancé. One of the men, Jones, remains bitter about his breakup with the young woman. When the lawyer interviewed Jones, he described the young woman as flirtatious, with a bit of a wild, rebellious streak. He related a story of having gone with her to a party and, after she had been gone for some time, discovering her in a room upstairs on a bed with Smith, a mutual friend, with some of her clothes off. Jones says he is willing to testify and doubts very much that the alleged victim was raped. In a second interview with the defendant, he admitted to the lawyer that his first story was false and that he indeed had forced the

pp. 930–32. Smith notes that while the allegations were so shocking that other cops broke the proverbial "blue wall of silence" and testified against the defendant, the public outrage was such that "[t]hose in charge clearly needed at least some of the officers involved to go down," and if the defendant was convicted, he faced a lengthy prison sentence where he would likely be at significant risk of being assaulted by other prisoners." Id. at 939. Under these circumstances, Smith argues that the defendant deserves vigorous representation, and it is not for the defense lawyer to worry about the harm to others or to be less than zealous in defending her client based on her own personal moral scruples about appealing to the biases and prejudices of the jury. Id. at 951–54.

young woman to have sex against her will. He refuses to consider pleading guilty to a lesser charge. Now what?

The point of calling Jones as a witness is to play to an ancient and pernicious stereotype: that women who are raped often invite the assault by flirting or dressing provocatively and that previous sexual promiscuity by women indicates a future propensity to lead men on.

> [I]n rape cases, it is always the victim who is on trial. The fact that she was willing to have sex with past lovers will be used to show that she wants it with violent strangers as well; the sexist *idée fixe* of the vengeful and accusatory bitch who is trying to get a man in trouble will suffice to throw a burden of proof on her that she did *not* consent to sex.[45]

Even if the defendant is ultimately convicted, the experience of testifying at trial, being cross-examined about her past sexual behavior, and sitting through the innuendo-based testimony of Jones will be humiliating. Other rape victims, observing the effects of the process on the complaining witness, may be deterred from reporting sexual assaults. For this reason, many jurisdictions have enacted so-called rape shield statutes that prohibit the introduction of evidence in a rape prosecution of the sexual history of the complaining witness. However, these statutes only prohibit the introduction of irrelevant sexual history evidence, and where there is a plausible consent defense, experienced criminal defense attorneys are usually able to introduce the evidence. Suppose the defense lawyer could get the evidence introduced – as an ethical matter, *should* the lawyer do it?

David Luban argues from that premise that "the criminal process must ensure that rape victims can step forward to accuse their assailants without their own sexuality being turned into the centerpiece of the trial" to the conclusion that a criminal defense lawyer must stop short of "allowing cross-examination that makes the victim look like a whore."[46] The concerns about abuse of state power, poverty and marginalization, and the unreliability of evidence that would ordinarily justify the zealous representation of criminal defendants must be balanced against the problem of perpetuating violence by men against women. Defenders of a strong conception of adversarial ethics may concede the harm to women who are forced to

---

[45] David Luban, *Lawyers and Justice* (Princeton: Princeton University Press 1988), p. 151.
[46] Luban, *supra*, p. 151.

endure a humiliating cross-examination at trial, but they insist that the only object of their special ethical concern is their client facing the possibility of a significant deprivation of liberty. Abbe Smith, for example, discusses Lord Brougham's speech and the modern progressive critique of zealous advocacy.[47] Progressives who would otherwise be sympathetic with criminal defenders are concerned about the collateral damage inflicted by Brougham-style advocacy on women, gay-lesbian-bisexual-transgender (GLBT) people, racial minorities, and other socially disempowered groups. Smith's response – itself from a progressive perspective – is that it is appropriate that a lawyer be concerned about marginalized people, but that concern should be expressed one client at a time, through the value of loyal and zealous representation of defendants. "It is simply wrong to place an additional burden on criminal defense lawyers to make the world a better place as they labor to represent individuals facing loss of liberty or life," she writes.[48] As in the conservative defense (by Charles Fried) of professional neutrality, the progressive critique of criminal defense shows that legal ethics can cut across conventional political categories in interesting ways. Ethics need not reduce to politics.

Going back to the three-step argument set out in Chapter 2,[49] what is the relevant value on the morality side of the bridge supporting a vigorous defense in this case, including the introduction of testimony and cross-examination that might result in the humiliation of the alleged victim? Consider Luban's appeal to the value of human dignity, grounded in human subjectivity – being a moral agent means having a first-person perspective on the world and thus having a story to tell. The reliance on dignity as a foundational value seems to tell against the argument given by Luban earlier (on the professional ethics side of the bridge) that lawyers should not be ethically permitted to shift the focus of a rape trial to the sexuality of the complaining witness.[50] The discussion of deceptive

---

[47] See Smith, *supra*, pp. 951–52.   [48] Smith, *supra*, p. 952.

[49] (1) Define, specify, and explain the significance of a moral value; (2) show that the value in step (1) entails a principle of professional ethics; (3) test the resulting theory against cases.

[50] See Katherine R. Kruse, "The Human Dignity of Clients," *Cornell Law Review* 93: 1343–64 (2008), p. 1346 ("it is unclear how lawyers are supposed to resolve conflicts when upholding the client's human dignity by giving voice to the client's subjectivity amounts to an assault on the human dignity of another").

stories suggests that an ethical duty to tell the client's story, which is entailed by Luban's conception of human dignity, requires the lawyer to introduce evidence in support of the client's story, even if the lawyer believes the client's story is false. If the violation of the moral duty of truthfulness is permitted here, then the lawyer may similarly be permitted to violate what would ordinarily be a moral obligation not to humiliate others.

8   Prosecutors

> In the criminal justice system, the people are represented by two separate yet equally important groups. The police who investigate crime and the district attorneys who prosecute the offenders. These are their stories.

Anyone who has turned on a television set in the past twenty years, anywhere in the English-speaking world, has heard the voiceover introduction of the long-running and endlessly replayed series *Law and Order*. (Admit it – you heard the "chung CHUNG" sound in your head when you read those lines.) But notice something strange in those familiar words: *The people* are represented by prosecuting attorneys. The assistant district attorneys shown investigating the facts, talking to witnesses, and trying cases in the courtroom have a boss – an elected or appointed political official – but, in theory, their *client* is an abstraction called "the people" or, in Commonwealth countries, the Crown. Criminal cases in these nations are captioned *R v. Defendant*, with the "R" standing for Rex or Regina – king or queen. Prosecutors claim to act in the name of the sovereign or society as a whole, seeking to punish offenses against the common good. That makes them different from most other lawyers who work on behalf of an identifiable client whose interests may differ from the common good. Although in theory they represent the public interest, prosecutors are employed by the state. All lawyers are, in principle, "officers of the court," meaning that their authority is derived in some way from that of the judicial system. Prosecutors are, in addition, subject to the direction of government officials. In most common law countries, the Director of Public Prosecutions or the Crown Attorney is an appointed position. (As in so many things, the United States is an outlier, and the chief prosecutor in many cities and counties is an elected office.) Just as lawyers representing a corporation in principle represent the shareholders acting through an elected board of directors, prosecuting attorneys represent all citizens, acting through some combination of elected and appointed political officials.

Numerous technical issues arise concerning the legal obligations of prosecutors. For example, must they disclose evidence to the defendant and his lawyer that would tend, if believed, to negate the guilt of the accused? Must a prosecutor call all credible material witnesses? How much certainty must a prosecutor have in the guilt of the accused before filing charges or seeking an indictment? What happens when a prosecutor subsequently discovers evidence tending to show that someone was wrongfully accused? These and related questions are addressed in the rules of professional conduct promulgated by bar associations (and, in the United States, by state courts).[1] Judicial decisions, statutes, and regulations also impose legal obligations on prosecutors.[2] In keeping with the theme of this book, however, this chapter analyzes the duties of prosecutors as a matter of ethics, seeking to connect moral considerations with professional ethics. It explores these issues through the discussion of a case involving the conflict between personal ethics, the norms of hierarchical organizations, and the rule of law.

---

[1] See, e.g., Western Australia Barristers' Rules § 88(a) ("A prosecutor must call as part of the prosecution's case all witnesses . . . whose testimony is admissible and necessary for the presentation of all of the relevant circumstances."); Code of Professional Conduct for British Columbia, Rule 5.1–3, Commentary ("The prosecutor . . . should make timely disclosure to defence counsel or directly to an unrepresented accused of all relevant and known facts and witnesses, whether tending to show guilt or innocence."); Bar Council of India, Rules on Professional Standards, Rules on an Advocate's Duty Toward the Client, Rule 6 ("An advocate appearing for the prosecution of a criminal trial should conduct the proceedings in a manner that it does not lead to conviction of the innocent. An advocate shall by no means suppress any material or evidence, which shall prove the innocence of the accused."); American Bar Association Model Rules of Professional Conduct, Rule 3.8(h) "When a prosecutor knows of clear and convincing evidence establishing that a defendant . . . was convicted of an offense that the defendant did not commit, the prosecutor shall seek to remedy the conviction."). For an excellent overview of the law governing Canadian prosecutors, see Michael Code, "Ethics and Criminal Law Practice," in Alice Woolley et al., eds., *Lawyers' Ethics and Professional Regulation* (Markham, Ont.: LexisNexis 2008).

[2] For example, in the United States, a defendant may obtain a new trial if the prosecution failed to disclose evidence or information that would have been material to the defense – that is, which might have led the jury to acquit the defendant. *Brady v. Maryland*, 373 U.S. 83 (1963).

8.1 Ministers of justice

Official statements of the duties of prosecuting attorneys, by both courts and bar associations, emphasize their role as "ministers of justice."[3] One might ask what exactly that means and what duties are imposed on ministers of justice that are not part of the ethics of lawyers generally. After all, many lawyers who represent private clients would say their role has something to do with justice.[4] The most general answer is that prosecutors are required to aim more directly at the ends of justice, including determining the truth and ensuring that participants in the legal process are treated fairly, whereas other lawyers are permitted to act in ways that only indirectly foster the ends of justice. For example, in a leading case, the Supreme Court of Canada said:

> [I]n our law, a criminal prosecution is not a contest between individuals, nor is it a contest between the Crown endeavouring to convict and the accused endeavouring to be acquitted; but it is an investigation that should be conducted without feeling or animus on the part of the prosecution, with the single view of determining the truth ... [P]rosecuting counsel should regard themselves rather as ministers of justice assisting in its administration than as advocates.[5]

An "advocate," as the court understands it, may aim at the interests of her client – "the accused endeavouring to be acquitted" – whereas a minister of justice must aim at the "single view" of ascertaining the truth. The defense lawyer's job is to advocate any available legal and factual ground for acquittal of the client. If the client is guilty and therefore an acquittal is unjust – well, so be it. It is not the job of the lawyer representing a client to seek justice. Rules of professional conduct for prosecutors, by contrast, emphasize that prosecutors must assist the court in determining the truth.[6]

---

[3] See, e.g., *Berger v. United States*, 295 U.S. 78, 88 (1935).

[4] See, e.g., William H. Simon, *The Practice of Justice* (Cambridge, Mass.: Harvard University Press 1998), p. 2 (beginning with "the values of justice that lawyers believe provide the moral foundations of their role").

[5] *R. v. Boucher*, [1954] S.C.J. No. 54, 110 C.C.C. 263 at 272 (internal quotations, citations, and alterations omitted).

[6] See, e.g., New South Wales Barristers' Rules § 82 ("A prosecutor must fairly assist the court to arrive at the truth, must seek impartially to have the whole of the relevant evidence placed intelligibly before the court, and must seek to assist the court with adequate submissions of law to enable the law properly to be applied to the facts.").

They should think of themselves as more like public officials than as representatives of private parties.[7] As a result, their obligation is described as exhibiting "controlled zeal" in attempting to convict the defendant.[8] Being a minister of justice means having objectives other than those defined by an actual client to whom one can look for instructions. It means, instead, being guided by the value of justice.

Not only must prosecutors aim directly at justice, but, in doing so, they also must contend with disagreement about what justice requires.[9] Unlike defense lawyers who are agents of their clients, prosecutors have constituencies.[10] The plural word here, constituencies, is important. Prosecutors represent "the people" (or the public interest reified as "the Crown"). The idea of "the people" is an abstraction, but *people* have interests and positions and may disagree with other people. Crime victims and members of social groups that feel they are being unfairly targeted by law enforcement officials have very different interests vis-à-vis the criminal justice system. The prosecutor must somehow reconcile these sometimes conflicting interests and act in the interests not of her immediate political superiors but in the interests of the people generally.

As an example of justice as a contestable standard, consider this observation from Paul Butler, an African-American law professor and former prosecutor, about the threat posed by both criminals and the police in minority neighborhoods:

> Young black men are the most frequent victims of crime and the most likely
> to be charged with crimes . . . You walk through your hood and you glare at
> the dope boys on the corner, who make your community unsafe. Then, when
> the squad car slowly rolls by, and the cops take a good look at you, you glare

---

Other Australian states have the identical rule – see, e.g., Western Australia Barristers' Rules § 82 and Victoria Barristers' Rules § 134.

[7] See, e.g., Law Society of Upper Canada [Ontario] Rules of Professional Conduct, Rule 4.01(3), Commentary ("When engaged as a prosecutor, the lawyer's prime duty is not to seek to convict but to see that justice is done through a fair trial on the merits. The prosecutor exercises a public function involving much discretion and power and must act fairly and dispassionately.").

[8] Alice Woolley, *Understanding Lawyers' Ethics in Canada* (Markham, Ont.: LexisNexis 2011), pp. 278–80.

[9] R. Michael Cassidy, "Character and Context: What Virtue Theory Can Teach Us About a Prosecutor's Ethical Duty to 'Seek Justice,'" *Notre Dame Law Review* 82: 635–97 (2006).

[10] R. Michael Cassidy, "Some Reflections on Ethics and Plea Bargaining: An Essay in Honor of Fred Zacharias," *San Diego Law Review* 48: 93–110, p. 95.

at them, too ... In the segregated neighborhood in Chicago where I grew up, blacks made the same claims about law enforcement that they do now. The times that my neighbors were not complaining about how the police treated them, they were complaining that the police were never there when they needed them.[11]

Justice, for Butler and his neighbors, includes both being treated fairly by police and being protected by the police from crime. Lack of justice may be evident in the indifference of police to black-on-black crime, as well as in the aggressiveness of police officers toward residents of these neighborhoods, particularly young African-American men. Butler decided to become a prosecutor "to help victims, and not be one – of the police or of another black man" and to work for "law enforcement interventions that actually work to keep communities of color both safe and free."[12] As this example shows, justice is what philosophers call an essentially contested concept.[13] Working out the meaning of justice, and thus the content of the prosecutor's ethical duty to seek justice, requires one to assign weights or priorities to different components of justice, such as security, respect for dignity, freedom from arbitrary harassment, and protection of rights. Others may assign different weights or priorities, however. These are not mere differences in taste or preference but represent different *rational* rankings of the components that make up the concept of justice. As a result, "there are disputes, centered on [the concept of justice] which are perfectly genuine: which, although not resolvable by argument of any kind, are nevertheless sustained by perfectly respectable arguments and evidence."[14] Lawyers may argue endlessly over what justice requires, but no rational resolution of this

---

[11] Paul Butler, "How Can You Prosecute Those People?," in Abbe Smith and Monroe H. Freedman, eds., *How Can You Represent Those People?* (New York: Palgrave MacMillan 2013), p. 16. For a similar account of the fear inspired by police officers in a minority neighborhood in Chicago, see Ta-Nehisi Coates, "The Gangs of Chicago," *The Atlantic* (Dec. 18, 2013) ("What people who have never lived in these neighborhoods must get, is that, like the crooks, killers, and gangs, the police are another violent force that must be negotiated and dealt with. But unlike the gangs, the violence of the police is the violence of the state, and thus unaccountable to [these neighborhoods].").

[12] Butler, *supra*, p. 17.

[13] See W. B. Gallie, "Essentially Contested Concepts," *Proceedings of the Aristotelian Society* 56: 167–98 (1956). The concept/conception distinction employed by Rawls and Dworkin, referred to in Chapter 2, is based on Gallie's notion of essentially contested concepts.

[14] Id., p. 169.

debate is possible because doing justice means attending to its various component values, such as public safety and respect for individual rights, none of which can be reduced to other values.

Prosecutors make discretionary decisions at every stage of the proceedings: which suspects to investigate and prosecute, what charges to bring, whether to offer a plea bargain, and what sentence to recommend to the court. At each stage, the prosecutor has considerable power despite being formally subject to legal and institutional controls. For example, in many US states and in the federal criminal system, a defendant has the right to be prosecuted only after indictment by a grand jury.[15] Although grand juries are no longer employed in the United Kingdom, the right has deep roots in English common law, and is believed to be a constraint on the arbitrary power of state officials to arrest and detain citizens. Under grand jury procedure, a prosecutor must present evidence tending to show probable cause, meaning (roughly) information sufficient to support a reasonable person's belief that the defendant committed the crime charged. The trouble with grand jury procedures from the defendant's point of view, however, is that only the prosecutor presents evidence, and the prosecutor is not required to present evidence that would tend to support the defendant's claim to be innocent.[16] As a result, grand juries are widely believed to function only as a rubber stamp on the prosecutor's decision to bring charges against the defendant. The former chief judge of the highest court in New York State once proposed to abolish grand juries in the state because, as he put it, a competent prosecutor could get a grand jury to indict a ham sandwich.[17]

Charging decisions and offering to accept a guilty plea to a lesser offense are similarly committed to the discretion of prosecutors. The same facts may be consistent with a relatively minor crime and a more serious offense.[18] In one of the classic articles on criminal defense, Barbara

---

[15] See US Constitution, amendment V ("No person shall be held to answer for a capital, or otherwise infamous crime, unless on a presentment or indictment of a Grand Jury . . . "). This provision of the Fifth Amendment has not been incorporated into the Fourteenth Amendment and is therefore not applicable to state criminal procedure. Many states, however, have their own constitutional or statutory grand jury rights.

[16] *U.S. v. Williams*, 504 U.S. 36 (1992).

[17] See Marcia Kramer and Frank Lombardi, "New Top State Judge: Abolish Grand Juries and Let Us Decide," *New York Daily News* (January 31, 1985).

[18] *U.S. v. Batchelder*, 442 U.S. 114 (1979).

Babcock tells the story of her client, Geraldine, who was prosecuted for her third offense of possessing heroin. The prosecutor in that case could have charged Geraldine with simple drug possession, but instead opted to charge her as a dealer and seek a lengthy mandatory sentence; he later refused a guilty plea to a simple possession charge, forcing Geraldine to go to trial.[19]

Prosecutors are instructed to make these discretionary decisions according to the ethical obligation to serve justice. Yet, as we have seen, justice is an essentially contested concept. Pursuing the maximum penalties against Geraldine is a response to one component of the concept of justice – that is, the public concern about the effects of the drug epidemic on public safety.[20] Meting out severe punishments to drug dealers is arguably one way to promote security and order. A different component of justice would emphasize restoring the social equilibrium that has been disturbed by the crime.[21] The justification for punishing crimes may be deeply related to the fair play principle supporting the obligation to obey the law (see Chapter 5). The criminal law enforces rules that are set up for the mutual benefit of everyone in society. For everyone to benefit from the rules of the criminal law, individuals must accept a burden of self-restraint "over inclinations that would, if satisfied, directly interfere or create a substantial risk of interference with others in prescribed ways."[22] Geraldine's defense lawyer portrayed her as a victim of her "horrendous childhood and of the toll on the development of her personality from many years of heroin addiction."[23] She may simply have lacked the capacity to exercise self-restraint over antisocial inclinations, even on the assumption that her drug habit creates a substantial risk of interference with the interests of others. If that portrayal is accurate (and, of course, a prosecutor may rightly be skeptical of

---

[19] See the updated version of Babcock's article, which is clearer about the prosecutor's decision making: Barbara Babcock, "'Defending the Guilty' After 30 Years," in Smith and Freedman, *supra*, p. 6.

[20] In the late 1960s and early '70s, the time period covered by Babcock's article, American politics was dominated by the public's near-hysteria about crime and lawlessness in the streets. Richard Nixon's successful 1968 campaign for President was focused on a "law and order" message. See, e.g., Dennis D. Loo and Ruth-Ellen M. Grimes, "Polls, Politics, and Crime: The 'Law and Order' Issue of the 1960s," *Western Criminology Review* 5: 50–67 (2004).

[21] See, e.g., David Johnston, *A Brief History of Justice* (Malden, Mass.: Wiley-Blackwell 2011), pp. 76–77 (discussing Aristotle's theory of corrective justice).

[22] Herbert Morris, "Persons and Punishment," *The Monist* 52: 475–501 (1968), p. 477.

[23] Babcock, *supra*, p. 7.

the stories told by defense lawyers, for reasons given in Chapter 7), then perhaps a discretionary charging decision should take into account the reasons Geraldine deserves something less than the most severe punishment. One can imagine reasonable prosecutors disagreeing about what should be done with Geraldine's case. Significantly, these are disagreements about the requirements of justice itself, because the law governing the conduct of prosecutors gives them discretion to decide what charges to pursue and whether to offer a plea bargain before trial.

Because prosecutors are instructed to use their legally conferred discretion to seek justice, some of the issues concerning the conflict between law and morality are irrelevant to understanding the ethics of this special role that lawyers can perform. If the law governing prosecutors directs them to act on considerations of justice then there is no tension between law and morality, no "role differentiation," because law incorporates morality.[24] The nature of justice as an essentially contested concept means there will be long-running debates about whether a particular exercise of discretionary judgment was just or unjust; that is simply the nature of a pluralistic concept such as justice. But the conflict between different conceptions of justice is different from the conflict that is the principal subject of this book – that between legal obligations and morality. Morality is, for the most part, incorporated within the role of prosecutor. Going back to the bridge structure from Chapters 1 and 2, the moral ideal of justice is reflected directly in a principle of professional ethics; that is, the directive that prosecutors should exercise their discretion toward the end of ensuring that justice is done.

There may be cases, however, in which the legal requirements of the role of prosecutor do conflict with morality. One illustration is the following case, in which a prosecutor disobeyed the requirements of his role, at least as defined by his supervisors, because he believed the values of truth and justice required it. In some ways, this case comes full circle back to the wrongful conviction case with which this book opened. It is different, however, because the lawyer in the first wrongful conviction case was representing another defendant. The lawyer in the following case is the prosecutor – a minister of justice – who believed justice required more from

---

[24] Joseph Raz would challenge the order of analysis in the text. Rather than asking whether law incorporates morality, he would begin with the priority of morality over law and ask whether law can ever exclude morality. See Joseph Raz, "Incorporation by Law," *Legal Theory* 10: 1–17 (2004).

him than his role would permit. As you read this case, think about this question: Which lawyer (or both, or none) acted rightly, and why?

8.2   Hero or traitor?

The case involves the Manhattan District Attorney's office, in New York City, known around the world through its fictional portrayal in *Law and Order*. Daniel Bibb was an attorney in the actual Manhattan DA's office.[25] He was fairly senior and well respected – the type of lawyer to be trusted with difficult and sensitive assignments. He was asked to review a case in which new evidence had come to light suggesting that someone had been wrongfully convicted of a crime. The original prosecution arose out of a shooting at a nightclub. Apparently one of the bouncers had ejected a patron and, in the process, punched him in the face. The patron decided to come back and get revenge, and at 3:30 a.m., two men got out of a car and opened fire, killing the bouncer. Eyewitnesses identified two men, Olmedo Hidalgo and David Lemus, as the shooters. Lemus had bragged to a woman about having committed the murder; she told a friend, who informed the police. However, a detective working on a different case heard from an informant that the nightclub shooting had actually been committed by Joey Pillot and Thomas "Spanky" Morales. The detective informed the Manhattan DA's office of this information but was told that the informant was mistaken because clear evidence pointed to Lemus and Hidalgo.[26] Furthermore,

---

[25] For the history of the case see David Luban, "The Conscience of a Prosecutor," *Valparaiso University Law Review* 45: 1–31 (2010). Luban's account of the case is based on publicly available information, as well as on communications with some of the participants. It is important to remember when considering a case like this, however, that some of the facts may not be disclosed without violating a lawyer's professional obligation of confidentiality. This obligation continues after the representation of a client has ended. All common law legal systems impose a duty of confidentiality on lawyers. See, e.g., ABA Model Rules, *supra*, Rule 1.6, Comment [20]; Solicitors' Regulation Authority [England and Wales] Code of Conduct 2011, Chapter 4; Federation of Law Societies [Canada], Model Code of Professional Conduct, Rule 3.3. It overlaps to some extent with legal professional privilege (called attorney–client privilege in the United States and solicitor–client privilege in Canada), but there are differences in applicability not relevant to this discussion.

[26] As Luban notes, the detectives and prosecutors were well aware that snitches sometimes lie. Luban, *supra*, p. 5. The incentives to minimize one's own responsibility and exaggerate the guilt of others are quite clear. As a result, one should be careful not to

another police officer had also heard that the killings had been committed by "Joey" and "Spanky," but when he followed up, he confused the nickname "Spanky" with another man, *Franky* Figueroa, who had been in prison on the night of the murders. The officer therefore concluded that the tip about Joey and Spanky must have been wrong and communicated this information to the DA's office.[27] At trial, the jury considered the evidence presented, convicted Hidalgo and Lemus of murder, and sentenced them to prison for 25 years to life.

Subsequently Joey Pillot and Spanky Morales were arrested for unrelated crimes. The prosecutors in that case, wishing to use Pillot's testimony against Morales, granted him immunity from prosecution from anything he told them. Among other things, Pillot said he and Morales had committed the nightclub shooting several years previously, for which Lemus and Hidalgo were convicted. Prosecutors at the DA's office, however, believed that even if Pillot and Morales had *also* been involved, it did not mean Lemus and Hidalgo were innocent because the testimony at trial had been consistent with the possibility that others had been present at the time of the shootings. Daniel Bibb was asked to conduct an investigation and report back to his supervisor at the Manhattan DA's office with a recommendation. After interviewing more than sixty people, Bibb became convinced that Hidalgo and Lemus were not involved at all. As for why Lemus had bragged about his participation in the killings, he said it was to impress a woman who "liked the gangster type and thugs"; he wanted to show that "he was a tough guy and a player, not just a 'knucklehead with a bus pass.'"[28] Other lawyers in the office, however, contended that Morales and Pillot had acted together with Lemus and Hidalgo to perform the killing. There was no dispute that the four men had grown up in the same neighborhood and hung around in the same bars. As other lawyers in the DA's office pointed out, a jury did believe beyond a reasonable doubt that Lemus and Hidalgo had been involved.

assume that the tip incriminating Pillot and Morales was necessarily truthful. See, e.g., Steven M. Cohen, "What Is True? Perspectives of a Former Prosecutor," *Cardozo Law Review* 23: 817–28 (2002). Interestingly, the author of the latter article was formerly in the Manhattan DA's office and, after he left to become a defense lawyer, represented Lemus and Hidalgo in the subsequent prosecution by Bibb. See Luban, *supra*, p. 6.

[27] Luban, *supra*, p. 4 n.21.   [28] Luban, *supra*, p. 7.

A judge ordered a new trial for Lemus and Hidalgo. Bibb's supervisor ordered him to continue to argue that Lemus and Hidalgo were guilty while also prosecuting Morales for the murder. (Because of the immunity agreement with Pillot, the prosecutors could not charge him with the crime.) An applicable rule of professional conduct requires prosecutors to investigate to determine whether a defendant was wrongfully convicted upon learning of "new, credible, and material evidence" suggesting that the defendant did not commit the offense.[29] The new evidence suggested the involvement of additional persons – Morales and Pillot – but did not necessarily disprove the involvement of Hidalgo and Lemus. Lawyers in the DA's office conducted an investigation, and there was reasonable disagreement over what that investigation showed. Suppose there was a full and fair internal debate within the DA's office, at which all the evidence was presented by experienced lawyers. On consideration of all of the evidence and arguments, and taking into account the principle that "[t]he duty of the prosecutor is to seek justice, not merely to convict,"[30] supervising lawyers in the Manhattan DA's office concluded that seeking justice in this case required Bibb to make a vigorous effort to vindicate the prior convictions of Hidalgo and Lemus while also seeking to hold Morales accountable for his role in the killing.

Stop for a moment and think about what Bibb should do. He is personally convinced that Hidalgo and Lemus were not involved, and he is the lawyer who conducted the interviews with dozens of witnesses. There is nevertheless some reason to believe that Hidalgo and Lemus are in fact guilty, not the least of which is Lemus's own statement confirming his involvement in the killing. Bibb's supervisors have ordered him to proceed and, in particular, to seek to obtain new convictions against Hidalgo and Lemus. Think about the following three questions:

1. *Practical*: What options does a lawyer have in this situation?
2. *Professional ethical*: What does the role of lawyer and, specifically, the role of prosecutor require?
3. *Moral*: All things considered, what should Bibb do?

---

[29] ABA Model Rules, *supra*, Rule 3.8(g).
[30] American Bar Association Standards Relating to the Administration of Criminal Justice, The Prosecution Function, Standard 3-1.2(c).

8.2.1 Practical solutions

A lawyer appears to have several options in this situation: (i) The first is to simply do what he was ordered to do. This option does not necessarily reflect an abdication of responsibility on the part of the prosecutor. Rather, it may simply be a concession to the reality that prosecutors are only a part of a complex system and are subject to pressures exerted by numerous institutional actors, each with its own agenda:

> In the criminal justice system, prosecutors must contend with multiple actors with competing claims in the drama – including the victim, police officers, the defendant, and other witnesses. The prosecutor must also maintain good working relationships with numerous stakeholders in the system – including the judge, other court personnel, law enforcement agencies, and informants. Prosecutors face external political pressure from a concerned public and the press, and internal pressures from a boss who is typically an elected public official.[31]

The facts in a case may also be ambiguous. In this case, conflicting testimony was given by witnesses who may have had motives to lie.[32] Bibb had one view of the evidence and his supervisors another.

(ii) The second option would be to make a further appeal within the DA's office. The problem states that there was a full and fair internal debate about the matter, and the facts that are known about the actual case suggest that Bibb vigorously made his case to supervising attorneys in the office.[33] But, in other cases, a lawyer may incorrectly assume that a decision of a supervisor is final when in fact it may have been possible to persuade the supervisor of the wisdom of a different course of action. All lawyers, including those in private practice, are required to consult with their clients about decisions to be made by the lawyer.[34]

(iii) The third option is to resign, either asking to be taken off the case and be replaced by another attorney or resigning altogether from the

---

[31] Cassidy, *supra*, p. 652.

[32] See, e.g., Luban, *supra*, p. 9 n.52 (reporting that one witness who incriminated Spanky Morales in the shooting may have done so to get revenge after Spanky, her husband's brother, raped her while her husband was serving in the military in Iraq).

[33] Luban, *supra*, pp. 8–9.   [34] Restatement (Third) of the Law Governing Lawyers § 20(1).

DA's office.[35] As Bibb points out, however, resigning from the case would not ensure that justice was done, because, in all likelihood, he would have been replaced by other lawyers in the office who would have dutifully carried out their assignment.[36] Furthermore, the perceived insubordination of refusing to prosecute Lemus and Hidalgo might have led to Bibb being fired from the office – not an attractive option where, as Bibb said, "I have a wife, three children, and a mortgage and college tuition to pay and could not afford to be out of work."[37]

8.2.2   Duties as a matter of professional ethics

Chapter 7 considered the ethical issues arising for criminal defense lawyers and the principle of zealous advocacy for the accused. As noted at the beginning of this chapter, however, the duties of prosecuting attorney are different as a matter of professional ethics. The fundamental obligation of a prosecutor is not to serve as a zealous advocate but as a representative of the public interest – a "minister of justice," as it is sometimes said.[38] The trouble with that statement of the prosecutor's responsibility is that, as noted previously, the requirements of justice are not self-defining. One might therefore ask whether a subsidiary principle of professional ethics might be that, in making decisions about what justice requires, a lawyer ought to take direction from his or her supervisors, at least in the case where the supervisor's direction represents a reasonable resolution of an arguable question of professional ethics.[39] In particular, when a prosecutor is direc-ted to act in the interests of "the people," it would make sense to delegate

---

[35] See, e.g., ABA Model Rules, *supra*, Rule 1.16(b)(4) (permitting lawyer to withdraw from representation where "the client insists upon taking action ... with which the lawyer has a fundamental disagreement"). There is no separate rule governing withdrawal by prosecutors.

[36] Luban, *supra*, p. 13.   [37] Id.

[38] "A prosecutor has the responsibility of a minister of justice and not simply that of an advocate." ABA Model Rules, *supra*, Rule 3.8, Comment [1].

[39] In the American law governing lawyers, there is an interesting resolution of this issue. Every lawyer is personally responsible for complying with the rules of professional conduct – there is no "Nuremberg defense" of merely following orders. See ABA Model Rules, *supra*, Rule 5.2(a). However, a lawyer is not subject to discipline if he or she acts at the direction of a supervisory lawyer if (and only if) the supervisory lawyer's direction represents a "reasonable resolution of an arguable question of professional duty." *Id.*, Rule 5.2(b).

decision-making authority to an appointed or elected political official.[40]
In this case, in light of the conflicting evidence, including the contradictory
statements by Lemus (first, to the woman he was trying to impress, that he
was involved in the shooting, and second, to police, that he was merely
bragging and trying to sound like a tough guy), a lawyer might reasonably
decide *either* to continue to try to hold Lemus and Hidalgo responsible or to
work to rectify their wrongful conviction. Thus, the "who decides?" question might be resolved, *as a matter of professional ethics*, in favor of deference
to the instructions of supervising attorneys. Even so, that does not resolve
the issue as a matter of morality.

8.2.3 Moral obligations: what comes across the bridge?

Professional ethics and the chain of command within a government
agency do not exhaust the content of morality. A lawyer remains a *moral
agent* even when acting in a professional capacity – as a lawyer and as a
participant in a complex, hierarchically organized institution. Sometimes
morality requires people to step outside of their role obligations and do
the right thing, quite apart from what their professional obligations
require. At the time of the writing of this book, there is active public
debate in the United States over the disclosures by Edward Snowden
concerning spying by the National Security Agency (NSA), an intelligence
agency specializing in the monitoring of electronic communications.[41]
Snowden worked for the NSA as a contractor and had a top-secret security
clearance. As a matter of the ethics of his own profession (providing
information technology services to government agencies) and the terms
of his employer's contract with the government, Snowden clearly had an
ethical obligation of confidentiality. Yet he believed he had an overriding
moral obligation to reveal illegal activities by the NSA, including systematic violations of federal law prohibiting wiretapping without obtaining a
warrant. The documents disclosed to journalists by Snowden showed that

---

[40] See Luban, *supra*, pp. 23–24 (quoting legal ethics scholars emphasizing that the head of
the DA's office acts on behalf of the people).

[41] For overviews of the story, see Barton Gellman, "Edward Snowden, After Months of NSA
Revelations, Says His Mission's Accomplished," *Washington Post* (Dec. 23, 2013);
James Bamford, "They Know Much More Than You Think," *New York Review of Books*
(Aug. 15, 2013).

the NSA had been illegally obtaining access to email and cellular phone records of citizens and noncitizens alike. Public opinion, not surprisingly, is divided, with some seeing Snowden as a hero and others considering him a traitor. His disclosures revealed extensive law-breaking by the government and invasions of the privacy rights of American citizens, but also (according to the government) compromised intelligence gathering efforts that have prevented another disaster on the scale of the September 11, 2001, terrorist attacks. Did Snowden act rightly by violating his professional obligation of confidentiality to defend what he believed are the fundamental rights of privacy and the limitation of government power? These are the issues confronting lawyers who must contend with the conflict between professional ethical obligations and the moral requirements that apply to them as human beings.

Even good organizations, such as the Manhattan DA's office,[42] can occasionally function badly. Public safety, policing, and crime issues can occasionally dominate regional or national elections, and lawyers within a prosecutor's office may feel tremendous political pressure to demonstrate that they are putting dangerous people in jail and keeping law-abiding citizens safe from crime. In addition, there are psychological effects that tend to make it difficult for people acting in groups to admit error and resist pressures to conform.[43] Conversely, there are also psychological effects that can make individuals overconfident in the correctness of their own judgments.[44] Organizational cultures may make it easier or more difficult for individuals to comply with their ethical obligations. In light of these considerations, what should be the responsibility of individuals when confronted with a case of institutional failure?

In the case we are considering here, the prosecutor, Daniel Bibb, did something extraordinary. As David Luban characterizes it, he "threw" the case. That is, he tried to ensure that the prosecution would be unsuccessful

---

[42] The Manhattan DA's office has a reputation for, by and large, playing fair and taking seriously the duty of prosecutors to serve as ministers of justice. Other state prosecutors, such as the Orleans Parish District Attorney's office in New Orleans, Louisiana, are known for their win-at-all-costs mentality. See, e.g., Emily Bazelon, "Playing Dirty in the Big Easy," *Slate* (Apr. 18, 2012).

[43] See, e.g., Philip Zimbardo, *The Lucifer Effect: Understanding How Good People Turn Evil* (New York: Random House 2008).

[44] See, e.g., Daniel Kahneman, *Thinking, Fast and Slow* (New York: Farar, Straus & Giroux 2011), pp. 252–58.

in its effort to convict Hidalgo and Lemus. As Bibb himself said, "I did the best I could to lose."[45] He spoke with defense attorneys concerning the evidence he had accumulated during the investigation of the case and its implication for the defense. He also put pressure on witnesses who were reluctant to show up and testify that Hidalgo and Lemus were not involved. Bibb also prepared defense witnesses for the questions he would ask them in cross-examination. (The practice of preparing witnesses to give testimony is, in general, permitted in the United States although prohibited in other common law jurisdictions.[46]) He did not seek to undermine their credibility when they testified for the defense, as he ordinarily would have as a lawyer for the prosecution.[47] As Bibb saw it, he was acting consistently with his obligation as a minister of justice by ensuring that truthful evidence was presented to the court. As his detractors saw it, he took upon himself the responsibility that properly was vested in the elected head of the DA's office.

One's reaction to the Daniel Bibb case (or to the Edward Snowden case) may depend as much as anything on one's temperament, worldview, or attitude toward rules and the hierarchical structures of authority, and one's preference for gradual, incremental change or more radical reform. These attitudes, in turn, may be connected with more fundamental beliefs about human nature and political associations.[48] Supporters of Bibb and Snowden might emphasize the primacy of individual conscience and the capacity of each individual to reason about what is in the common good.[49] Critics might observe the contestability of concepts like justice and note

---

[45] See Benjamin Weiser, "Doubting Case, a Prosecutor Helped the Defense," *New York Times* (Jun. 23, 2008).

[46] See, e.g., Code of Conduct of the Bar of England and Wales, Rule 705(a) ("A barrister must not rehearse, practise or coach a witness in relation to his evidence"). The Canadian and Australian positions appears to be a middle ground between that of the US and the English rule. See, e.g., Woolley, *supra*, pp. 187–90 (Canada); New South Wales Professional Conduct and Practice Rules 2013, Rule 24 (identical language and rule numbering in Queensland).

[47] See Luban, *supra*, pp. 11–13.

[48] See, e.g., Yuval Levin, *The Great Debate: Edmund Burke, Thomas Paine, and the Birth of Right and Left* (New York: Basic Books 2014).

[49] Simon, for example, says my analysis of the Bibb case reveals an authoritarian impulse. See William H. Simon, "Authoritarian Legal Ethics: Bradley Wendel and the Positivist Turn," *Texas Law Review* 90: 709–26 (2012), pp. 711–12.

the partial, limited perspectives that individuals have with respect to the common good. Prosecutors cannot avoid grappling with the essential ambiguity lurking in ideas like justice and the common good because their ethical obligations require them to take these values into account. Even cases that are not as dramatic as Daniel Bibb "throwing" the prosecution may involve the attempt by lawyers to harmonize competing conceptions of justice. Discretionary decisions, such as whether to prosecute, what offenses to charge, and how to negotiate a plea bargain, all directly engage with the essentially contested concept of justice. In this way, the ethics of prosecutors bears a much closer resemblance to the ethics of other public officials than to the ethics of other lawyers. As the next chapter will show, however, it is not *only* prosecutors who have to deal with uncertainty and disagreement. Lawyers representing the parties in noncriminal disputes also have obligations that are not simply to advocate zealously for a client, but which must also take into account the interests of others and perhaps even justice.

9 Civil litigation

9.1 The different ethical worlds of civil and criminal lawyers

Lawyers do many things other than prosecuting and defending criminal cases. This chapter, and those that follow, considers the lawyer's ethical duties in these other contexts. Interestingly, when thinking about those ethical issues, lawyers often have in mind the paradigm of the criminal defense lawyer as the model of ethical lawyering. Consider this critique of the rules of professional conduct from an ethical point of view:

> It used to be, and around the turn of the century it was, that the rules expressly stated that the lawyer's obligation to the client in litigation was to represent the client with warm zeal. Now, in the latest incarnation of the rules, the words "warm zeal" are dropped out. Instead, [the current rule of professional conduct] says (in essence) "we really mean warm zeal, but we talk about professionalism and competence and so on because we are afraid that if we say warm zeal, people will think that means you need to be a zealot on behalf of your client, and nobody likes zealots." So in the name of softening up the rules and softening up the image of the profession, the warm zeals are a threatened species. They are clubbing the warm zeals to death to make coats for rich people.[1]

Can you tell what kind of law this critic practices? The lawyer, Michael Tigar, is a passionate and talented defender of unpopular clients accused of crimes (and of the practice of criminal defense). Clubbing baby zeals is a

---

[1] Michael E. Tigar, "Litigators' Ethics," *Tennessee Law Review* 67: 409–24 (2000), p. 411. The language of "warm zeal" is from American Bar Association Canons of Professional Ethics, Canon 15. The Canons of Ethics were adopted in 1908 and continued as the official statement of the ABA on professional ethics until the adoption, in 1969, of the Model Code of Professional Responsibility.

funny line, but the concern about making coats for rich people shows that Tigar is really thinking about representing powerless individuals facing the dehumanizing machinery of the state, even though he talks more broadly about representing clients in litigation. Warm zeal may be an appropriate gloss on the principle of partisanship in the context of criminal defense, but it is problematic in other contexts of practice, including the representation of disputing parties in civil litigation.

Chapter 3 briefly mentioned the difference between common law and civil law legal systems. The relevant distinction here is *within* a common law legal system, between criminal and civil litigation – that is, disputes between two or more parties that may in principle be resolved by a trial even if most disputes are settled by agreement of the parties before trial. Unlike criminal cases, which are brought by a prosecuting attorney in the name of the sovereign, civil lawsuits are generally initiated by a private party – an individual or a corporation. They do not seek to punish an offender but to enforce some type of legal right. The remedy sought is generally money damages or a direction, called an *injunction*, to do or not do something. Civil lawsuits may arise in contexts including accidents and personal injury (governed by the law of torts), performance and breach of contractual agreements, workplace discrimination or unfair labor practices, divorces and child custody disputes, environmental pollution, unfair competition, the protection of intellectual property such as patents and copyrights, and so on. The parties in noncriminal litigation do not have the same rights as criminal defendants, which are often set forth in constitutional documents.[2] Civil litigants do have rights to a fair trial and, in some cases, to a trial by jury, but there is nothing like the extensive protection afforded to criminal defendants. In particular, in most cases, there is no right for a client who cannot afford a lawyer to be represented by a lawyer paid for by the state, as there is for criminal defendants accused of serious crimes.[3]

---

[2] The New Zealand Bill of Rights Act 1990, for example, guarantees criminal defendants the right to a speedy trial, the presumption of innocence, the privilege against compelled self-incrimination, and the right to confront prosecution witnesses, among other rights. See § 25. Section 11 of the Canadian Charter of Rights and Freedoms and Article 6 of the European Convention on Human Rights, which provide similar protections.

[3] In the United States, a Supreme Court case called *Gideon v. Wainwright*, 372 U.S. 335 (1963), establishes the right of indigent defendants to have defense counsel appointed

The question to be considered in this chapter is whether the legal distinction between civil and criminal litigation makes an *ethical* difference. The image of the lonely individual facing the resources, technology, and wrath of the modern state is a powerful one, and it is a natural inference to a set of ethical principles for lawyers that emphasize single-minded loyalty, devotion, fearlessness, doggedness, and independence – all the qualities that are summed up in Tigar's phrase "warm zeal." Many people come to understand or even admire lawyers who resolutely defend people accused of even the worst crimes. Do you feel the same way about a lawyer for XYZ Corporation, which was disappointed that a promised shipment of 1,000 widgets was not delivered on time, resulting in delayed production of gizmos and in lost profits? It seems less noble somehow to argue about the allocation of the risk of loss in a contract or to quibble over the interpretation of words like "as soon as practicable." Yet lawyers in civil cases are also protecting the rights of their clients and ensuring that disputes are resolved fairly on their merits and in an orderly manner. The parties in civil lawsuits may not be facing jail time or the death penalty, but serious interests may nevertheless be at stake. The most important categorical distinction is that the state is not seeking to deprive a citizen of liberty in a civil case. One question to be considered in this chapter is whether that distinction carries as much ethical weight as lawyers believe it does. Sometimes the plight of clients in civil litigation is just as compelling as that of criminal defendants. To return to one of the themes from Chapter 6 on legal injustice, if you believe the law is sometimes (or always) an instrument of oppression, its application in civil cases can be just as oppressive as in criminal prosecutions.

The ethical analysis in this chapter is organized around two civil cases. One involves the representation of a poor client in her dealings with a state housing authority. The second is an intellectual property dispute between a start-up company and a patent holder. The cases seem to have little in common except that they fall on one side of the criminal/civil divide. As you read the cases, think about whether the duties of the lawyers are the same. If you believe they are different, should they vary according to the

and paid for by the state. The term "civil *Gideon*" has therefore come to be a shorthand way of referring to the movement to broaden the right to appointed counsel to civil matters in which comparable important interests are at stake. See, e.g., Rebecca Aviel, "Why Civil *Gideon* Won't Fix Family Law," *Yale Law Journal* 122: 2106–24 (2013).

justice or the legal merit of the client's case? (Both cases are set up so that they have very little legal merit.) How much creativity on the part of lawyers is justified if there appears to be a moral case for a right that is not recognized by the law?

The first case involves a client represented by a legal aid clinic. These clinics, which exist in many countries, provide legal assistance to clients in civil matters who cannot afford a lawyer and where there is no legal right to a lawyer paid for by the state. Lawyers in a legal aid clinic in Tel Aviv represent tenants in disputes with their landlords.[4] Many of the clients of the clinic are poor, unemployed, and Arab, meaning that they exist at the margins of Israeli society. Although public housing assistance is available to people with incomes below a certain threshold, conservative governments have cut back on the amount of benefits available and have tightened up eligibility criteria.[5] At the same time, however, an economic boom has increased rents throughout the country. As a result, housing assistance often does not cover the full rent owed, even in public housing, where recently adopted government policies have adjusted rent payments to more closely track the private market. As a result, many residents are evicted due to unpaid rent, and these residents need legal services to help them deal with the eviction proceedings.

Anitta is a woman in her late 20s, recently divorced from her husband, a drug addict who was physically abusive toward her during their marriage. She had gotten married early in life and has never worked outside the home. As a single mother of two children, Anitta qualified for income-assistance and housing benefits, but the combined benefits were not sufficient to cover her rent payments and prescription medication needed to help her daughter deal with severe asthma. As a result, she was forced to move three times in the past two years, causing great disruption to her children's schooling. Faced with the possibility of being evicted from her fourth apartment, Anitta was desperate. She learned that a nearby public housing building had a vacant apartment, so she and her family simply broke the lock and moved in. She used what furniture she had to create a modest but comfortable home for herself and her daughters.[6] When she received an eviction

---

[4] This case is taken from Neta Ziv, "Lawyers Talking Rights and Clients Breaking Rules: Between Legal Positivism and Distributive Justice in Israeli Poverty Lawyering," *Clinical Law Review* 11: 209–39 (2004), modified slightly.

[5] Id., pp. 217–18.   [6] Id., pp. 221–22.

notice from the state housing agency, demanding that she immediately terminate her illegal occupation of the apartment, she sought representation from lawyers at the legal aid clinic. The lawyers filed a motion to dismiss the eviction proceeding, claiming that evicting Anitta would violate a basic, constitutional right to housing. The Supreme Court of Israel has never decided that there is a constitutional right to housing, but the lawyers believe Anitta's situation would be a good test case if the court were inclined to establish such a right. (If asked to assess the merits candidly of the constitutional challenge, the lawyers would admit that it is highly unlikely to be successful.[7]) At the same time, filing the constitutional challenge would delay Anitta's eviction for several years. The lawyers also filed an administrative petition with the Ministry of Housing, seeking an adjustment in the amount of Anitta's housing benefit. The lawyers are fairly certain that the petition will be denied, based in part on Anitta's unlawful occupation of a public housing unit, but, again, they are counting on the resolution of the administrative petition, through multiple levels of review, to give her more time in the apartment. They also hope the delay will give Anitta additional leverage in negotiations with the public housing authority.

An explicitly "politicized" conception of lawyering (see Chapter 6) might contend that Anitta's lawyers are ethically permitted to employ the strategy of filing numerous motions and petitions, with very little likelihood of success on the merits, in order to delay her eviction. The case does share many features with the typical criminal defense representation, including an impoverished client contending with an unfeeling bureaucracy. But does that mean her lawyers are entitled to represent her with the same "warm zeal" that is appropriate in a criminal proceeding? As the lawyer who supervised the legal aid clinic concedes, civil "[l]awyers have been repeatedly accused of abusing the legal system by meticulous and superfluous use of needless, exhausting procedures."[8] Lawyers for the public housing authority contend that, although Anitta is genuinely needy, there are

---

[7] See id., p. 235 n.74 (noting that the Supreme Court held that the Basic Law "explicitly recognizes the right of property, but not social rights such as housing, education, health, and minimal subsistence"). The strategy of the lawyers was therefore to argue that the right to housing was an aspect of the constitutionally guaranteed right of human dignity.

[8] Id., p. 233.

other families with even greater need, and they are entitled to the apartment that Anitta is illegally occupying. May the legal aid lawyers representing Anitta respond with the principle from Lord Brougham, that they need not regard "the alarm, the torments, the destruction which he may bring upon others"? The Brougham principle is most clearly applicable where the "others" in question are themselves represented by counsel, especially in the context of criminal defense, where the state employs law enforcement personnel, investigators, and forensic experts in addition to prosecuting attorneys. In this case, however, the other needy families are unlikely to have their own lawyers, and their interests will go unrepresented in the conflict between Anitta and the housing authority. In the euphemistic language of the military, their interests are "collateral damage" in the battle between two represented parties. The lawyers believe Anitta deserves a decent place to live and create a stable life for her children. From this politicized perspective, it makes a great deal of difference whether they are ethically permitted to advocate only for the rights Anitta actually has as a matter of law, which in this case would not allow her to remain in the apartment, or whether the principle of partisanship also permits them to raise challenges and defenses they reasonably believe are nonmeritorious for the purpose of delaying Anitta's eviction.

If you believe Anitta's lawyers are justified in turning her eviction proceeding into the Jarndyce and Jarndyce case from *Bleak House* in order to keep her in her apartment, consider your reaction to the following case. The blandly named InfoTech, Inc., is a patent assertion entity – colloquially, a patent troll. Its business model is to acquire patents from bankrupt companies, often failed technology startup companies. Rather than licensing the patents to other companies who produce and market the technology, InfoTech waits for an invention that allegedly infringes a patent it owns to come to market. It then surfaces and demands a hefty licensing fee for using the technology, with the threat that it will sue the company for patent infringement if it does not pay the licensing fee. Experienced patent lawyers estimate that the cost of defending the preliminary stages of a patent infringement lawsuit is $1 million, and the costs can climb to $2.5 million if a trial is required. InfoTech has recently targeted developers of software applications ("apps") for Apple and Android smartphones and tablets. The apps use technology licensed by Apple and Google that allows users to make purchases within the application. InfoTech contends that, although it may have licensed the technology to Apple and Google, it must be separately licensed by any app developer intending to use it.[9] Many app developers are small startup businesses. They generally rely on their founders' capital contributions, hoping to develop technology that is sufficiently promising to attract venture capital financing. InfoTech knows that because the small developers cannot afford to defend an infringement case, they are likely to pay the demanded licensing fees. A law firm represents InfoTech on a contingent fee basis, as permitted by US law. Under its contingent fee agreement, the firm receives 40 percent of the licensing fees paid by app developers to InfoTech. All of the lawsuits filed by InfoTech have settled, so there are no judicial decisions determining whether the use by app developers of the in-app purchasing technology infringes InfoTech's patent.

Does it make a difference that Anitta's lawyers are representing a poor, vulnerable individual while the lawyers for InfoTech are helping a company whose business model is threatening litigation against small entrepreneurs? Should it make a difference to the ethical evaluation? On a politicized perspective, the answer would be yes; the more traditional approach, from the perspective of political liberalism, would emphasize that Anitta does not have a legal right to the relief her lawyers are seeking. The housing case was written to make the legal claims on behalf of Anitta a bit dodgy; the lawyers will not be held in contempt of court or otherwise sanctioned for making them, but the constitutional challenges are highly unlikely to succeed on their merits. The patent cases against the startup companies are more likely meritorious, although one might argue that they are an abuse of the patent system, which is intended to create incentives for innovation and the development of useful technology. Even if the infringement claims have some likelihood of success on the merits, the companies who settle these cases do so mostly because of the expense of defending an infringement case.

The issue here is to determine which features of Anitta's case and the patent case make a difference to the ethical duties and permissions of the lawyers representing their clients in civil litigation. Potentially relevant features on the morality side of the bridge include, in Anitta's case, her

---

[9] This problem is based on the description of Lodsys LLC on the website of the Electronic Freedom Foundation. See Julie Samuels, "App Developers: Lodsys is Back: It's Time to Beat This Troll" (April 3, 2013), available at https://www.eff.org/deeplinks/2013/04/app-developers-lodsys-back.

powerlessness, the justice of her cause, and the importance of establishing a general right to housing; in the patent troll case, pertinent issues are the injustice of allowing a patent holder to hold up the release of useful technology until it is paid off and the apparent sleaziness of InfoTech's business model. The relevance of these features depends on the extent to which you favor a politicized conception of legal ethics or one that is grounded in rule of law considerations. A politicized approach, at least from a progressive political perspective, would distinguish the two cases by assuming that Anitta's cause is just and that patent trolling is sleazy. Thus, as a matter of professional ethics, lawyers would be justified in filing a blizzard of motions to delay Anitta's eviction. On the other side, an approach beginning with rule of law would contend that the Standard Conception, with its principles of partisanship, neutrality, and nonaccountability, is derived from underlying moral values such as equality and human dignity but that lawyers do not act directly on them. Instead, they play a role in a process set up to determine what rights citizens ought to have in respect of housing or intellectual property.

The argument for the centrality of their clients' legal rights (as distinct from their moral positioning) to the ethical duties of lawyers begins with the possibility of disagreement about justice. Consider Anitta's case as an example. Most readers would agree that she has experienced misfortune in her life, deserves to be treated with compassion, and ought to be able to create a stable environment for her children. In short, one wishes to say that Anitta has rights, as a matter of morality and perhaps also as a matter of law. But what legal rights does she have and against whom? And what do those rights entail? To have a right means that some aspect of one's interests or well-being is a sufficient reason (all else being equal) to hold another person to a duty with respect to the rights-holder.[10] The duty may simply be that of noninterference. Anitta has the negative right not to be mistreated by others on account of her status as a woman, poor, and Arab. Controversially, moral and legal rights may lead to positive duties on the part of others. For example, a person may have positive rights to the assistance of others if that person is in a situation of great need, and the risks and costs of giving that assistance are low for the other party.[11] Rights

---

[10] Joseph Raz, "Rights-Based Moralities," in Jeremy Waldron, ed., *Theories of Rights* (Oxford: Oxford University Press 1984), p. 183.

[11] See, e.g., Michael Walzer, *Spheres of Justice* (New York: Basic Books 1983), p. 33.

of this type often depend for their recognition on a political community. So-called second-generation human rights recognize claims by citizens to the economic and social conditions necessary to live decent lives as the equals of other citizens. No one can exercise whatever rights she may have without an adequate share of the essentials for a reasonably healthy life; hunger and destitution are incompatible with social and political equality.[12] Anitta may therefore argue that she has a moral and legal claim-right, correlative with duties on the part of the community as a whole, to be provided with adequate housing.[13]

The extent to which other members of the political community ought to contribute toward the just distribution of resources so that other citizens can have a decent life, and the best means of ensuring that people are adequately cared for while at the same time not creating incentives for dependency and free-riding, are, of course, some of the most vigorously contested political issues in modern democracies. One may agree that Anitta deserves some public support while remaining agnostic about a number of subsidiary social, political, and economic questions. For example, government intervention in the housing market to provide free or reduced-cost housing may distort the market and lead to undesirable collateral consequences. Many economists contend, for example, that rent control regulations benefit existing tenants at the expense of future tenants and lead to an overall decline in the quantity and quality of available rental housing.[14] The housing ministry cited the problem of other families who had an even greater need for housing, suggesting an inevitable scarcity in the supply of public housing. The difficulty in Anitta's case arises when one seeks to specify what duties are correlated with a right to housing. Practical problems such as scarcity combine with normative disagreements over issues such as how to determine the priority among competing applicants for available housing units.

---

[12] See generally Jeremy Waldron, "Two Sides of the Coin," in *Liberal Rights* (Cambridge: Cambridge University Press 1993), pp. 5–10.

[13] The classic treatment of the correlativity of rights and duties, distinguishing different types of rights according to the duties with which they are paired, is Wesley Newcomb Hohfeld, "Fundamental Legal Conceptions as Applied in Judicial Reasoning," *Yale Law Journal* 26: 710–70 (1917).

[14] See, e.g., Edgar O. Olson, "Is Rent Control Good Social Policy?," *Chicago-Kent Law Review* 67: 921–45 (1991).

Similar issues arise in the patent case: The term "patent troll" suggests a negative evaluation of the client's conduct, but the more neutral term "nonpracticing entity" covers many companies who purchase portfolios of patents. Defenders of nonpracticing entities argue that they contribute to a secondary market in intellectual property rights, one that helps small inventors monetize their intellectual property.[15] Also, by aggregating many smaller patents into portfolios, they redress the imbalance in resources between small investors and large technology companies. Few small startup companies have the capacity to bring an infringement lawsuit, but if they can transfer their patent rights to a different owner with greater resources, it may deter potential infringers. As the founder of several startup technology companies writes:

> I have become very accustomed to having larger companies copying my
> start-ups' products and technology, and in the process blithely
> ignoring each of my start-ups' patent rights. Either they were assuming
> that we would just "go away" or that we would never have the where-
> with-all to properly enforce our patents. I am sure they believed that if
> the worse came to pass and we ended up in court with them, they would
> simply use their resources to find some obscure prior art, or they might
> acquire some patents that we were unwittingly infringing so as to force
> some sort of cross-license deal, or simply drag the whole process out so
> long that we would run out money and energy. All of this in order to
> avoid having to license off us, or buy us or simply respect our patent
> rights and not compete with us. From a start-ups' perspective, the
> emergence of patent brokers and patent trolls has meant that all patents,
> even those of a start-up, need to be taken far more seriously because one
> can never be sure who will end up owning or enforcing them.[16]

Nonpracticing entities also may serve as brokers, ultimately leading to the technology being brought to market by companies with the resources to translate the inventor's idea into a practical application.

The point is not to argue that Anitta is entitled to stay in the apartment or that the patent troll should be allowed to sue the app developers. Rather, the point is that reasonable people may disagree about what rights people and

---

[15] See, e.g., Paul Schneck, "Not So Scary After All: In Defense of Patent Trolls," *Forbes* (Feb. 1, 2013).

[16] Ian Maxwell, "In Defense of Patent Trolls," *IP Strategy* (May 29, 2013), available at http://ipstrategy.com/2013/05/29/in-defense-of-patent-trolls/.

institutions ought to have with respect to each other. "Pluralism and reasonable disagreement are uneliminable features of the political landscape
in modern constitutional democracies."[17] As noted in Chapter 1, pluralism
is not the same thing as moral relativism. It is, instead, a claim about the
diversity of human goods, ends, and values.[18] Moral philosopher David Ross
gave a list of prima facie duties – that is, those obligations that would be
binding if there were no competing obligations – but went on to note that
these obligations are often in conflict. Ross's list includes duties arising
from promises, obligations of reparation for harms done, duties of gratitude
arising from services provided, duties of beneficence that are grounded in
"the mere fact that there are other beings in the world whose condition we
can make better," and the duty not to injure others.[19] The conflicts among
these values cannot easily be resolved because they arise from different
perspectives, are formally unlike, and appeal to a diversity of underlying
considerations. More recently, John Rawls gave an explanation of the pluralism of reasonable comprehensive religious, philosophical, and moral doctrines with reference to what he called the burdens of judgment.[20] These
include the difficulty in assessing the empirical evidence that bears on a
course of action; disagreement regarding the weight of various competing
considerations; the vagueness and indeterminacy of many of our concepts
such as good, rights, and justice; and the differences between the experi-
ences and perspectives of people who have lived very different lives.

Theoretical accounts of law and society often begin with a hypothetical
state of nature. (Recall the discussion of Locke's social contract theory in
Chapter 4, for example.[21]) The trouble is, one could not begin to conceptu-
alize the cases of Anitta and the patent troll in a true state of nature because
the very idea of rights to state-subsidized housing and the protection of
intellectual property are themselves dependent upon a complex system of
political and legal institutions. Nevertheless, to the extent you can do this,

[17] Tim Dare, *The Counsel of Rogues? A Defence of the Standard Conception of the Lawyer's Role*
(Farnham, Surrey: Ashgate 2009), p. 61.

[18] See, e.g., Thomas Nagel, "The Fragmentation of Value," in *Mortal Questions* (Cambridge:
Cambridge University Press 1979), p. 128.

[19] W. D. Ross, *The Right and the Good* (Oxford: Oxford University Press 1930), p. 21.

[20] John Rawls, *Political Liberalism* (New York: Columbia University Press 1993), pp. 55–58

[21] See also Scott J. Shapiro, *Legality* (Cambridge, Mass: Harvard University Press 2011),
pp. 155–56 ("I begin with the oldest trick in the book. I . . . drop [a bunch of people] into
the 'state of nature' and describe their various reasons for creating a legal system.").

try to imagine a very general problem fitting roughly with the facts of one of these cases: Either someone is a poor, single mother who needs a decent place to live, or someone has developed a useful piece of technology but is charged with having stolen it from its true inventor. What should be done in this situation? One possibility is to let the parties to the dispute try to work things out, but, even in an ideal world without transaction costs and strategic behavior, the existence of pluralism and disagreement mean that we cannot expect that people will be able to reason, deliberate, and persuade each other into agreement concerning the rights and duties they ought to have. An alternative would be to submit the dispute to a neutral decision maker with a reputation for wisdom, one whose decision the parties will regard as binding – a kind of protojudge or arbitrator. If that is the strategy employed, one would expect similarly situated parties to pay attention to the decision rendered by the protojudge because if they found themselves in a similar dispute, they might able to predict what would happen if the case was referred to the same decision maker. The crucial step from a prelegal state of nature to a legal system is the recognition that everyone would be better off if they had a way to determine in advance what any decision maker would decide if a dispute arose. This would require that decision makers give reasons justifying their decisions, that these reasons refer to general characteristics of the parties, and that decision makers follow past decisions as long as the reasons applied in the same way to the dispute they were considering.

State-of-nature stories can be a bit contrived, but they identify an important feature of modern legal systems: Legal systems enable people to deal with each other, plan their actions, and form stable expectations about what others will do, notwithstanding Rawls's burdens of judgment. Even though people may disagree as a first-order moral matter about the extent of subsidizing housing rights someone ought to have and what priority someone like Anitta should have over other needy families, it may be much easier to agree on the rights that have actually been conferred by a legislature, administrative agency, or judge. Rather than reasoning through all of the moral, economic, and practical questions pertaining to housing policy, people can simply consult the (hypothetical) constitution, Housing Act, regulations promulgated by the Ministry of Housing, and court decisions issued in housing cases. As Scott Shapiro argues, the authority of law is related to the function of law in solving a crucial social problem:

Given the complexity, contentiousness, and arbitrariness of modern life, the moral need for plans to guide, coordinate, and monitor conduct [is] enormous. Yet, for the same reasons, it is extremely costly and risky for people to solve their social problems by themselves, via improvisation, spontaneous ordering, or private agreements, or communally, via consensus or personalized forms of hierarchy. Legal systems, by contrast, are able to respond to this great demand for norms at a reasonable price.[22]

Law stands in for the chaotic, cumbersome process of trying to reason one's way through a complex moral or practical problem. In doing so, it creates reasons for people and institutions to act in particular ways. An app developer may have to pay InfoSys the licensing fees it demands *because* InfoSys is the holder of a piece of property created by the legal system, called a patent, which gives it the right to demand that the app developer stop using patented technology. And the government may force Anitta and her children to vacate the apartment because the right to occupy it is created by the laws governing public housing, which may give higher priority to another family.

One way of understanding the role of lawyers on the professional ethics side of the bridge is that lawyers do good to the extent that they enable clients to understand, assert, and protect the rights that have been assigned to them by the legal system. Arguably, lawyers are wrongdoers in professional ethics terms if they engage in conduct that has the effect of denying or interfering with the rights that have been allocated to citizens by the law. One way of denying rights would be to represent a client incompetently, causing the client to lose the opportunity to assert a right she otherwise would have had.[23] A lawyer might do this because of inexperience or

---

22 Shapiro, *supra*, p. 172. Here is a quick review of Chapter 4 on the nature of law. Shapiro calls himself a positivist. He defends the Moral Aim Thesis, that "the fundamental aim of the law is to rectify the moral deficiencies associated with the circumstances of legality." Id., p. 213. The circumstances of legality are just those conditions described in the text – i.e., a community with complex problems requiring coordination and settlement. Given Shapiro's claim that "[t]he law is *morally valuable* ... because we face numerous and serious moral problems whose solutions are complex, contentious, and arbitrary," id., p. 396, I cannot see why he does not bite the bullet and locate his theory within the natural law tradition. What do you think?

23 One of the standard examples in American law is *Togstad v. Vesely, Otto, Miller & Keefe*, 291 N.W.2d 686 (Minn. 1980). In that case, the lawyer negligently caused the client to believe she did not have a valid medical malpractice claim against the surgeon who had mistreated her husband. Because the client thought she did not have a good claim,

inattention or because of a conflict of interest between the client's case and the representation of another client. In a case where the lawyer caused the client to lose the benefit of a right conferred by the legal system, the lawyer would be subject to ethical criticism for failing to fulfill a core function of the role. The remainder of this chapter considers the possibility of a different type of ethical wrongdoing by lawyers. What if a lawyer represents her own client in litigation in a way that either yields the client more than he was entitled to under the law or else causes another person (not the client) to lose something the other person was entitled to under the law? Both Anitta's case and the patent troll case were written to suggest this kind of ethical analysis. One may have had the intuition that the lawyers in those cases were abusing or manipulating the legal system by doing things that were lawful in one sense yet resulted in benefits to their clients that the law was not intended to provide. The following section considers this interesting problem of legal ethics.

9.2   Abusive litigation and the problem of legal realism

The principle of partisanship instructs lawyers to pursue their clients' objectives up to the limits of the law. In an early critique of the Standard Conception, David Luban raised an important jurisprudential problem: When a lawyer is instructed to act for the client up to the limits of the law, are the "limits of the law" understood to mean what a lawyer would predict would bring down some sort of legal penalty on the client, such as a sanction for filing an abusive lawsuit, or what legal officials would do when interpreting the law in good faith? Both of these glosses on the limits of the law owe something to the jurisprudential movement of the 1920s and '30s, originating in the United States, called *legal realism*.[24] The most general form of the legal realist thesis is that judges decide cases based on something

---

she did not file a lawsuit, and the statute of limitations ran out on her claim. She was then legally barred from suing the surgeon. When she later found out about the lawyer's negligence, she sued him, and recovered from the lawyer the amount she would have recovered from the surgeon but for the lawyer's negligence.

[24] For a collection of the classic articles in the legal realist movement see William W. Fisher III, et al., eds., *American Legal Realism* (Oxford: Oxford University Press 1993). The name "American" legal realism is not intended to convey parochialism but to distinguish this movement from the quite different school of Scandinavian legal realism.

other than authoritative rules set out in precedent cases and statutes.[25] The target of the realists was legal formalism, the thesis that there are right answers to legal questions that can be determined by simply consulting the applicable legal sources.[26] Writing several decades after the realists, H. L. A. Hart offered a devastating critique of formalism in *The Concept of Law*. One of his seemingly simple insights is actually quite powerful: "Particular fact-situations do not await us already marked off from each other, and labeled as instances of the general rule … nor can the rule itself step forward to claim its own instances."[27] Hart's famous example marries a claim about the relationship between meaning and language with a thesis about the law and adjudication. It shows that the law *itself* does not fully determine the scope of its application but must be applied to cases by judges in ways that may involve a certain amount of creativity or judgment.

Suppose a statute says, "No vehicles in the park." Does this apply to bicycles, skateboards, helicopters flying overhead, an ambulance rushing to save a heart attack victim in the park, a gardener using a riding lawn mower, a decommissioned army jeep mounted atop a war memorial, and so on?[28] Hart notes that language, by its nature, has an open texture.[29] A word may have a core of settled meaning, but there may also be a penumbra of debatable cases.[30] Driving a car through the park for no good reason is clearly within the core of settled meanings of the rule, "no vehicles in the park." A bicycle is a debatable case. It resembles the core instance of a car in some ways – it has wheels, it is a means of transportation, it goes fast, and potentially can be a hazard to pedestrians – but in other instances it is distinguishable (lack of noise and pollution, for example). Hart therefore contends that legal formalism must be false because a judge necessarily, because of the relationship between language and meaning, has *discretion* in

---

[25] See, e.g., Brian Leiter, "Legal Realism," in Dennis Patterson, ed., *A Companion to Philosophy of Law and Legal Theory* (Oxford: Blackwell 1996), p. 261.

[26] See, e.g., Shapiro, *supra*, pp. 240–42.

[27] H. L. A. Hart, *The Concept of Law* (Oxford: Oxford University Press, 2d. edn., 1994), p. 126.

[28] For the example of the war memorial, see Lon L. Fuller, "Positivism and Fidelity to Law: A Reply to Professor Hart," *Harvard Law Review* 71: 630–72, p. 663.

[29] Hart, *supra*, p. 128.

[30] The core and penumbra terminology is from H. L. A. Hart, "Positivism and the Separation of Law and Morals," *Harvard Law Review* 71: 593–629, p. 607.

applying a general rule to the facts of particular cases.[31] A judge has to take into account something other than the text of the statute in order to determine whether a bicycle is similar to the core instance of a car in relevant respects. The criteria of relevance "depend on many complex factors running through the legal system and on the aims or purpose which may be attributed to the rule."[32] If the purpose of the rule is to eliminate noise and preserve the park as an oasis of calm, it would make no sense to refuse permission to place a jeep on a war memorial. Bicycles are still a hard case, though, because they are quiet but fast-moving; they do not contribute to noise, but they might be a hazard to people who want to stroll or allow their children to play in the park. The law is therefore *indeterminate* with respect to the bicycle case because of the vagueness of the word "vehicle" in the statute.[33]

In practical terms, the vagueness and open texture of language means judges have a great deal of latitude for creativity. If judges necessarily must decide cases based not on the law but on the facts, along with a healthy dose of extralegal reasoning concerning what would be fair or just in the case, then how can one criticize a judge, in legal terms, for reaching either of two inconsistent results? A judge who allows bicycles under the "no vehicles" statute and one who prohibits them from the park evidently disagree about the proper balance of uses to which the park may be put. Neither one, however, can be said to have gotten the law wrong. Nevertheless, vagueness and open texture do not mean anything goes. At some point, an interpretation of the statute would strain language to its breaking point. A judge who upheld a fine issued to a skateboarder for violating the "no vehicles" statute would probably be acting wrongly. Although a bicycle may be a close case, it is highly implausible that a skateboard is an instance of the general concept of a vehicle. On the other hand, only the most rigid, doctrinaire judge would uphold a fine issued to the driver of an ambulance who crossed the park to reach a heart attack victim. Although an ambulance is clearly a vehicle, the statute must be understood as containing an implied exception for emergencies. Additional indeterminacy therefore results from the possibility that a statute will be interpreted not to apply even to a case covered by its plain language.

---

[31] Hart, *supra*, p. 127.   [32] Hart, *supra*, p. 127.   [33] Id., pp. 130–31.

The legal realists made the problem of indeterminacy central to the philosophy of law.[34] Legal realism also poses a problem that goes all the way to the foundations of legal ethics.[35] The Standard Conception says that lawyers should serve as advocates for their clients up to the limits of the law (the principle of partisanship), not taking into account the interests of non-clients or the public interest (the principle of neutrality), and they should not be subject to moral criticism for doing so (the principle of nonaccountability). As Luban noted, however, there is an ambiguity in the notion of the limits of the law. "Every lawyer," he writes, "knows tricks of the trade that can be used to do opponents out of their legal deserts," such as using procedural maneuvers to delay proceedings and increase the cost of litigation or filing non-meritorious lawsuits on the assumption that the opponent would prefer to settle the claim inexpensively than to incur the cost of defending the case all the way through trial.[36] (These tricks should sound familiar from Anitta's case and the patent troll problem.) Using these "tricks of the trade" is arguably within the limits of the law because the tricks are themselves provided for by law. The various procedural devices that lawyers use to prolong litigation are a creature of the rules of procedure that structure the adversarial system of adjudication. Bribing or threatening witnesses is clearly outside the bounds of the law on any understanding of the nature of law, but a realist lawyer would see nothing wrong with filing a series of motions solely for the purpose of causing delay as long as the lawyer had sufficient confidence that she would not be subjected to legal penalties for doing so. Luban calls this understanding of the limits of the law Low Realism, to distinguish it from the High Realist claim that the content of the law is determined by human officials interpreting authoritative rules in good faith.[37]

In a recent defense of a modified version of the Standard Conception, Tim Dare similarly recognizes the problem posed by legal realism for legal ethics. He contends that lawyers do, in fact, have an obligation to "pursue the client's interests aggressively and single-mindedly all the way up to the

---

[34] For example, the notion of judicial discretion subsequently became central to the Hart-Dworkin debate concerning legal positivism. For a helpful overview, see Shapiro, *supra*, pp. 261–65.

[35] See David B. Wilkins, "Legal Realism for Lawyers," *Harvard Law Review* 104: 468–524 (1990).

[36] David Luban, *Lawyers and Justice* (Princeton: Princeton University Press 1988), p. 75.

[37] David Luban, "The Lysistratian Prerogative: A Response to Stephen Pepper," *American Bar Foundation Research Journal* 1986: 637–49, pp. 646–47.

limits of the law."[38] But this does not mean the lawyer is entitled to "pursue any advantage obtainable for their client through the law."[39] Dare accepts the principle of zealous advocacy, but distinguishes between what he calls mere zeal and "hyper-zeal." Mere zeal, which is ethically required of lawyers, is the effort to act on behalf of clients in ways that they would be unable to do for themselves without expert assistance in order to obtain for clients the rights that have been allocated to them by the legal system.[40] A merely zealous lawyer will advocate for a client up to the limits of what the law in fact establishes as that client's legal rights. Dare accepts Hart's thesis of the indeterminacy of language – he is no formalist – and understands that the law may be moderately indeterminate. He also acknowledges that there may be close cases in which judges and lawyers might reasonably disagree about what the law requires. Nevertheless, the law is not radically indeterminate and, even if there is not a right answer to a question of law in every case (e.g., "Is a bicycle a vehicle?"), some answers may be worse than others, and some may be flat-out wrong. As for how we know which answers are better or worse than others, Dare says we simply must do what lawyers and judges do: "putting arguments, consulting precedents and statutes, drawing out implications of the point of particular bodies of law, and so on."[41]

Using either Luban's or Dare's categories, the principle of partisanship can be understood as follows:

Luban	Dare	Partisanship requires a lawyer to …
Low Realism	Hyper-zeal	Use "tricks of the trade," if necessary, to obtain any advantage for the client that the law can be made to give
High Realism	Mere Zeal	Obtain for the client those rights that have been allocated to them by legal institutions

Luban and Dare are both claiming that it is possible, at least in principle, to identify what legal rights a client actually has and to differentiate these rights from incidental benefits that might be obtainable under the law by a clever lawyer.[42] In the housing rights case, the problem stipulates that the

---

[38] Dare, *supra*, p. 75.   [39] Id., p. 76.   [40] Id., p. 77.   [41] Id., p. 82.

[42] I refer to these collateral benefits as windfalls and differentiate them from entitlements. See W. Bradley Wendel, *Lawyers and Fidelity to Law* (Princeton: Princeton University Press 2010), pp. 73–76. Thus, I accept the Low Realism/High Realism or hyper-zeal/mere zeal distinction.

constitutional and housing authority challenges filed by Anitta's lawyers
are highly unlikely to succeed on the merits. It would take a lot more
background in law itself, as opposed to the ethics of law, to be able to
analyze a complex issue of constitutional or administrative law, but most
lawyers and judges would agree that, in many cases at least, it is possible to
distinguish between what a client is entitled to on the merits of the law and
those collateral advantages that may be obtained through the use of legal
proceedings. Luban and Dare further argue that this distinction makes a
normative difference; that is, that lawyers may permissibly advocate up to
the limits of the law as understood in High Realist terms – that is, be merely
zealous on behalf of their clients – but that it is not ethically permissible to
obtain an advantage that is simply one the law may be made to give.

We are therefore left with two issues, one normative, the other descriptive. The normative issue is why the principle of partisanship should depend
on whether the advantage obtainable for a client is a genuine legal right
as opposed to an incidental benefit. The concern here is that requiring the
lawyer to temper her advocacy on behalf of a client might make the lawyer
into a double agent. On the one hand, the lawyer is an advocate for the
client's interests. On the other hand, the lawyer has to think like a judge and
determine whether the client has a genuine legal right to something or
whether the client's objective is merely an incidental benefit of advocacy.
Although this situation is not a technical conflict of interest under the law
governing lawyers, it nevertheless appears to involve a kind of divided
loyalty. The descriptive issue is whether the distinction between mere
zeal and hyper-zeal, or between genuine rights and incidental benefits, is
tenable: Can a lawyer or judge really tell the difference between a legal right
and an incidental benefit? If so, how?

9.2.1 Normative issue: why are lawyers limited to mere zeal?

In my view, this is by far the easier of the two issues to resolve. If you accept
that the law is determinate to some extent – that is, that there is a difference
between a genuine legal entitlement and a mere advantage that may be
obtained through the procedures of the legal system – then the ethical
question is why the principle of partisanship ought to be limited to obtaining genuine legal entitlements. To put the answer very bluntly, engaging in
hyper-zealous advocacy is cheating. Clients have been allocated certain

rights by political and legal institutions. The role of the lawyer is understood with reference to the purpose of the law, which is to allow people to live together and coordinate their activities notwithstanding the burdens of judgment. Because the lawyer's role obligations are defined institutionally, the lawyer is required to assist the client in ascertaining and protecting the rights she has been allocated by the legal system. The lawyer's job "is to act on the client's behalf, *relative* to the institutions of law. It is not their job to pursue interests that are not protected by law."[43] Lawyers may know how to use legal procedures to obtain something that is not the client's right but is something the client would like to have. But this is no different from a physician who might have access to narcotics or an accountant who is able to devise a complicated tax shelter. Expert knowledge can be used for ill as well as for good. Within the norms of legal ethics, appropriately under-stood, a lawyer is permitted to obtain for a client only those benefits allocated to the client by the law.

A variation on this argument focuses on the nature of the lawyer–client relationship. In legal terms, the lawyer is an agent of the principal, the client. Any principal–agent relationship involves a delegation by the princi-pal to the agent of power to act on behalf of the principal and often is created because the agent has some skill or opportunity that the principal lacks. If I owned a valuable painting and wanted to sell it, I might designate an auction house like Sotheby's as my agent for the sale of the painting. The auction house has distinctive expertise, which I lack, in valuing art and conducting a sale. It makes sense from my perspective to give Sotheby's the authority to sell the painting because using their expertise is a means to achieve my end of selling the painting. In a lawyer–client relationship, the principal similarly has an objective that can best be accomplished by dele-gating to an agent the authority to act on behalf of the principal. The client's end is something like ascertaining what rights she has or filing a lawsuit to protect or vindicate those rights. The client may have other ends, of course, such as making money or finding a place to live, but, *with respect to the legal system*, the relevant ends of the client are determining the content of her rights and taking lawful steps to secure them. The legal system is indifferent to nonlegal ends. Any actors whose roles are defined with reference to the institutions of the legal system, such as judges and lawyers, are concerned

---

[43] Dare, *supra*, p. 80.

only with those interests of the client that pertain to her legal rights. Lawyers are agents of their clients only with respect to those ends of their clients that make reference to rights allocated by the legal system.

Dare gives an example of the difference between the legal ends of a client – those that make reference to rights – and mere interests.[44] Modifying the example slightly to keep it within civil litigation, suppose a client has filed a claim with his property insurer for damages caused to the client's warehouse by a fire. A provision of the fire insurance policy excludes coverage for fires set intentionally. A witness observed the client setting fire to the warehouse to collect insurance proceeds and is prepared to testify on behalf of the insurance company that the fire was intentionally set. It would be in the client's interests if that witness disappeared. The client considers hiring two different agents: (1) a contract killer to eliminate the witness, and (2) a lawyer to sue the insurance company for a declaration that it has to pay on the fire insurance policy. Although the client's interests would be served either by killing the witness or suing the insurance company, pretty clearly it is not within the lawyer's job description, so to speak, to kill the witness. This example is exaggerated, but still makes the important point that, with respect to an actor whose role is defined with reference to a social institution, that actor's ethical responsibilities are themselves determined with respect to the function of the institution. As Dare writes:

> [T]he institutional rights of law structure the lawyer's responsibility.
> In their capacity as lawyer, they can and should respond to my request
> for help with these "extra-legal" interests [such as killing the witness] by
> pointing out that that is not their job. Their job is to act on the client's
> behalf, relative to the institutions of law.[45]

The distinction still holds in less dramatic cases. If Anitta's lawyers are able to gum up the works and delay her eviction for several years by filing constitutional and administrative challenges, they can be criticized for obtaining a mere collateral advantage for Anitta, not protecting her rights, *if and only if* the legal challenges lack merit. If they represent a plausible attempt to secure an existing right, or if they are a good faith effort to establish a new constitutional right, then Anitta's lawyers may, and should, file them. But if they are

---

[44] Dare, *supra*, p. 79.   [45] Id.

merely delaying tactics, filed with no hope of success on the merits, then the lawyers are abusing the procedures of the legal system to further their client's interests, but not her *lawful* interests. As a matter of the ethical responsibilities of lawyers, the law, interpreted in good faith, sets the boundary between what lawyers may seek to obtain for their client (the object of a merely zealous lawyer) and that which is a collateral advantage (the object of a hyper-zealous lawyer). For example, a provision of the rules of professional conduct for American lawyers states that it is impermissible to bring or defend a lawsuit or take a position with respect to a legal issue "unless there is a basis in law and fact for doing so that is not frivolous, which includes a good faith argument for an extension, modification, or reversal of existing law."[46] The rule goes on to exempt criminal defense lawyers from this requirement, permitting them to "defend the proceeding as to require that every element of the case be established." Civil litigators are different, however, and must take some responsibility for ensuring that their representation of a client stays within the bounds of those rights that have been allocated to clients by legal institutions.

That does not mean the lawyers are without some plausible moral justification for their actions. But they cannot rely on the pattern of justification considered here – that is, that the law has ethical significance because it represents a morally attractive way of solving a serious social problem arising from conflict and disagreement within a political community. In fact, as the lawyer who related Anitta's case has written, there is a tension between this conception of the ethical significance of law and extralegal values:

> [O]ur intuitive feeling is that at least *prima facie* the state does have a point in demanding law obedience in general, including in the public housing area. The need to set certain criteria for the distribution of public resources, the concern for growing lawlessness, the real need to repair apartments and the shortage of funding for this purpose – are all claims we tend to sympathize with, or at least find hard to renounce instantaneously. Lawyering in squatting cases thus requires public interest lawyers to wrestle with this initial inclination, but also to raise doubts about it being the sole paradigm through which one might approach, analyze, and judge such behavior.[47]

---

[46] American Bar Association, Model Rules of Professional Conduct, Rule 3.1.
[47] Ziv, *supra*, p. 213.

This is an important qualification. The argument given here for the authority of law may not be "the sole paradigm" through which we can evaluate the behavior of lawyers. Perhaps lawyers should be ethically permitted to act directly on extralegal values and considerations that have not been recognized by the legal system. These include historical disparities in resources that lead to present inequalities in access to housing, neoliberal policies that have drastically reduced state resources available for social welfare programs, and growing poverty.[48] To the great credit of Anitta's lawyer, she recognizes that arguing for the weakness, instability, and contingency of the law will undercut her own legitimacy as a lawyer; that is, as someone who is within the legal system and who asserts claims to legal rights for her client.[49] One cannot have it both ways, contending simultaneously that (1) there is something distinctive about one's role as a lawyer because it has to do with the rights allocated by the legal system, and (2) the legal system's claim to authority is weak and should be disregarded in a case in which the allocation of rights is unjust.

It is important not to overlook the resources that exist within the law for bringing about legal change. Lawyers are not restricted to bringing lawsuits where the basis for their client's claim is already well established. A lawsuit can seek to continue the evolution of some line of legal doctrine, expand a right that was recognized in an embryonic form in a prior case, overrule a precedent that has become obsolete through social change, or even recognize an entirely new type of claim. Professional folklore highlights turning points in the law where a judge decisively changed the *status quo ante*. Every American lawyer, for example, can tell the story of how the Supreme Court overruled its prior decision in *Plessy v. Ferguson* that "separate but equal" school facilities for black and white children did not violate the Equal Protection Clause of the US Constitution.[50] After a long, dogged, and carefully mapped-out strategy of filing lawsuits challenging segregation in higher education and other government institutions, civil rights lawyers brought the lawsuit that culminated in the Supreme Court's ruling in *Brown v. Board of*

---

[48] Id., p. 216.

[49] Id., pp. 216–17. See also id., p. 229 (noting that the acceptance of category distinctions such as landlord/tenant and the past distribution of resources that has led to some people being landlords and others being tenants is "a prerequisite to enter the legal field").

[50] 163 U.S. 537 (1896).

Education that the "separate but equal" doctrine was no longer good law and that states were no longer permitted to maintain segregated schools.[51] It cannot be the implication of any theory of legal ethics, as applied to civil litigation, that civil rights lawyers behaved unethically in filing constitutional challenges to segregation after the *Plessy* case was decided.[52]

For the most part, judges will give some latitude to lawyers to bring lawsuits seeking legal change. As long as the lawyers identify some basis for their argument that the new case should be treated differently from the old case – including social change or a factual distinction between the cases – a judge is unlikely to impose legal sanctions for filing a nonmeritorious lawsuit. This does not mean that anything goes, and the law may at some point become well enough settled that there is no plausible basis for challenging it. If there is room to seek the extension, modification, or reversal of existing law or establishment of new law,[53] however, an ethical lawyer may bring a lawsuit. I know nothing about Israeli law, but from the description of the representation of Anitta, it appears that there is some ground to contend that the right of human dignity, enshrined in the Basic Law, could be interpreted to include a right to housing, even though the Supreme Court had previously denied that there is a separate, freestanding right to housing in the Basic Law. If this ground does exist, then Anitta's lawyers can hardly be criticized for seeking to establish this new constitutional right while at the same time keeping Anitta and her children in the apartment.

9.2.2   Descriptive issue: what, if anything, imparts determinacy to the law?

In the background of the discussion of Anitta's case is a claim about the determinacy of law. Although the problem simply stipulates that the

---

[51] 347 U.S. 483 (1957).

[52] Remember step 3 of our three-step argument structure from Chapter 2 – test the results of the theory against cases? The normative conclusion that the lawyers challenging segregation were acting properly, even heroically, is so well established that a theory with a contrary conclusion would be highly unlikely to be accepted.

[53] This language is from Rule 11 of the (US) Federal Rules of Civil Procedure, which empowers judges to impose sanctions against lawyers who file any pleadings, motions, or other papers without an adequate factual and legal basis.

constitutional challenges are unlikely to be successful, this is the sort of judgment experienced lawyers could make. Indeed, much of the distinctive expertise of lawyers consists of making determinations concerning the likelihood that a particular claim or defense will be successful if asserted. Judgments about the likelihood of success tend not to be binary. Lawyers are accustomed to thinking in rough probabilistic terms, not quantified, but potentially arranged on a continuum like this:

Nonmeritorious |-(1)---(2)--(3)-----(4)------(5)--(6)-| Meritorious

1. Almost certainly a loser. Getting close to a case in which a judge might impose sanctions on a lawyer for bringing a frivolous lawsuit.
2. A real long shot. Not sanctionable but very unlikely to succeed. Probably a waste of time and money from the client's perspective.
3. Some chance of success. May be worth a shot, from the client's perspective.
4. A close call; could go either way.
5. Pretty good claim, but with a few identifiable weaknesses. Not a sure thing, but more likely than not to succeed.
6. Almost a sure thing – a slam-dunk, as American lawyers (and basketball fans) would say.

It is difficult to get much more precise than this. Lawyers and judges use terms such as a "colorable" legal argument or one that is "nonfrivolous" to describe position (2) on the continuum. A regulation of the US Treasury Department relating to tax shelters permits lawyers to advise on the use of a tax-avoidance device if it has a "realistic possibility of being sustained on the merits,"[54] and the American Bar Association has said that lawyers can advise a client to take a position on a tax return as long as there is a "reasonable basis in law" for the position.[55] That language suggests something falling between (3) and (4) on the continuum.

As for how lawyers make these judgments, that is a subject in itself. It is the distinctive professional expertise that is acquired in law school and in the course of training and socialization in practice. One might

---

[54] Treasury Department Circular 230, 31 C.F.R., Subtitle A, Part 10, § 10.34.
[55] American Bar Association, Standing Committee on Professional Ethics, Formal Ethics Opinion 85–352 (1985).

contend that legal reasoning is a craft, like architecture, design, painting, playing a musical instrument well, and engaging in close reading and criticism of literary works. It is the nature of a craft that is difficult to theorize in non–craft-dependent terms.[56] I recently struggled to explain to a group of nonmusicians what was meant by the idea of "phrasing" and why Frank Sinatra, Etta James, and Willie Nelson are all known as singers with excellent phrasing. A definition such as "subtle shifts in emphasis and timing that create the shape of a vocal line" is helpful only if one has already listened to enough performances that it is possible to grasp metaphorical ideas like a musical "line" and to understand how a performer could exercise creativity within the limits of the structure of the song. You can probably come up with examples like this from some activity in which you are experienced. The point is, legal reasoning is like that. Without being "inside" a craft such as music or legal reasoning, it difficult to appreciate how it could be performed well or poorly. Expertise at many practices is constituted, in part, by knowing when it is done well. It cannot be reduced to rules that are independent of participating in the practice.

This is a somewhat controversial approach to explaining the determinacy of law, relying as it does on the virtue ethics tradition beginning with Aristotle's *Ethics*. In the Aristotelian tradition, every activity aims at a characteristic end or good. An excellence or virtue is some characteristic that enables someone who participates in a practice to realize its characteristic end. The exercise of a virtue demands judgment, which is a trait of character, and is not reducible to the mechanical application of rules.[57] "The exercise of a virtue exhibits qualities which are required for sustaining a social role and for exhibiting excellence in some well-marked area of social practice."[58] Good lawyers are those who aim at the characteristic end of law that, if you accept the functional account given in this chapter, is to allocate rights and responsibilities to citizens in a political community. Virtues are

---

[56] See Wendel, *supra*, Chapter 6.

[57] See Aristotle, *Nicomachean Ethics*, 1.7, 1097a (W. D. Ross and J. O. Urmson trans. 1984); Alasdair MacIntyre, *After Virtue* (Notre Dame, Ind.: University of Notre Dame Press, 2d edn., 1984), pp. 14–51.

[58] MacIntyre, *supra*, p. 187.

formed within a community, so a good lawyer is also one whose judgment reflects the community's judgment about the rights that citizens have.[59] The next chapter considers a different context in which the exercise of judgment is central to ethical lawyering – namely, counseling clients about the law, not representing them in civil or criminal litigation.

---

[59] MacIntyre, *supra*, p. 151. If you object to the Aristotelian account of legal reasoning, a different modern account (which I believe nonetheless has a great deal in common with the classical tradition) uses the idea of interpretive communities that discipline the activities of community members. See Stanley Fish, *Is There a Text in This Class? The Authority of Interpretive Communities* (Cambridge, Mass.: Harvard University Press 1982); Owen M. Fiss, *Objectivity and Interpretation, Stanford Law Review* 34: 739–63 (1982). If you believe legal determinacy is the property of something else, such as language (notwithstanding Hart's critique in the *Concept of Law*) or political morality (following Ronald Dworkin's "right answers" thesis), we are engaged in a jurisprudential debate that is far beyond the scope of an introductory text on legal ethics … but a very good one to have!

10   Counseling clients

10.1   A good barista is hard to find

Your client is a company that operates a chain of successful boutique cafes and coffee shops in the four largest cities in New Zealand (Auckland, Wellington, Christchurch, and Hamilton).[1] The president of the company, who is also the majority stockholder, asks you to draft an employment contract to offer to applicants. She is particularly concerned that new staff might stay with the company for a year or two, to develop relationships with customers and suppliers and skills as coffee purchasers, roasters, baristas, and managers, before leaving and setting up in competition. The coffee business, your client explains, depends crucially upon close personal and professional relationships with customers and suppliers, and upon the special skills of good baristas and coffee roasters.

The president of your client company has heard about the use of restraint-of-trade (sometimes called noncompete) clauses in employment contracts. She has come to your office with a sample contract, prepared by the New Zealand Employers and Manufacturers Association (EMA). The sample contract includes an explanation by the EMA of various clauses and the reason for including them. Regarding restraint-of-trade clauses, it says:

> Deterrence is a good reason for including restraint-of-trade clauses in your employment agreements. Sometimes this may be the only reliable reason for including such a clause in your employment agreements; most restraint-of-trade clauses have been found unenforceable when tested in court.

"Deterrence," says the president, "is exactly what I want. I want you to draft the strongest possible clause. I want it to specify that, in consideration for a

---

[1] This example is borrowed, with gratitude, from Professor Tim Dare of the University of Auckland.

generous salary, the people I hire will agree not to have any role in the coffee industry anywhere in New Zealand for four years after they stop working for me."

You point out that such a clause would almost certainly be unenforceable and that if it were challenged in court a judge would conclude that a company has no right to include such a sweeping restraint. "Do you mean it's illegal?" asks the president. You respond that this may be putting it too strongly. Although one could imagine a contract that would be illegal in the sense of violating the criminal law (say, one for the delivery of a shipment of cocaine), in this case, saying that there is no right to include the restraint-of-trade clause is merely a matter of a court refusing to enforce it. You further suggest, however, that there are practical reasons to favor a more moderate clause. "While a court could strike down the entire contract, it is more likely that they will either modify the unreasonable provision and enforce it as modified, or strike it altogether, thus leaving you with no restriction on your ex-employee competing with you. Wouldn't it be better to include a more moderate clause, which a court might accept, rather than running the risk that a court would strike it entirely?" The president is unpersuaded. "I know all of that," she says, "and I'm not prepared to budge on the content of the contract. I want you to use your legal skills to draft this contract with the clause I request. Even if there is a risk that a court may not enforce it, it sure does look legal, and intimidating, so anyone I hire will think twice about competing with me." The coffee company is a valuable client, and the market for legal services is competitive. You know that if you say no to the president, she may take her business down the street to another more pliant lawyer.

After the president leaves, you begin thinking about the ethics of the situation. The rules of professional conduct applicable to lawyers in New Zealand state two duties that appear to bear on the president's instructions:

- A lawyer must use legal processes only for proper purposes. A lawyer must not use, or knowingly assist in using, the law or legal processes for the purpose of causing unnecessary embarrassment, distress, or inconvenience to another person's reputation, interests, or occupation.[2]
- A lawyer must not advise a client to engage in conduct that the lawyer knows to be fraudulent or criminal, nor assist any person in an activity

---

[2] Lawyers and Conveyancers Act (NZ) 2008, Lawyers: Client Conduct and Care Rules § 2.3.

that the lawyer knows is fraudulent or criminal. A lawyer must not knowingly assist in the concealment of fraud or crime.[3]

Under applicable law, it would not be a crime, nor a civil fraud, to draft a contract with a clause the lawyer knows or reasonably believes to be unenforceable. But what is the effect of the requirement in the rule that legal processes should be used only for "proper purposes"? Is the lawyer using the law for the purpose of causing unnecessary inconvenience to another person's interests or occupation if she includes the unenforceable clause?[4]

Notice that the president is seeking to manipulate the content of the contract to obtain something to which the company does not have a legal right. She is trying, in essence, to coerce employees into continuing employment with the company even though they have a legal right to go elsewhere. In all likelihood, the coffee company will be able to get away with paying lower wages because employees believe they are prohibited from working for competitors. (The president says she intends to compensate employees generously, but perhaps once they are locked in to employment the company will take a hard line on future increases in pay.) The lawyer did not suggest the use of the restraint-of-trade clause, however. Generally, the client instructs the lawyer on the objectives of representation, but, in this case, it was the president who brought up the idea of using the aggressive contract provision. If the client would not be subjected to legal penalties for including the clause in the contract (regardless of whether it would be enforceable if asserted against the former employee), then the lawyer is arguably offering only neutral, technical advice to assist the client in

---

[3] Id. § 2.4.

[4] The leading text on lawyers' ethics in New Zealand suggests that the rule should be interpreted along the lines of the distinction set out in Chapter 9, between mere zeal and hyper-zeal or rights and collateral advantages. "There will be cases where clients wish to avail themselves of some legitimate legal machinery, but where the motive for employing the law is at odds with the purpose of the law." Duncan Webb, *Ethics: Professional Responsibility and the Lawyer* (Wellington: Butterworths 2000), § 13.5, p. 353. The reference to the motive of the client is potentially problematic, however, because clients may seek to defend their legal rights for many reasons, some admirable, some not, and it would be burdensome for the lawyer to determine the client's motivation. It should be possible to determine the content of the law without reference to the subjective mental states of parties who assert legal rights. As a matter of ethics, as opposed to jurisprudence, lawyers might conceivably be held to a standard of acting only on behalf of rightly motivated clients, but this position appears to be a minority view.

implementing a lawful objective. At least that is one way of understanding the application of the Standard Conception to the situation of client advising.

10.2 Lawyers outside the courtroom: the ideal of independent judgment

Leaving aside any questions about legal liability,[5] what is the lawyer's *ethical* duty in this situation? You may be tempted to say something along the lines of, "to advocate zealously for the client's desired outcome, within the limits of the law." Many lawyers, in fact, give that as a shorthand summary of the ethical duties of lawyers in all situations. A lawyer may even have been inspired by the rhetoric of Lord Brougham and would contend that he or she must take no need of "the alarm, the torments, the destruction which he may bring upon others," including employees of the coffee shop who believe they are unable to change jobs. Notice, however, a difference between this example and the cases discussed previously. The lawyer here is not representing a client in a litigated matter before a court or any other sort of tribunal. There is no opposing lawyer presenting legal arguments or evidence that would support the other side's point of view. Most importantly, there is no judge and no procedure for obtaining an impartial resolution of uncertainty regarding the facts and law. In essence, the lawyer in this problem is acting as both advocate and judge.

The problem assumes that a broad, sweeping restraint-of-trade clause would likely not be upheld by a court. This is the sort of thing lawyers are expected to know. A business lawyer who advises many clients like the coffee company will probably have seen many similar cases go to court and will probably have a fairly reliable sense of how aggressively one party to a contract can assert its rights before a contractual provision will be invalidated. One of the things clients pay for is the experience and judgment of their lawyers. The lawyer is not giving moral advice but is merely pointing

---

[5] The problem was written to make it unlikely that the lawyer would be subject to liability for malpractice. In a different case, if the client was unaware of the risk that the restraint-of-trade provision would be invalidated, with the attendant increase in the expense and hassle of litigation, the lawyer may be liable for failing to inform the client of these risks. See Paul D. Carrington, "Unconscionable Lawyers," *Georgia Law Review* 19: 361–94 (2002), pp. 384–85.

out that the contract clause desired by the president is very likely to be struck down if challenged by the employee. One might therefore argue that there is, and ought to be, a kind of ethical division of labor between a lawyer and client. The lawyer's job is to provide technical information about the law based on the lawyer's training and experience. The ethical aspect of that function is to use reasonable skill and diligence to provide competent advice. Here, the lawyer fulfills that duty when she tells the client that the contract provision is unlikely to be upheld. If the lawyer's advice were mistaken, we could criticize her for not doing her job well; absent some evidence of carelessness, however, all one can say is that the lawyer did what a good lawyer should do – she gave her client sound legal advice. As for the moral decision making in this situation, it is for the client and the client alone. The lawyer has no business second-guessing her client's moral decisions. Moreover, she has no special expertise in moral matters, so why would the client pay for that kind of advice?

There is a long tradition in legal ethics challenging this technocratic view of the lawyer's duties. This contrary tradition emphasizes that the duty of lawyers is to say to their clients, where appropriate, "Yes, the law allows you do that, but don't do it. It's a rotten thing to do."[6] This ideal, which is often labeled *professionalism*, includes a conception of the lawyer's duty as a wise counselor, not merely someone who has technical proficiency with the law. Professional counseling is meant to be holistic, encompassing all aspects of the client's situation, including economic, strategic, public relations, and moral aspects. Lawyers are not mouthpieces or tools of their clients, but enjoy substantial independence from clients. The most prized attribute of a professional lawyer is judgment, refined over years of experience getting to know not only the applicable law but also the client's goals and values. At the core of the ideal of judgment is the obligation of lawyers to serve the public good through the representation of clients, either by discouraging their clients from acting in ways that are unjust or contrary to the public interest or, more positively, by seeking to establish mutually beneficial cooperative arrangements.[7]

---

[6] Mary Ann Glendon, *A Nation under Lawyers* (New York: Farrar, Straus and Giroux 1994), p. 35 (quoting Archibald Cox).

[7] See William H. Simon, *The Practice of Justice* (Cambridge, Mass.: Harvard University Press 1998), pp. 128–32 (describing the conception of professionalism associated with Louis D. Brandeis, a corporate lawyer and later US Supreme Court Justice).

Former Yale Law School dean Anthony Kronman is a leading contemporary proponent of this view. He has written that the hallmark of ethical lawyering is the exercise of judgment or what he calls "practical wisdom."[8] Exercising professional judgment on behalf of clients means having the capacity to view the client's position sympathetically but also with detachment. Detachment requires *independence* – not, in this case, the independence of the bar from the state (although that is important, too), but independence of the lawyer from her client. The lawyer must appreciate the client's point of view without necessarily endorsing it, while also seeing things from the standpoint of others and taking into account their own interests and commitments.[9] The lawyer is a loyal representative of clients, but he is also a public-spirited professional who acts to preserve the integrity of the framework of laws and legal institutions within which the interests of clients may be realized.[10] Unlike the ideal of zealous advocacy, that (at least in its hard-core Lord Brougham version) instructs lawyers not to take the interests of others into account, the ideal of professional judgment does not make things easy for lawyers who are called upon to balance competing interests even while serving clients. Independence is what dignifies law as a profession, not a mere business or trade.

In less lofty terms, the exercise of independent professional judgment means that the lawyer in our example should endeavor to understand the coffee company's legitimate interest in maintaining long-term employment relationships while also making an effort to feel the pull of the interests of employees in their freedom to change jobs if they choose. The lawyer also must reconcile the client's economic interests with the constraint of the lawyer's professional role, which may require the lawyer to refuse to draft a contract provision that would be unenforceable. There is no formula or algorithm for making this kind of ethical choice. Kronman chose the word *judgment* to convey the Aristotelian idea of practical wisdom (*phronesis*) as a virtue or character trait, shaped through education, training, and experience.[11] Not everyone is equally qualified to offer independent judgment. Some lawyers are better than others. One of the criticisms of Kronman's call for a return to the virtue of practical wisdom as the ethical ideal for lawyers was its seemingly inherent elitism. As exemplars of his ideal, Kronman

---

[8] Anthony T. Kronman, *The Lost Lawyer: Failing Ideals of the Legal Profession* (Cambridge, Mass.: Harvard University Press 1993).

[9] Id., pp. 69–70.   [10] Id., p. 364.   [11] Id., p. 41.

chose a number of "lawyer-statesmen" who had alternated periods of government service with practice in elite law firms.[12] But there is no reason to believe that excellence in the exercise of judgment on behalf of clients is limited to former government officials who become name partners of law firms. Perfectly ordinary lawyers, in small towns and big cities everywhere, can acquire the distinctive expertise of deliberating well about cases, seeing them as instantiations of conflicting values, approaching the client's situation with sympathy and detachment, and ultimately making wise decisions for their clients.[13] Perhaps no one would use the label "statesman" to describe a solicitor in the Auckland CBD with a modest practice representing local businesses, but that lawyer may nevertheless have acquired the capacity, through long experience representing clients, to provide the kind of advice that would best harmonize the interests of the client with the public interest.

Another critique of Kronman's proposal of judgment as an ethical ideal for lawyers is pragmatic: The conditions under which many lawyers can acquire the experience necessary for the exercise of practical wisdom may no longer exist. Lawyers representing large corporate clients no longer serve as generalist advisors dealing with all aspects of the client's business. Instead, lawyers employed directly by the company (referred to as "in-house" counsel) handle much of the company's routine business. When it is necessary to retain an "outside" law firm, it is usually for a specific matter – either a litigated dispute or a transaction such as a merger. Outside lawyers have accordingly become highly specialized, with expertise primarily in one type of practice, such as employment litigation, environmental compliance, defending shareholder lawsuits, mergers and acquisitions, real estate finance, asset securitization, and so on. The market for legal services is also much more competitive than it once was. Instead of long-term relationships between corporate clients and their outside law firms, clients now put new business out for a competitive bidding process, referred to (in the sexist term used in the industry) as "beauty contests," in which law firms go head-to-head on price and expertise. Paradoxically, the long-term nature of the lawyer–client relationship helped secure the lawyer's independence from the client. If a lawyer told a client "no," the client was less likely to take its business to another law firm. Not only was it not

---

[12] Id., pp. 11–12, 283.   [13] Id., pp. 361–63.

generally done, but it might have signaled to other actors in the market-place that the client was up to something a bit dodgy. Today, however, it is not unusual for clients to retain dozens of outside law firms for work on a variety of matters and to regard any firm as potentially replaceable. The costs of saying "no" are therefore much higher; the result may be the loss of the client's business. Given the internal competitive pressures within law firms, with partners scrambling to justify their share of the firm's profits,[14] the incentives are to acquiesce in the client's objectives as long as they do not violate the law.

In the sector of the market serving individual clients, lawyers face new competitive pressures resulting from deregulation of the market (in some countries, most notably the United Kingdom) and the widespread adoption of digital information technology.[15] In the United Kingdom, the Legal Services Act of 2007, based on a report prepared by Sir David Clementi, led to the abandonment of much of the traditional regulation of the divided profession in England and Wales by the Law Society and the Bar, for solicitors and barristers, respectively.[16] The result has been the threat of competition from lawyers employed by existing providers of other consumer services (referred to in the United Kingdom as "Tesco Law" after a large supermarket chain).[17] One fear of High Street lawyers is that Tesco lawyers will act like any other employee of a large corporation as opposed to understanding themselves as members of a learned profession. Will clients go to Tesco Law seeking independent professional judgment? Alternatively, clients may not go to law offices at all but will instead rely on online document preparation services such as LegalZoom for routine legal matters. An organization such as LegalZoom, set up to make efficient use of information technology, is unlikely to provide the kind of independent professional

---

[14] For a fascinating account of a lawyer at an elite law firm who succumbed to this competitive pressure and was ultimately convicted of bankruptcy fraud, see Milton C. Regan, Jr., *Eat What You Kill: The Fall of a Wall Street Lawyer* (Ann Arbor: University of Michigan Press 2004). Regan's book also provides a helpful overview of the competitive pressures discussed in this paragraph.

[15] See Richard Susskind, *The End of Lawyers? Rethinking the Nature of Legal Services* (Oxford University Press, 2008).

[16] See John Flood, "Will There Be Fallout from Clementi? The Repercussions for the Legal Profession after the Legal Services Act 2007," *Michigan State Law Review* 2012: 537–65.

[17] See, e.g., Neil Rose, "'Tesco Law' – Not the Big Bang, But it Will Change the Face of Legal Services," *The Guardian* (March 25, 2011).

judgment that is the hallmark of professionalism. It is almost inconceivable that a client's computer will come to the conclusion, "Yes, the law lets you do that, but don't do it. It's a rotten thing to do."

None of these pragmatic arguments responds to Kronman in ethical terms. Independence and professional judgment would remain ethical ideals even if it is increasingly difficult for lawyers to fulfill them. (Honesty remains an ethical ideal even if it would be very tempting to lie and get away with it.) An ethical critique of Kronman's conception of professionalism would have to emphasize a different ethical value. To go back to our bridge structure, Kronman identifies "the public interest" as the relevant foundational moral value (step 1) and argues that it entails a duty within professional ethics to exercise professional judgment to harmonize the interests of the client and the public interest (step 2). But is the public interest the right foundational value? What happened to the values of loyalty to clients and protecting the dignity and autonomy of clients? To continue the evaluation of Kronman's argument about the centrality of practical wisdom to professional ethics, we will relax one of the assumptions in the problem that opened this chapter.

10.3   Constructions of clients

As initially written, the president of the coffee company was imagined as a hard-nosed businessperson who cared little for the interests of her employees. That caricature highlights some ethical issues that may arise for lawyers, but it is by no means a fair representation of all clients. Clients have values, too, and they are not always the values of Ebenezer Scrooge. Many clients are motivated to do the right thing, not just to see how much they can get away with. More to the point, a lawyer may not know in advance what her client's values are, and it would be a mistake to assume that the client necessarily wants advice on how to walk right up to the edge of the line between permissible and unlawful conduct.[18] The conception of legal ethics that emphasizes loyalty, partisanship, and zealous advocacy may tacitly presuppose that clients are always interested only in maximizing their self-interest. If the problem in this chapter is revised so that the client did not suggest the

[18] Katherine R. Kruse, "Beyond Cardboard Clients in Legal Ethics," *Georgetown Journal of Legal Ethics* 23: 103–54 (2010).

restraint-of-trade clause but merely asked the lawyer for advice about the business's contracts with employees, the lawyer might fail to serve the client's objectives if she assumes the company wants to make it as difficult as possible for employees to change jobs. Suppose the lawyer had used the aggressive, broad, restraint-of-trade clause with other business clients who were pleased with the results (i.e., greater retention of employees). The lawyer might believe that the coffee company president would desire the same contractual arrangement. Unknown to the lawyer, however, the president may have different attitudes toward both the terms of the employment relationship (she may prefer to be less aggressive in protecting the rights of the company, believing it will be good for employee morale) and the company's stance toward the law (she may not want to do something that would be disallowed if challenged in court). The lawyer should therefore begin by having an open-ended conversation with the president to learn what she hopes to achieve in the company's employment contracts.

Ironically, Kronman's alternative, which encourages the lawyer to seek a position that harmonizes the client's interests and the public interest, may also lead lawyers to treat their clients as caricatures. The ideal of the lawyer as wise counselor may tacitly assume that clients are less capable than their lawyers of making moral judgments. Kronman warns against lawyers understanding their professional role in narrowly instrumental terms. The picture of legal ethics he is criticizing gives the lawyer two responsibilities in this case: (1) to give the president accurate information about the legal consequences of using the restraint-of-trade clause (in this case, that it would likely be invalidated if challenged), and (2) to "implement whatever decision the client makes, so long as it is lawful"; it is the client who "does all the real deliberating" about what the client's goals should be and whether they are worth pursuing.[19] This division between ends and means is reflected in the American law of lawyering (which probably has counterparts in other common law systems), which recognize it both as a matter of rules of professional conduct and the generally applicable law of agency.[20] Kronman argues, in

---

[19] Kronman, *supra*, p. 123.

[20] American Bar Association Rules of Professional Conduct, Rule 1.2(a) ("a lawyer shall abide by a client's decisions concerning the objectives of representation and ... shall consult with the client as to the means by which they are to be pursued"); Restatement (Third) of the Law Governing Lawyers § 21 (summarizing agency law on the allocation of decision-making authority between lawyers and clients). The problem in this chapter

opposition to this view, that "most lawyers would ... agree that their responsibilities to a client go beyond the preliminary clarification of his goals and include helping him to make a deliberatively wise choice among them."[21] Thus, the lawyer in the problem should not merely ask the president of the coffee company what kind of employment contracts she would like to have, but also should attempt to steer her toward a wise decision. Does that mean one that *the lawyer considers* to be wise? Or is it the decision that is *in fact* wise? If there is disagreement over what is in fact wise, whose view of the wisdom of the client's ends should prevail – the lawyer's or the client's? These are all questions that must be addressed if one believes the lawyer's role includes going beyond a narrow, instrumental conception of the lawyer's expertise as primarily involving technical knowledge and experience with the law and seeks to broaden it to providing practical wisdom and assisting the client in making wise choices about ends.

The view criticized by Kronman is not only recognized by law, but it appeals to a value on the morality side of the bridge that has a great deal of resonance in a liberal democratic society. Telling lawyers that they are responsible for harmonizing the interests of their clients with the public interest (or justice, or morality, or whatever) risks interfering with client autonomy. On the assumption that the client is a competent adult, shouldn't she be free to decide for herself whether it is right or wrong to take a hard line in contractual relationships with employees? In other words, Kronman's conception of wise counseling casts the lawyer in a paternalistic role. Professionals such as lawyers, physicians, and psychotherapists act paternalistically when they make decisions that the patient or client has a right to make for him- or herself.[22] One could therefore criticize Kronman and support the means/ends division of labor in the professional

is set in New Zealand, and I think the rules of professional conduct there would support the same analysis, although it is not quite as clear from the face of the rules. See Lawyers and Conveyancers Act (NZ) (2008), Lawyers: Client Conduct and Care Rules, Preface, informing clients that, "[w]hatever legal services your lawyer is providing, he or she must ... discuss with you your objectives and how they should best be achieved." See also Duncan Webb, *Ethics: Professional Responsibility and the Lawyer* (Wellington: Butterworths 2000) §5.3 (discussing contract and fiduciary duties owed by the lawyer to the client).

[21] Kronman, *supra*, p. 129.

[22] See David Luban, "Paternalism and the Legal Profession," *Wisconsin Law Review* 1981: 454–93, p. 458.

relationship by stressing the necessary connection between the moral value of autonomy and a principle of professional ethics that avoids paternalism. Kronman at this juncture has two options.[23] He could either appeal to a different value on the morality side of the bridge (step 1 of the argument), or he could deny that the conception of professional ethics he supports has the effect of unduly interfering with autonomy (a variation on step 2 in the argument). He may plausibly do both.[24]

First, on the morality side of the bridge, Kronman may concede that autonomy is an important value in a liberal democracy, but it is by no means the only value that matters when one is considering the duties of public officials or professionals whose actions have an impact on the public interest. Autonomy may be only instrumentally valuable. That is, all else being equal, it is a good thing when people act autonomously, but there is no moral value in an autonomously chosen immoral act.[25] Consider the example from Chapter 4, of someone who borrowed money in a time of desperate need and then refused to pay it back later, having made a fortune in the interim. I believe most people would make a kind of rough, pretheoretical moral judgment that the borrower acted wrongly by not paying back the debt. The fact that the borrower made an autonomous choice not to repay the debt does not change the evaluation. Granted, if someone had held a gun to the borrower's head and said "I'll shoot you if you repay that debt," the failure to repay would be excused. But just because we do not blame people when they act under coercion, the inverse principle does not hold. Making a free, uncoerced decision to do wrong is still wrong. In the domain of morality – again, not considering the question of whether there are good reasons for a legal system to recognize rights – merely having a right to do something does not justify that act:

> If an action appears arbitrary or capricious, if, for example, I stand on my
> head for a week facing west in a public place, or marry somebody I loathe, or

---

[23] Remember the structure of the three-step argument in Chapter 2: (1) define, specify, and explain the significance of a moral value; (2) show that the value in step (1) entails a principle of professional ethics; (3) test the resulting theory against cases.

[24] Again, the purpose of this discussion is not to persuade you one way or the other regarding Kronman's theory of legal ethics but to illustrate how these positions may be taken apart and criticized.

[25] See David Luban, "The Lysistratian Prerogative: A Reply to Stephen Pepper," *American Bar Foundation Research Journal* 1986: 637–49, p. 639.

burn my stock certificates in a fit of pique, or vote randomly in a general election, my action when questioned is not made to appear one iota more reasonable or defensible, nor is a spectator the slightest bit more likely to understand why I did it, when I reply, "I had a right to do it; I was exercising my right."[26]

The role of lawyer and its characteristic duties as a matter of professional ethics must therefore be connected with some value other than autonomy on the morality side of the bridge.

Although Kronman does not make this connection explicitly, he seems to be appealing to something that is central to the natural law tradition, namely, the common good of the political community.[27] He refers to the ideal of public-spiritedness and argues for a conception of legal ethics in which lawyers should internalize an attitude of civic-mindedness and be capable of setting aside concerns for the private interests of their clients.[28] He also relies on the existence of a sentiment of political fraternity – that is, bonds of sympathy that exist among members of a political community notwithstanding the differences of opinion concerning the aims and ambitions of the community that otherwise set citizens apart from each other.[29] If the common good and political fraternity are important moral and political values, then lawyers might understand their role as contributing to their realization. Indeed, this is the connection envisioned by Kronman. The central principle of his conception of legal ethics is the exercise of judgment or practical wisdom in the representation of clients. He contends that practical wisdom ought to take into account the public interest. "[W]hat makes one judgment wiser than another when the alternatives cannot be measured on any common scale of value is its tendency to promote political fraternity."[30] In the coffee company example, the lawyer would not be

---

[26] Jeremy Waldron, "A Right to Do Wrong," *Ethics* 92: 21–39 (1981), p. 28. Waldron does argue that having a moral right may entail a duty of noninterference by others, but this conception of autonomy does not help the proponent of the Standard Conception of legal ethics. The bridge structure requires that a value on the morality side entail a principle of professional ethics. If all a moral right generates is a duty of noninterference, it does not support a duty as a matter of professional ethics for lawyers to defend the client's autonomy, which is generally understood as the principle of partisanship.

[27] See, e.g., Mark C. Murphy, *Natural Law in Jurisprudence and Politics* (Cambridge: Cambridge University Press 2006), pp. 61–63; John Finnis, *Natural Law and Natural Rights* (Oxford: Oxford University Press 1980), pp. 154–56.

[28] Kronman, *supra*, pp. 127, 141–43.   [29] Id., p. 93.   [30] Id., p. 97.

acting paternalistically toward her client because the client, as much as the lawyer, has an obligation to consider the common good. The president may *want* to keep her employees on a short leash (depending on how the problem is specified), but a want or an interest is different from a value.[31] One person may justifiably interfere with the liberty of another where the first knows the second is about to give in to a desire that would result in a violation of her values.

Kronman seeks to make the legal profession the guardians of the public interest, not because clients do not also have a reason to care about the public interest, but because lawyers, through training and experience, may be better than clients at determining what the public interest requires in a particular case. Lawyers have a distinctive expertise that consists of deliberating well about cases.[32] They help their clients do better at something clients already have a reason to do – namely, to determine what action is consistent with the public interest. A lawyer who followed Kronman's conception of legal ethics would understand the president's request for advice in this case as aimed at getting the right balance among all the competing values that are implicated by the employment contract, including the company's interest in a stable, well-trained workforce and the employees' interest in earning reasonable compensation and having the flexibility to change jobs.

Second, on the professional ethics side of the bridge, Kronman may rely on a distinction between representing a client as an advocate, in litigation, and counseling a client in a matter unrelated to a litigated dispute. When a lawyer is representing a client in litigation, it is essential that the lawyer consider only the interests of the client and not be concerned about "the alarm, the torments, [and] the destruction" caused to others. (This is the principle of neutrality, from the Standard Conception.) It is the job of the institutions and procedures of the adversary system to ensure that the public interest and the interests of others are protected. The interests of crime victims are represented, in essence, by the prosecuting attorney, and, in civil cases, the opposing party usually has its own lawyer. As for witnesses who may be harassed or humiliated by questions from a lawyer, rules of evidence prohibit abusive questioning, and the trial judge may step in to limit it. Interpretation of the law is the role of the judge who makes

---

[31] Luban, pp. 471–73.   [32] Kronman, *supra*, p. 362.

decisions after considering the submissions of lawyers for both sides. Decisions of the trial court are subject to review by courts of appeal, again after briefing of the issues by the parties' lawyers. It makes sense to identify autonomy as the foundational value in litigation because there are so many institutional mechanisms to ensure that the interests of all parties have been fairly considered before a final judgment is reached. In the advising context, however, where there is no opposing lawyer, no judge, no rules of evidence and procedure, and no possibility of appeal, it is plausible to say that the lawyer may be required to balance the client's interests with the public interest.

The practice of counseling clients reveals an ambiguity in the Standard Conception of legal ethics. On the Standard Conception, lawyers are supposed to be partisan representatives, seeking to further their clients' lawful interests, and be neutral with respect to the interests of others who would be affected by the representation. The open term, so to speak, in the Standard Conception is the interests of clients. Clients may desire to act in a public-interested way or at least to consider the interests of others who would be affected by their actions. The president of the coffee company may prefer a happy, motivated workforce over employees who feel legally bound not to seek other employment opportunities. This might be the case in litigation, as well as in the context of client advising. For example, suppose the lawyer drafts the contract with the sweeping restraint-of-trade clause. Now suppose one of the company's best coffee roasters decides to leave and open her own independent coffee shop in a location that is not in direct competition with one of the company's shops. At that point, the president has a second choice: Either to sue on the contract, knowing that a lawsuit is unlikely to be successful but hoping that the former employee might settle to avoid the expense of litigation, or to wish the former employee well and hire a replacement.

Lawyers are trained to spot and analyze legal issues, anticipate risks, and propose solutions that protect the client's legal interests. At all stages of representation, lawyers should be aware that their training creates the risk of objectifying clients – that is, treating them as merely an aggregation of legal interests without considering whether, as moral agents and possibly members of overlapping social communities with those affected by their actions, they have interests that are not congruent with the full extent of the rights they may have under law. Even if the restraint-of-trade clause were enforceable, the president may choose not to employ it. Kronman's conception of legal ethics as practical wisdom would instruct the coffee company's lawyers to consider the public interest as well as the client's interests. His proposal can come off sounding grandiose, as if lawyers are supposed to reason like high-ranking government officials only without the usual mechanisms of political accountability to check their power. (It does not help that Kronman continually refers to the "lawyer-statesman" ideal.) Calling on lawyers to be civic-minded obscures the extent to which the representation of clients in perfectly ordinary matters, such as the coffee shop employment contract, implicates the interests of others, which the client may herself care about. Even a lawyer who adheres to the standard conception of legal ethics should remember that faithful client service depends on being able to ascertain the client's actual interests, not a hypothetical set of objectives that happen to line up with the client's legal rights.

In one context, it can be difficult to treat the client as a flesh-and-blood person with genuine human interests because the client is not, in fact, a real person. The representation of formally organized business entities, particularly publicly held corporations, relies on the legal fiction that corporations are "persons" in the sense of being independently existing entities who have the right to own property, make contracts, sue and be sued, assert certain legal rights, and do other things that are characteristic of being actual persons.[33] The next chapter, concluding our review of legal ethics in particular contexts of practice, considers the ethical issues arising from the representation of entity clients.

---

[33] You may have noticed that the president is the majority shareholder of the coffee company. The detail was added so that, for the purposes of the ethical analysis in this chapter, the president and the company could be considered equivalently the client of the lawyer. The situation would be more complicated if the president were acting as an agent of shareholders who themselves were represented by a board of directors.

11 Representing corporations: lawyers as gatekeepers?

11.1 Up in the air

LVP, Pty., is an Australian manufacturer of advanced lithium cobalt oxide batteries for electric cars, located in Newcastle, New South Wales. Recently, it developed a battery for aerospace use and won a contract to supply BoeBus, a multinational aircraft manufacturer, with batteries for use on its new jetliner.[1] Largely due to this contract, LVP has turned around its financial performance and is beginning its second profitable year. You are the general counsel of LVP. One evening at dinner, an engineer with the company, who is an old friend from your university days, confided to you that she feared the worst. She was convinced that the batteries may be prone to a condition called thermal runaway, which would cause them to overheat and even catch fire under some circumstances. Although the batteries passed all applicable design and safety standards when LVP won the contract with BoeBus, the company's recent tests caused the engineer to believe that thermal runaway could occur if unusual demands were placed on the airplane's electrical power system. The new BoeBus plane includes advanced electrical systems that might place heavy loads on the batteries. An in-flight fire, particularly the kind of rapidly accelerating fire character- istic of lithium-ion batteries, would almost certainly have catastrophic consequences. Your friend said she had informed the company's president of the research but had been told not to discuss it with anyone else.

The next day, you mentioned to the president that you had heard of problems with the batteries. The president stated that, although it was the

---

[1] This problem is adapted from a problem in an article by former US Court of Appeals Judge John Ferren, "The Corporate Lawyer's Obligation to the Public Interest," *Business Lawyer* 33: 1253–69 (1978). Any resemblance to problems experienced by the Boeing 787 is purely coincidental.

case that a majority of the engineering staff believed there was a danger of thermal runaway, a minority of the staff, including some of the most experienced engineers, believed the new tests showed no danger or, at worst, were inconclusive. The president emphasized that the batteries met all legal safety requirements imposed by aviation authorities in the European Union and North America. He also stated that changes to the composition of the batteries were being considered so that, in due course, any problem – which he believed not to exist in any event – would undoubtedly be resolved. You suggested informing customers, including BoeBus, of the adverse test results and promising to replace batteries already in service with the newly developed batteries, but the president objected strongly. He referred not only to conflicting interpretations of the test results but also to the recent turnaround in the financial performance of the company, the fact that 25 percent of company sales were now to BoeBus, and the employment by LVP of a substantial number of people in a community that had been experiencing economic hardship before LVP opened a production facility there. The president urged you to let the matter lie.

Under Australian law,[2] which is similar in all relevant respects to company/corporate law throughout the common law world, major decisions affecting the corporation are made by a board of directors. The directors are elected by shareholders who are the owners of the company. As it happens, a regular meeting of the board of directors was scheduled for the week following the disclosure by the engineer. As general counsel, it is your duty to report to the board of directors on legal issues concerning the company. You therefore informed the board of what the engineer had told you about the thermal runaway problem. The president then addressed the board and said, "I appreciate _____ raising all concerns related to safety, but I can assure the board that the possibility of thermal runaway has been thoroughly investigated by the engineering staff, who ran a series of additional tests and concluded that there is no reason to believe there is a safety issue. As you know, we are always improving our products, and a new line of batteries is being developed that will have even greater margins of safety protection. We believe no action is warranted at this time." The board deliberated and decided to do nothing. The chairman of the board instructed you to "consider the matter closed."

---

[2] Corporations Act (2001). See also Christine Parker and Adrian Evans, *Inside Lawyers' Ethics* (Cambridge: Cambridge University Press 2007), ch. 9.

The more you thought about the board's decision, the more troubled you became. Your family had lived for a time in the United States when you were a child, and you will never forget the experience of gathering with your primary school class to watch the launch of the American space shuttle *Challenger*, carrying the first teacher ever to travel in space. As millions of schoolchildren watched in horror, the *Challenger* exploded in a gigantic fireball a few minutes after takeoff. Subsequent investigation determined that engineers at one of the aerospace contractors that built the solid-fuel rocket boosters for the shuttle had expressed concerns about the performance of a crucial part in the unusual cold-weather conditions forecast for the morning of the launch. Senior managers at the company and officials at the American space agency overrode their concerns, however, and ordered the launch to proceed.[3] One of the concerns motivating the launch was the concern about the substantial economic costs of canceling the launch and of the perception that the agency was inefficient. You believe the president and board of directors may be so focused in using the economic success of the aviation batteries to continue the transformation of the company that they have not given due regard to safety considerations. You believe your friend in the engineering department is careful, well-informed, and not prone to overstating risks.

You are well aware of the duty of confidentiality owed to your client. Under the solicitors' rules of New South Wales, without client authorization, you are prohibited from disclosing confidential information unless the communication falls within one of the exceptions to the professional duty.[4] The duty of confidentiality, along with all the other rules of professional conduct, apply to so-called "in-house" lawyers who are employed by a corporation.[5] You already know that the client will not consent to disclosing information about the batteries to its customers, including BoeBus, because both the president and the board of directors instructed you to consider the matter closed. (You also know the president is close friends with several members of the board and that the board is likely to support any decision

[3] See Diane Vaughan, *The Challenger Launch Decision: Risky Technology, Culture, and Deviance at NASA* (Chicago: University of Chicago Press 1996).

[4] Law Society of New South Wales, *Professional Conduct and Practice Rules 2013 (Solicitors' Rules)*, Rule 9.

[5] Law Society of New South Wales, Corporate Lawyers Committee, *Handy Hints for In-House Counsel* (2012); Parker and Evans, *supra*, pp. 212–13.

made by the president, including sacking the company's general counsel.) An exception to the confidentiality rule permits disclosure "for the purpose of preventing imminent serious physical harm to the client or to another person."[6] Obviously, a crash resulting from an in-flight fire would lead to serious harm, but is the harm "imminent"? Your worst nightmare is that there is an airplane somewhere in the world taking off right now with a battery that might catch fire, but you have no information suggesting that this is the case – only that there is a risk of thermal runaway, and, as for how severe that risk is, it is disputed by engineers. Some leaders of the Australian bar emphasize the ethical obligation of corporate lawyers to consider broader conceptions of the public interest, not only narrow legal questions.[7] Of course, your primary ethical obligations are to your client, the company, and you had never previously considered disclosing confidential information, even when you suspected company employees of wrongdoing. As the company's lawyer, it is your job to handle those sorts of problems within the company, without involving government regulators. But this feels different. What do you do?

11.2   Lawyers as gatekeepers and whistle-blowers

Suppose there was a crash of a BoeBus airplane, the cause of which was traced to an in-flight fire started by a battery manufactured by your client. If evidence were developed that lawyers for the company knew about the safety problems but did nothing, do you have any doubt that there would be a public outcry? Outrage might properly be focused on the company and its senior management, but there might be plenty of blame to go around, including severe criticism of lawyers who knew of the danger and took no steps to protect people who relied on the safety of their company's products. When the misdeeds of powerful corporations are revealed, one naturally wants to know whether professional advisors knew of the misconduct and tried to do anything to stop it. For example, after a series of bank failures in the United States in the 1980s that were linked with both corrupt managers and lax oversight by government regulators, a federal judge

[6] N.S.W. *Solicitors' Rules, supra*, Rule 9.2.5.

[7] See Parker and Evans, *supra*, pp. 216–17, 238–39 (discussing the efforts of an asbestos manufacturing company to divest itself of liability for personal-injury claims filed by victims of asbestos-related illnesses).

famously commented on the failure of the attorneys (and accountants) who were hired to advise the bank:

> Where were these professionals . . . when these clearly improper transactions were being consummated?
>
> Why didn't any of them speak up or disassociate themselves from the transactions?
>
> Where also were the outside accountants and attorneys when these transactions were effectuated?
>
> What is difficult to understand is that with all the professional talent involved (both accounting and legal), why at least one professional would not have blown the whistle to stop the overreaching that took place in this case.[8]

The judge's choice of words, "blowing the whistle," was provocative, and the aftermath of the collapse of the savings and loan industry (i.e., small, local banks originally intended to accept deposits from individuals and make loans to finance the purchase of homes) witnessed a sometimes acrimonious struggle over the role lawyers should play when advising corporate clients. Lawyers perceived that they were being asked to play a new role – that of gatekeeper – which would require them to take active steps to prevent their clients from committing financial frauds or other types of wrongs or at least not remain passive after learning of ongoing wrongdoing by a client.

The judge's choice of words, "blowing the whistle," was provocative, and Whistle-blowing and gatekeeping are different things, strictly speaking. Whistle-blowing refers to an actor within an organization making a public disclosure of wrongdoing by the organization. When an attorney learned that his client, a manufacturer of medical devices, planned to ship defective kidney dialysis machines to a customer in the developing world "who buys only on price" and reported the proposed sale to a government regulator, thus blocking the shipment, that attorney was acting as a whistle-blower.[9] Blowing the whistle is an extraordinary event, comparable to civil disobedience (see Chapter 6), in which a professional normally subject to an ethical duty of confidentiality determines that the need to protect the interests of nonclients or the public interest is sufficiently compelling that violating the professional ethical duty of confidentiality is required. Gatekeeping, by contrast, is not extraordinary. It is what many lawyers (and

---

[8] *Lincoln Saving & Loan Association v. Wall*, 743 F. Supp. 901, 920 (D.D.C. 1990).
[9] *Balla v. Gambro, Inc.*, 584 N.E.2d 104 (Ill. 1991).

other professionals, such as public accountants, and institutions, such as ratings agencies) do on a daily basis. Gatekeepers are actors who "serve investors by preparing, verifying, or assessing the disclosures that they receive."[10] For example, ratings agencies evaluate the creditworthiness of the issuers of securities. At least in the United States, many institutional investors are prohibited from holding securities that have not been rated as "investment grade" by a recognized ratings agency. Similarly, corporate attorneys who are not comfortable with the representations made by a client in a securities registration statement may withhold approval by declining to file the registration with the Securities and Exchange Commission (SEC).[11] To be effective gatekeepers, lawyers or other professionals must be independent to some extent from the clients who retain them because the basic professional ethical obligation of a gatekeeper is to withhold consent from a transaction that does not satisfy the standards necessary to earn consent, approval, or a rating.[12] In most cases, a gatekeeper discharges its obligation by simply refusing consent, as opposed to a whistle-blower, who discloses wrongdoing publicly or to a government agency.

---

[10] John C. Coffee, Jr., "The Attorney as Gatekeeper: An Agenda for the SEC," *Columbia Law Review* 103: 1293–1316 (2003), p. 1296.

[11] The landscape of securities fraud liability for secondary actors such as lawyers and accountants is complicated in the United States following two Supreme Court cases called *Central Bank* and *Stoneridge*. For a careful treatment see *Pacific Investment Management Company LLC v. Mayer Brown LLP*, 603 F.3d 144 (2d Cir. 2010). I make no representations of expertise in the law of securities fraud in Australia, Canada, the United Kingdom, or elsewhere. The discussion in the text is intended merely to exemplify an approach to regulation of the legal profession and to set up the ethical analysis of the lawyer's role as gatekeeper, not to analyze the liability of law firms for securities fraud.

[12] Coffee, *supra*, p. 1297. Even lawyers who are critical of expanded gatekeeping obligations concede that many routine lawyering tasks quite appropriately call on lawyers to serve as gatekeepers:

> [U]nder typical contractual arrangements, securities issuances cannot go forward without a host of opinions from the attorneys involved, including opinions that give negative assurances with respect to disclosure. Even a litigator is a gatekeeper who typically makes a representation of due inquiry and colorable merit when he or she signs a pleading.

Evan A. Davis, "The Meaning of Professional Independence," *Columbia Law Review* 103: 1281–92 (2003), p. 1283.

The organized bar has always fought hard against any obligations that would interfere with what it saw as the fundamental role of lawyers – namely, standing between the client and the state. After a high-profile corporate fraud case in the 1970s, lawyers expressed consternation that enforcement efforts by the SEC would have the effect of "chang[ing] lawyers from client-defenders into whistleblowers and policemen." As Susan Koniak, a long-time critic of lawyer passivity in the face of client wrongdoing, observed, "[i]t is difficult to overstate the vehemence of the bar's reaction to the SEC complaint; references to the return of King George [III] were commonplace, and the rhetoric suggested that the liberty of all Americans was at stake."[13] The bar similarly protested when, following the financial accounting scandals at Enron and other American corporations, the SEC proposed regulations to give additional weight to the corporate attorney's obligation to serve as a gatekeeper.[14] One bar leader, a partner at a firm representing financial institutions and other large corporations, criticized the proposed regulations by appealing to "the role of the legal profession as an independent bulwark between individuals or organizations and the political branches of government."[15] Although this partner did not mention the return of King George III, he did worry about the bar being regulated by the Department of Justice. "It would be much harder to resist either gentle or firm governmental pressure if the government's lawyers decided how the bar in general or you, as an attorney, in particular, should behave."[16] The partner's argument appeals to the value of independence, but it also depends on the centrality of loyalty to one's client as the foundational value in professional ethics. It harkens back to Lord Brougham's declaration (see Chapter 3) that the lawyer "knows but one person in all the world, and that person is his client."

Notice, however, that there might be something awry in the partner's argument. It begins with the undoubtedly important ideal, in the context of criminal defense representation, of the independence of the legal profession as a safeguard of the liberty of individuals against overreaching by an all-powerful state – "an independent bulwark between individuals or

---

[13] Susan P. Koniak, "When the Hurlyburly's Done: The Bar's Struggle with the SEC," *Columbia Law Review* 103: 1236–80 (2003), p. 1249.

[14] See, e.g., Lawrence J. Fox, "The Fallout from Enron: Media Frenzy and Misguided Notions of Public Relations Are No Reason to Abandon our Commitment to Our Clients," *Illinois Law Review* 2003: 1243–59.

[15] Davis, *supra*, p. 1281.   [16] Id., p. 1291.

organizations and the political branches of government." But the argument then makes what philosophers call a category mistake by assuming that the properties of one subset of the legal profession (i.e., the ethical principles of the criminal defense bar) are necessarily shared by all members of the legal profession. Quite simply, many features of the criminal defense lawyer's ethical rights and duties will not translate into other contexts without modification. We have already seen that lawyers who represent clients in noncriminal litigation do not have the same ethical latitude as criminal defense attorneys to assert groundless legal claims.[17] For example, criminal defense lawyers may seek permission from the court to withdraw if they believe there are no nonfrivolous grounds for reversing the defendant's conviction, and, if they do seek permission to withdraw, they are required to accompany that request with a brief setting forth "anything in the record that might arguably support the appeal."[18] By contrast, a lawyer representing a client in an appeal from a civil judgment is potentially subject to court sanctions for pursuing a frivolous appeal.[19] It is certainly the case that the ethics of criminal defense lawyers should be grounded on the role of the defense bar in standing between the individual and the state. The ethics of other types of lawyers may stand on a different foundation.

To make some progress in this seemingly intractable debate, let us once again use the three-step argument from Chapter 2, which aims at justifying principles of professional ethics:

1. Define, specify, and if necessary explain the significance of a moral value.
2. Show that the value in step 1 entails a principle of professional ethics.
3. Test the resulting theory against cases.

Remember, too, that the method of reflective equilibrium aims to find a satisfactory fit between theory and practice. Thus, we may want to work backward from observations about the way lawyers represent corporations in practice and seek a theoretical justification that accounts for our intuitions about what duties lawyers ought to have as a matter of professional ethics. Alternatively, we can begin with normative considerations that we believe ought to be taken into account in structuring the ethical duties of

---

[17] See American Bar Association, Model Rules of Professional Conduct, Rule 3.1.

[18] *Anders v. California*, 386 U.S. 738, 744 (1967). *Anders* was modified in some respects by *Smith v. Robbins*, 528 U.S. 259 (2000), but the differences are not relevant here.

[19] Federal Rules of Appellate Procedure, Rule 38.

professionals. For instance, the protection of investors from financial frauds or the protection of the traveling public from airplane crashes caused by faulty batteries are goals that may bear on the duties imposed on lawyers representing corporations.

At the risk of oversimplifying, imagine a debate between two sides, the gatekeepers and the hired guns. The gatekeepers are those, like Susan Koniak or the federal judge quoted earlier, who believe that lawyers ought to refuse to provide assistance to their clients in committing an unlawful or harmful act. They see their ethical obligations as akin to those of accountants or securities ratings agencies. If a client is engaging in wrongdoing, the ethical obligation of a lawyer is, at the very least, not to lend assistance and to withdraw from the representation if necessary. If those steps are not sufficient to prevent the harm, however, in extreme cases. a lawyer may also have to consider blowing the whistle – that is, disclosing the contemplated wrongdoing with the aim of preventing it from occurring. On the other side, the hired guns are those who understand their ethical obligations as akin to those of criminal defense lawyers or at least civil litigators. They adhere to some form of the Standard Conception of legal ethics (see Chapter 3). That is, their most important duties are those that run to their client and include loyalty and the stringent maintenance of confidentiality (the principle of partisanship) and, to a significant extent, not taking into account the interests of others (the principle of neutrality). Within the confines of the lawyer–client relationship, a lawyer is encouraged to attempt to dissuade the client from going forward with an action the attorney believes is potentially unlawful or harmful. If the client insists, despite the lawyer's advice, however, the lawyer must not disclose any information relating to the representation. First consider the (somewhat fanciful and exaggerated) arguments of each side, and then we can map them onto the three-step structure.

11.2.1   Gatekeepers

There are two ways to defend an ethical obligation not to assist client wrongdoing. The first is conceptual. The word "law" is the first half of "lawyer." The only way to give an intelligible account of the distinctive nature of the role of *lawyer* is with reference to the law. Otherwise, lawyers are no different from other types of advisors, such as business consultants. There is nothing wrong with business consultants, but they lack the distinctive role of advising clients and representing them *with reference to the law*. Sometimes the participation of lawyers is necessary for a client to commit unlawful acts, as in the transactions through which some senior managers at Enron defrauded investors of billions of dollars.[20] It would be conceptually incompatible with the lawyer's role for legal assistance to be used to violate the law. To do so would be like an architect designing a building that fell down or an engineer building a car that failed to run; these failings go to the heart of what it means to be a professional with a distinctive role and special ethical rights and duties.

The second argument for gatekeeping responsibilities is not conceptual but normative. Granting that, in the airplane batteries case, there is no clear violation of law, it may be stretching the conceptual argument to contend that lawyers who were not involved in the underlying wrongdoing have an obligation to disclose the client's misconduct. But lawyers have always understood themselves as being more than mere mouthpieces for their clients. Lawyers are public citizens with a special responsibility for the administration of justice. The public interest must be at the heart of any plausible conception of legal ethics. A lawyer who sat passively while the client allowed potentially dangerous component parts to be incorporated into passenger airplanes would be, in effect, subjecting people to substantial safety risks even though the lawyer was not personally involved in the client's decision making.[21] Lawyers are also moral agents who must accept personal responsibility for their acts, just as anyone else would; being a lawyer does not provide an exemption from the demands of ordinary morality.[22] If the result of the client's marketing of the batteries was a catastrophic accident, how could anyone have a clear conscience knowing that it would have been possible to prevent the accident by warning customers?

11.2.2   Hired guns

We agree that the distinctive ethical role of the lawyer is to represent clients within the law. But the gatekeepers' argument leaves out something extremely important – namely, any appreciation for the practical context

---

[20] Koniak, *supra*, pp. 1239–43.

[21] See, e.g., Deborah L. Rhode, *In the Interests of Justice: Reforming the Legal Profession* (Oxford: Oxford University Press 2000), p. 50.

[22] Id., pp. 17–20.

in which lawyers advise their clients and bring them into compliance with the law. Facts are seldom clear-cut in real life. The battery manufacturer does not come to the lawyer saying, "we know these batteries will catch fire in flight – what should we do?" Rather, the facts take the form of inconclusive test data and varying predictions by engineers. On one version of the facts, the batteries are dangerous; on another, they are as safe as any new and complex product can be. Judgments about risk are notoriously difficult for people to make, particularly with respect to rare events, and when the event in question is one that calls to mind vivid images of death and destruction (as in the case of the *Challenger* launch), people tend to assign extraordinarily high weights to miniscule probabilities.[23] Also, the law may be unclear or uncertain. The company may have a responsibility to disclose the test data showing possible in-flight failures to a regulatory agency, but it also may be that the law, properly interpreted, does not require disclosure. The client deserves to have the lawyer's best judgment about what it should do, one informed by all the relevant evidence and the law. But the process of deliberating about the facts and law requires that the client trust that the lawyer is on the same team, so to speak. People who work for the company cannot be constantly worrying that anything they say will be reported to government regulators.

Now consider these arguments in the three-step structure:

Step 1: define, specify, and if necessary explain
the significance of a moral value

By now, you should be alert to the possibility that a moral value is ambiguous or essentially contested. Recall the discussion of the prosecutor's duty to seek justice, discussed in Chapter 8. Justice may mean different things depending, for example, on whether one is considering the perspective of a crime victim, the defendant, residents of a crime-plagued neighborhood, or minority citizens subject to harassment by police officers. Instructing a prosecutor to do justice merely shifts the focus of the argument from professional ethics to the underlying moral value but does not provide any guidance for how these value conflicts should be resolved. The hired guns here make a similar appeal

---

[23] Daniel Kahneman, *Thinking, Fast and Slow* (New York: Farar, Straus & Giroux 2011), pp. 322–23.

to the ambiguity of the concept of the public interest,[24] and they point out that facts may also be uncertain. It can be tempting, with the benefit of hindsight, to assume that lawyers at Enron knew the company was engaging in fraudulent transactions or that the lawyer for the battery company knew of safety problems. In many cases, lawyers may have more or less well-founded hunches or suspicions but not knowledge or even a firm belief that wrongdoing is occurring. The hired guns therefore appeal not so much to a moral *value* but to the metaethical condition of value pluralism and the epistemological problem of uncertainty.

Step 2: show that the value in step 1 entails a principle
of professional ethics

If the hired guns are persuasive in their appeal to value pluralism and uncertainty, the principles of loyalty to one's client and confidentiality of lawyer–client communications follow naturally. As the US Supreme Court has stated, the purpose of professional confidentiality, including the attorney–client privilege, is "to encourage full and frank communication between attorneys and their clients and thereby promote broader public interests in the observance of law and administration of justice."[25] The desire to do justice is admirable, but for the lawyer to provide effective legal advice, it has to be clear that the lawyer's primary loyalty is to the client and that the lawyer is not some kind of double agent who is also working as an agent for the government.[26] The ethical principle of professional independence thus is an indirect way of promoting moral ends such as justice, the protection of investors, and public safety. The hired guns are keen to resist efforts to require lawyers to act directly on those moral ends. They are opposed to "damaging the independence of the bar in order to address even important social problems."[27] We have encountered this argument again and again: Lawyers should play their role within the system,

---

[24] See, e.g., Austin Sarat, "The Profession Versus the Public Interest: Reflections on Two Reifications," *Stanford Law Review* 54: 1491–99 (2002), p. 1498 (arguing that the public interest is only a makeweight in any argument – it is something "to which no one can rightly be opposed" – but it lacks content).

[25] *Upjohn Corp. v. United States* 449 U.S. 383 (1981).

[26] See Fox, *supra*, p. 1247 ("[O]ur rules on confidentiality, in the end, create a far better society than any [the gatekeepers] envision by turning lawyers into cops.").

[27] Davis, *supra*, p. 1291.

serve their clients effectively and keep their confidences, and trust the legal system as a whole to look after the interests of nonclients and the public interest.

The gatekeepers have a response at this stage in the argument. They contend that the hired guns are preoccupied with the notion of independence from government regulators but have paid insufficient attention to the importance of independence from their clients. Loyalty and confidentiality are principles of professional ethics, but so is providing candid advice that the client may not want to hear. Remember the discussion in Chapter 10 of Kronman's view, that professionalism means more than simply providing technical assistance to clients? Good lawyers also provide wise counsel, practical wisdom, and independent judgment. All of these things require some distance from one's client, so that the lawyer can give impartial advice. A leader of the corporate bar stated this ideal in a 1974 speech:

> [I]n securities matters (other than those where advocacy is clearly proper) the attorney will have to function in a manner more akin to that of auditor than to that of the attorney. This means several things. It means that he will have to exercise a measure of independence that is perhaps uncomfortable if he is also the close counselor of management in other matters, often including business decisions. It means he will have to be acutely cognizant of his responsibility to the public who engage in securities transactions that would never have come about were it not for his professional presence. It means that he will have to adopt the healthy skepticism toward the representation of management which a good auditor must adopt.[28]

A healthy skepticism toward management is the antithesis of "warm zeal" and devotion to one's client, but it may be required because the lawyer represents clients within the law.

In the case of the battery manufacturer, the lawyer may wish to advise the client, "Yes, the law lets you [say nothing about the adverse test results], but don't do it. It's a rotten thing to do."[29] Loyalty is a good thing, but *excessive* loyalty may cause a lawyer to lose sight of the distinctiveness of the role of representing clients with respect to the law. As the discussion of

[28] Quoted in Coffee, *supra*, p. 1299.
[29] Mary Ann Glendon, *A Nation under Lawyers* (New York: Farrar, Straus & Giroux 1994), p. 35 (quoting Archibald Cox).

Low Realism and High Realism in Chapter 9 showed, there is a difference between the client's interests and the client's legal rights. Principles of professional ethics must be able to account for this difference. The gatekeepers might say that the problem with the argument of the hired guns is its inability to distinguish between representing the client with respect to its interests and advising the client on its legal rights.

Step 3: test the resulting theory against cases

What would be the right thing to do in the case of the battery manufacturer? If you believe it is to disclose the adverse test results to customers or regulators, how do you respond to the hired guns' concern about uncertainty and the importance of maintaining a relationship of trust and confidence between attorney and client? If the law does not require disclosure, is it the lawyer's place – and not that of the president or the board of directors – to make these decisions? If, on the other hand, you believe the lawyer should remain silent, are you giving up on the ideal of the lawyer as a public-spirited professional concerned with more than merely providing technical expertise in the law? What about the lawyer's conscience? Lawyers remain moral agents even when acting in a professional capacity. If there is an accident caused by the company's batteries, it may be cold comfort to the lawyer that the legal system indirectly promotes the objective of public safety. There is no clear answer here. The gatekeeper versus hired gun debate has been so persistent because each side appeals to features of the professional role that seem essential. The hired guns emphasize the agency structure of the lawyer–client relationship, with the client instructing the lawyer in general terms and the lawyer providing technical expertise. The gatekeepers respond that the lawyer–client relationship is different from other agency relationships in its inextricable connection with the law. The lawyer's authority extends only to promoting the client's *lawful* interests. To which the hired guns respond that determining the scope of the client's lawful interests takes place in circumstances of uncertainty, partial information, and ambiguity; it is essential that clients trust that their lawyers will give them the benefit of the doubt and not "blow the whistle" without justification. To which the gatekeepers respond that sometimes blowing the whistle is justified and is the only way to protect the public from harm. And so it goes.

11.3   Chain of command

We have not yet discussed one feature of the problem facing the lawyer for the battery manufacturer, namely, the directive of the president and the chairman of the board of directors to take no further action. Are those instructions entitled to any moral weight? When lawyers think about authority, they often have in mind the authority of law. Indeed, that was one of the major themes of Chapter 5 on legal obligation. Authority can take other forms, however, and one of its other manifestations is a hierarchical organization in which subordinates owe obligations of loyalty to superiors. Max Weber's classic theory of bureaucratic organizations emphasizes their capacity for carrying out complex tasks with "[p]recision, speed, unambiguity, ... continuity, discretion, unity, strict subordination, [and] reduction of friction and of material and personal costs."[30] Modern business corporations embody bureaucratic rationality but depart from some of its classic characteristics. Decision making in corporations is both hierarchical and decentralized. Power is centralized at the top, but tasks are delegated to subordinates in general terms, with the expectation that the subordinate will discern her boss's objectives and carry them out. In this type of organization, "details are pushed down and credit is pulled up."[31] Subordinates are expected to generate "successful results without messy complications" and feel enormous pressure to transmit good news up the hierarchy so that their boss can bask in the glory of the success.[32] In turn, bosses protect their subordinates and dole out privileges. Everyone within an organization understands the tacit rules, such as: Don't embarrass or publicly contradict your boss; never go around his or her back; tell your boss what he or she wants to hear; and if your boss wants something dropped, drop it.[33]

Unlike Weber's conception of bureaucracy, in which authority is impersonal and flows from the hierarchical nature of the organization, personal relationships are an essential component of authority within a corporation.[34] A loyal subordinate may expect protection from a high-ranking "rabbi" or "Godfather" within the company when mistakes are made and

---

[30] Max Weber, "Bureaucracy," in H. H. Gerth and C. Wright Mills, ed. and trans., *From Max Weber: Essays in Sociology* (Oxford: Oxford University Press 1946), p. 214.

[31] Robert Jackall, *Moral Mazes: The World of Corporate Managers* (Oxford: Oxford University Press 1988), p. 20.

[32] Id., pp. 21, 42–43.   [33] Id., pp. 19, 109–10.   [34] Id., pp. 133, 192.

"blame-time" comes. Without a protector, however, the subordinate may be the scapegoat who must be sacrificed to protect higher-ups.[35] Success, for the purposes of meting out rewards and blame, is measured by criteria that are themselves dependent on the social structure and personal loyalties within an organization.[36] Within this system, moral issues are perceived as ambiguous and conflicting with the overarching imperative to get things done.[37] "Bureaucracy transforms all moral issues into immediately practical concerns."[38]

A story about a health and safety problem, from a sociological study of ethical decision making within corporations, may help illustrate the collision between ethics and the structures of authority in organizations.[39] White (a pseudonym) was an occupational health manager in a large textile manufacturing company. One characteristic of textile plants is the incessant noise from weaving looms, and White became concerned that workers were experiencing severe hearing loss. He argued for the adoption of a program proposed by government regulators that would have involved strict enforcement of hearing protection requirements, as well as more extensive training for workers and managers. White subsequently found that his report and recommendations had been ignored. The problem was that he was an outsider relative to the social circles of managers who were the real decision makers in the organization. His immediate supervisor saw himself as an advocate for the interests of the textile industry against its numerous critics, and he was hostile to the proposed government regulations. White had not developed a patronage relationship with a powerful "Godfather" in the corporation who could have taken his concerns to senior management. Most damningly, he raised his concerns specifically as a moral issue, without linking them to the dominant values of the corporation (i.e., productivity and efficiency). "[I]ndependent morally evaluative judgments get subordinated to the social intricacies of the bureaucratic workplace."[40] By contrast, a more adept manager, Tucker, was able to head off a potential liability disaster by maintaining solidarity with his colleagues, signaling that he could be trusted not to talk about the problem outside the company and working within the network of social relationships through which things get done in a corporation.[41] Tucker understood,

---

[35] Id., pp. 85–90.   [36] Id., p. 45.   [37] Id., pp. 117–21.   [38] Id., p. 111.
[39] See id., pp. 101–05.   [40] Id., p. 105.   [41] Id., pp. 128–33.

and White did not, that moral issues must be translated into the institutional logic of the corporation.[42]

The point of this brief detour into the sociology of organizations is not that corporations are moral black holes. Managers are people, too, and they care about such values as honesty, fairness, and the safety of the users of their products. But just as lawyers have a distinctive moral universe, which in the Standard Conception is characterized by partisanship, neutrality, and nonaccountability, corporate managers may also give a special priority to certain values such as loyalty, trustworthiness, discretion, and respect for one's superiors:

> A moral judgment based on a professional ethic makes little sense in a world where the etiquette of authority relationships and the necessity for protecting and covering for one's boss, one's network, and oneself supercede all other considerations and where nonaccountability for action is the norm.[43]

The tacit norms that regulate life in a corporation exert a powerful influence on the way moral decisions are framed. The example of the battery manufacturer included a reference to the space shuttle *Challenger* launch decision, which has become a classic case study in business ethics and organizational decision making. In that case, engineers recommended against the launch at low temperatures, citing concerns about the performance of a critical safety feature. Senior managers at the company that built the solid-fuel rocket boosters said they had to make a "management decision." This had the subtle but powerful effect of focusing the deliberation on reasons to support a decision to launch the shuttle contrary to the usual default position in engineering that a launch should not proceed unless it was safe. In addition, the problem was framed as a management decision, not an ethical decision – that is, not as one that implicated the lives of the astronauts on the shuttle.[44] The "fading" of ethical considerations from the decision-making process is even more pronounced when the potential

---

[42] Id., p. 112 (defining institutional logic as "the complicated, experientially constructed, and therefore contingent, set of rules, premiums, and sanctions that men and women in a particular context create and re-create in such a way that their behavior and accompanying perspectives are to some extent regularized and predictable").

[43] Id., p. 111.

[44] See Max H. Bazerman and Ann E. Tenbrunsel, *Blind Spots: Why We Fail to Do What's Right and What to Do About It* (Princeton: Princeton University Press 2011), pp. 14–16.

victims are merely statistical abstractions, rather than actual people known to the decision makers.[45] Unlike the astronauts, who were very much public figures, the passengers threatened with harm in the battery example are unidentifiable victims.

Ethical decision making in organizations is not different *in principle* from an isolated moral agent deliberating about what she must do. The relevant values are the same. What is different is the pressure, often felt unconsciously, exerted on people within organizations to engage in wrongdoing. It is tempting to believe that large-scale organizational corruption is the result of "a few bad apples" – some unethical individuals who manage to bend others, reluctantly, to their will. Research in behavioral ethics has shown, however, that well-meaning people often fall easily into patterns of corruption, often without their knowledge.[46] Students contemplating a professional career may believe they will be able to resist the pressure to engage in wrongdoing, but they may not be aware of psychological processes that make it difficult to recognize ethical issues when they arise. For example, initial actions that are self-serving or unduly favorable to the organization and its goals are often committed under time pressure, without significant ethical deliberation.

> Many of the actions that begin cycles of corruption are the products of the intuitive judgment system, which means that they are rapidly arrived at, less than consciously considered, and unintentional in their ethical dubiousness. Further, they often are the product of pressure to make fast decisions.[47]

The rushed decision to launch the *Challenger* is a perfect example. Senior management had to decide quickly what to recommend to the space agency and, almost without thinking about it, referred to it as a management decision. Once a preliminary decision is made, it may tend to become locked

---

[45] Id., p. 98. The term "ethical fading" is from an important paper in behavioral ethics, Ann E. Tenbrunsel and David M. Messick, "Ethical Fading: The Role of Self-Deception in Unethical Behavior," *Social Justice Research* 17: 223–36 (2004).

[46] The best single, short, accessible paper describing these processes, by one of the pioneers of social psychology, is John M. Darley, "The Cognitive and Social Psychology of Contagious Organizational Corruption," *Brooklyn Law Review* 70: 1177–94 (2005). Another excellent overview is David Luban, "The Ethics of Wrongful Obedience," in *Legal Ethics and Human Dignity* (Cambridge: Cambridge University Press 2007).

[47] Darley, *supra*, p. 1183.

in through psychological mechanisms such as loss aversion, which causes people (again, unconsciously) to regard giving something up as significantly more painful than the pleasure they would associate with getting that thing.[48] Having committed to some extent to the launch decision, changing to a no-launch decision would involve a higher perceived cost than if managers had begun with a no-launch decision. Considerations of group loyalty may motivate individuals in the organization to go along with what they perceive is the course of action that has been decided by senior management and to go along with the moral perspective of the group.[49]

To conclude, we can return to the debate between the hired guns and the gatekeepers. Behavioral psychology suggests that professional independence may be extremely difficult to maintain because of subtle pressures to blend in to the culture of an organizational client.[50] The stories of White and Tucker show that it takes considerable skill to earn the trust of senior management, work through a network of peers and superiors, not be perceived as an officious busybody, and actually get things done within an organization.[51] The lawyer in the battery case may simply be marginalized in decision making if the president is determined not to notify customers of adverse test results. Lawyers should not assume at the outset that their clients are uninterested in candid advice, but, at some point, it may become clear that the client's managers are determined to ignore anything the lawyer says that is not in keeping with their own view of the best interests of the organization. At that point, the lawyer has an extremely difficult decision to make, comparable to the weighty moral issues of conscientious objection and civil disobedience considered in Chapter 6. It is the nature of role-differentiated professional ethics that it will sometimes conflict with the requirements of morality. One hopes this is not a regular occurrence in one's career, but lawyers with decision-making responsibilities in organizations may find themselves in the position of the lawyer in this problem.

---

[48] Kahneman, *supra*, pp. 292–94.

[49] Darley, *supra*, p. 1191. The classic work is Irvin Janis, *Victims of Groupthink: A Psychological Study of Foreign Policy Decisions and Fiascoes* (Boston: Houghton-Mifflin 1972).

[50] See Donald C. Langevoort, "The Epistemology of Corporate-Securities Lawyering: Beliefs, Biases, and Organizational Behavior," *Brooklyn Law Review* 63: 629–76 (1997).

[51] See Darley, *supra*, p. 1193 (discussing pressure in groups to avoid the social identity of "the naïve fool").

The discussion in the second half of this chapter has only scratched the surface of the rich, emerging literature on behavioral ethics. It would take another book of this length to do it justice. In an inherently practical discipline such as legal ethics, however, there should be more attention paid to the way ethical decisions are made in real-world settings such as law firms and corporate legal departments. All the conceptual clarity and knowledge in the world can only do so much when people must contend with overt and unconscious influences on their ethical decision making.

References

Primary sources

American Bar Association Model Rules of Professional Conduct
American Bar Association Standards Relating to the Administration of Criminal
    Justice
Australian Solicitors Conduct Rules 2012
Bar Council of India, Rules on Professional Standards
Federation of [Canadian] Law Societies, Model Code of Professional Conduct
Canadian Charter of Rights and Freedoms
Code of Professional Conduct for British Columbia
Code of Conduct of the Bar of England and Wales
Law Society of Upper Canada [Ontario] Rules of Professional Conduct
Malaysian Bar, Legal Profession (Practice and Etiquette) Rules 1978
New South Wales Barristers' Rules
New Zealand Bill of Rights Act 1990
New Zealand Lawyers Conduct and Client Care Rules 2008
Restatement (Third) of the Law Governing Lawyers (2000) [U.S.]
Solicitors Regulation Authority [England and Wales] Code of Conduct 2011
United States Constitution
Western Australia Barristers' Rules

Case law

Anders v. California, 386 U.S. 738 (1967)
Balla v. Gambro, Inc., 584 N.E.2d 104 (Ill. 1991)
Berger v. United States, 295 U.S. 78 (1935)
Boucher, R v., [1954] S.C.J. No. 54, 110 C.C.C. 263
Gideon v. Wainwright, 372 U.S. 335 (1963)
In re Holocaust Victims Assets Litigation, 319 F.Supp.2d 301 (E.D.N.Y. 2004)
Jones v. Barnes, 436 U.S. 745 (1983)

Lincoln Saving & Loan Association v. Wall, 743 F. Supp. 901 (D.D.C. 1990)

Pacific Investment Management Company LLC v. Mayer Brown LLP, 603 F.3d 144 (2d Cir. 2010)

Riggs v. Palmer, 22 N.E. 188 (N.Y. 1889)

Rondel v. Worsley, [1967] 3 All E.R. 993 (H.L.)

Togstad v. Vesely, Otto, Miller & Keefe, 291 N.W.2d 686 (Minn. 1980)

Upjohn Corp. v. United States 449 U.S. 383 (1981)

Zabella v. Pakel, 242 F.2d 452 (7th Cir. 1957)

Secondary sources

Alexy, Robert, *The Argument from Injustice* (Oxford: Oxford University Press, Bonnie Litschewski Paulson and Stanley L. Paulson, trans. 2002).

Amsterdam, Anthony, and Jerome Bruner, *Minding the Law* (Cambridge, Mass.: Harvard University Press 2000).

Applbaum, Arthur Isak, *Ethics for Adversaries* (Princeton: Princeton University Press 1999).

Aquinas, Thomas, *Summa Theologica*, in William P. Baumgarth and Richard J. Regan, eds., *Aquinas on Law, Morality, and Politics* (Indianapolis: Hackett, 2nd edn., 2002), pp. 10-69.

Arendt, Hannah, *Eichmann in Jerusalem* (New York: Viking 1963).

Aristotle, *Nicomachean Ethics*. W. D. Ross and J. O. Urmson trans., in J. L. Ackrill, ed., A New Aristotle Reader (Princeton, N.J.: Princeton University Press 1984).

Austin, John, *The Province of Jurisprudence Determined* (London: J. Murray 1832).

Aviel, Rebecca, "Why Civil *Gideon* Won't Fix Family Law," *Yale Law Journal* 122: 2106-24 (2013).

Babcock, Barbara, "Defending the Guilty," *Cleveland State Law Review* 32: 175-87 (1983).

Barrett, Edward F., "The Adversary System and the Ethics of Advocacy," *Notre Dame Lawyer* 37: 479-88 (1962).

Bazerman, Max H., and Ann E. Tenbrunsel, *Blind Spots: Why We Fail to Do What's Right and What to Do About It* (Princeton: Princeton University Press 2011).

Bazyler, Michael J., "Gray Zones of Holocaust Restitution: American Justice and Holocaust Morality," in Jonathan Petropoulos and John K. Roth eds., *Gray Zones: Ambiguity and Compromise in the Holocaust and Its Aftermath* (New York: Berghan Books 2005), pp. 339-59.

Berlin, Isaiah, "The Pursuit of the Ideal," in Henry Hardy, ed., *The Crooked Timber of Humanity* (Princeton: Princeton University Press 1990), pp. 1-19.

Binder, Guyora, "Critical Legal Studies," in Dennis Patterson, ed., *A Companion to Philosophy of Law and Legal Theory* (Malden, Mass.: Blackwell 1996), pp. 280–90.

Blackstone, William, *Commentaries on the Laws of England.* (Chicago: University of Chicago Press, 1979).

Bok, Sissela, *Lying: Moral Choice in Public and Private Life* (New York: Pantheon Books 1978).

Boon, Andrew, and Jennifer Levin, *The Ethics and Conduct of Lawyers in England and Wales* (Oxford: Hart, 2nd edn. 2008).

Burnett, D. Graham, *A Trial by Jury* (New York: Knopf 2001).

Butler, Paul, "How Can You Prosecute Those People?," in Abbe Smith and Monroe H. Freedman, eds., *How Can You Represent Those People?* (New York: Palgrave MacMillan 2013), pp. 15–27.

Carr, Albert Z., "Is Business Bluffing Ethical?," *Harvard Business Review* (Jan.–Feb. 1968): 143–53.

Carrington, Paul D., "Unconscionable Lawyers," *Georgia Law Review* 19: 361–94 (2002).

Cassidy, R. Michael, "Some Reflections on Ethics and Plea Bargaining: An Essay in Honor of Fred Zacharias," *San Diego Law Review* 48: 93–110 (2011).

Cassidy, R. Michael, "Character and Context: What Virtue Theory Can Teach Us About a Prosecutor's Ethical Duty to 'Seek Justice,'" *Notre Dame Law Review* 82: 635–97 (2006).

Clemmer, Christopher D., "Obstructing the Bernardo Investigation: Kenneth Murray and the Defence Counsel's Conflicting Obligations to Clients and the Court," *Osgoode Hall Review of Law and Policy* 1: 137 (2008).

Clermont, Kevin M., *Standards of Decision in Law* (Durham, N.C.: Carolina Academic Press 2013).

Cochran, Johnnie L., Jr., "How Can You Defend Those People?," *Loyola of Los Angeles Law Review* 30: 39–43 (1996).

Code, Michael, "Ethics and Criminal Law Practice," in Alice Woolley et al., eds., *Lawyers' Ethics and Professional Regulation* (Markham, Ont.: LexisNexis 2008).

Coffee, John C., Jr., "The Attorney as Gatekeeper: An Agenda for the SEC," *Columbia Law Review* 103: 1293–1316 (2003).

Cohen, Steven M., "What Is True? Perspectives of a Former Prosecutor," *Cardozo Law Review* 23: 817–28 (2002).

Cole, David, *No Equal Justice: Race and Class in the American Criminal Justice System* (New York: New Press 1999).

Coleman, Jules, "Negative and Positive Positivism," in Marshall Cohen, ed., *Ronald Dworkin and Contemporary Jurisprudence* (Totowa, N.J.: Rowman & Allanheld 1983), pp. 28–48.

Cooper, Austin, Q.C., "The Ken Murray Case: Defence Counsel's Dilemma," *Criminal Law Quarterly* 47: 41 (2009).

Cover, Robert M., *Justice Accused* (New Haven: Yale University Press 1975).

Crenshaw, Kimberle, "A Black Feminist Critique of Antidiscrimination Law and Politics," in David Kairys, ed., *The Politics of Law: A Progressive Critique* (New York: Pantheon Books, revised edn. 1990), 195–218.

Dagger, Richard, "Political Obligation," *Stanford Encyclopedia of Philosophy*, http:// plato.stanford.edu/entries/political-obligation/

Damaška, Mirjan R., *The Faces of Justice and State Authority* (New Haven: Yale University Press 1986).

Daniels, Norman, "Reflective Equilibrium," *Stanford Encyclopedia of Philosophy*, http://plato.stanford.edu/entries/reflective-equilibrium/

Dare, Tim, *The Counsel of Rogues? A Defence of the Standard Conception of the Lawyer's Role* (Farnham: Ashgate 2009).

Darley, John M., "The Cognitive and Social Psychology of Contagious Organizational Corruption," *Brooklyn Law Review* 70: 1177–94 (2005).

Dauer, Edward A., and Arthur Allen Leff, "Correspondence: The Lawyer as Friend," *Yale Law Journal* 86: 573–84 (1976).

Davis, Evan A., "The Meaning of Professional Independence," *Columbia Law Review* 103: 1281–92 (2003).

Dershowitz, Alan M., *Reasonable Doubts: The Criminal Justice System and the O. J. Simpson Case* (New York: Touchstone 1997).

Dworkin, Ronald, *Taking Rights Seriously* (Cambridge, Mass.: Harvard University Press 1977).

Dworkin, Ronald, *Law's Empire* (Cambridge, Mass.: Harvard University Press 1986).

Dworkin, Ronald, "Rights as Trumps," in Jeremy Waldron, ed., *Theories of Rights* (Oxford: Oxford University Press 1994), 153–67.

Ferren, John, "The Corporate Lawyer's Obligation to the Public Interest," *Business Lawyer* 33: 1253–69 (1978).

Finnis, John, *Natural Law and Natural Rights* (Oxford: Clarendon Press 1980).

Fish, Stanley, *Is There a Text in This Class? The Authority of Interpretive Communities* (Cambridge, Mass.: Harvard University Press 1982).

Fisher, William W., III, et al., eds., *American Legal Realism* (Oxford: Oxford University Press 1993).

Fiss, Owen M., "Objectivity and Interpretation," *Stanford Law Review* 34: 739–63 (1982).

Flathman, Richard E., "Legitimacy," in Robert E. Goodin, Philip Pettit, and Thomas Pogge, eds., *A Companion to Contemporary Political Philosophy* (Malden, Mass.: Wiley-Blackwell, 2nd edn. 2012), pp. 678–84.

Flood, John, "Will There Be Fallout from Clementi? The Repercussions for the Legal Profession after the Legal Services Act 2007," *Michigan State Law Review* 2012: 537–65 (2012).

Flood, John A., *Barristers' Clerks: The Law's Middlemen* (Manchester: Manchester University Press 1983).

Foot, Philippa, "The Problem of Abortion and the Doctrine of Double Effect," in *Virtues and Vices* (Berkeley: University of California Press 1978), pp. 19–32.

Fox, Lawrence J., "The Fallout from Enron: Media Frenzy and Misguided Notions of Public Relations Are No Reason to Abandon Our Commitment to Our Clients," *Illinois Law Review* 2003: 1243–59 (2003).

Frankena, William K., *Ethics* (Englewood Cliffs, N.J., 1963).

Freedman, Monroe, and Abbe Smith, *Understanding Lawyers' Ethics* (New Providence, N.J.: Lexis-Nexis, 4th edn., 2010).

Freedman, Monroe H., "Why It's Essential to Represent 'Those People,'" in Abbe Smith and Monroe H. Freedman, eds., *How Can You Represent Those People?* (New York: Palgrave MacMillan 2013), pp. 73–80.

Freedman, Monroe H., "The Lawyer's Moral Obligation of Justification," *Texas Law Review* 74: 111–18 (1995).

Freedman, Monroe H., *Lawyers' Ethics in an Adversary System* (Indianapolis: Bobbs-Merrill 1975).

Freeman, Samuel, "John Rawls – An Introduction," in Samuel Freeman, ed., *The Cambridge Companion to Rawls* (Cambridge: Cambridge University Press 2003), pp. 1–61.

Fried, Charles, "The Lawyer as Friend: The Moral Foundations of the Lawyer-Client Relation," *Yale Law Journal* 85: 1060–89 (1976).

Fried, Charles, *Contract as Promise* (Cambridge, Mass.: Harvard University Press 1981).

Fuller, Lon L., "Positivism and Fidelity to Law – A Reply to Professor Hart," *Harvard Law Review* 71: 630–72 (1958).

Fuller, Lon L., *The Morality of Law* (New Haven: Yale University Press, 2d edn., 1964).

Fuller, Lon L., and John D. Randall, "Professional Responsibility: Report of the Joint Conference," *American Bar Association Journal* 44: 1159–62, 1216–18 (1958).

Gallie, W.B., "Essentially Contested Concepts," *Proceedings of the Aristotelian Society* 56: 167–198 (1956).

Gilbert, Margaret, "Group Membership and Political Obligation," *The Monist* 76: 119–31 (1993).

Gilbert, Margaret, *A Theory of Political Obligation* (Oxford: Oxford University Press 2006).

Gilovich, Thomas, and Dale W. Griffin, "Judgment and Decision Making," in Thomas Gilovich, Dacher Keltner, and Richard E. Nisbett, eds., *Social Psychology* (New York: Norton, 2d edn., 2011), pp. 542–88.

Glendon, Mary Ann, *A Nation under Lawyers* (New York: Farrar, Straus and Giroux 1994).

Green, Leslie, "Law and Obligations," in Jules Coleman and Scott Shapiro, eds., *The Oxford Handbook of Jurisprudence & Philosophy of Law* (Oxford: Oxford University Press 2002), pp. 514–47.

Greenawalt, Kent, *Conflicts of Law and Morality* (Oxford: Oxford University Press 1989).

Harr, Jonathan, *A Civil Action* (New York: Random House 1995).

Hart, H. L. A., "Are There Any Natural Rights?," *Philosophical Review* 64: 175–91 (1955).

Hart, H. L. A., "Positivism and the Separation of Law and Morals," *Harvard Law Review* 71: 593–629 (1958).

Hart, H. L. A., *The Concept of Law* (Oxford: Oxford University Press, 2d edn., 1994) (with Postscript edited by Penelope A. Bulloch and Joseph Raz).

Hazard, Geoffrey C., Jr., *Ethics in the Practice of Law* (New Haven: Yale University Press 1978).

Hazard, Geoffrey C., Jr., "Quis Custodiet Ipsos Custodes?," *Yale Law Journal* 95: 1523–35 (1986) (book review).

Hazard, Geoffrey C., Jr., and Angelo Dondi, *Legal Ethics: A Comparative Study* (Stanford: Stanford University Press 2004).

Hazard, Geoffrey C., Jr., and Dana A. Remus, "Advocacy Revalued," *University of Pennsylvania Law Review* 159: 751–81 (2011).

Hohfeld, Wesley Newcomb, "Fundamental Legal Conceptions as Applied in Judicial Reasoning," *Yale Law Journal* 26: 710–70 (1917).

Horwitz, Morton, *The Transformation of American Law, 1780–1860* (Cambridge, Mass.: Harvard University Press 1977).

Hume, David, "On the Original Contract," in Ernest Barker, ed., *Social Contract* (Oxford: Oxford University Press 1947), pp. 147–66.

Hutchinson, Allan C., "Calgary and Everything After: A Postmodern Re-Vision of Lawyering," *Alberta Law Review* 33: 768–86 (1995).

Jackall, Robert, *Moral Mazes: The World of Corporate Managers* (Oxford: Oxford University Press 1988).

Janis, Irvin, *Victims of Groupthink: A Psychological Study of Foreign Policy Decisions and Fiascoes* (Boston: Houghton-Mifflin 1972).

Johnston, David, *A Brief History of Justice* (Malden, Mass.: Wiley-Blackwell 2011).

Joseph, Lawrence, *Lawyerland: What Lawyers Talk About When They Talk About Law* (New York: Farrar, Straus & Giroux 1997).

Kahneman, Daniel, *Thinking, Fast and Slow* (New York: Farrar, Straus & Giroux 2011).

Kant, Immanuel, *Grounding for the Metaphysics of Morals* (James W. Ellington, trans.) (Indianapolis: Hackett 1981).

Kelman, Mark, *A Guide to Critical Legal Studies* (Cambridge, Mass.: Harvard University Press 1987).

Kennedy, Duncan, *A Critique of Adjudication {fin de siècle}* (Cambridge, Mass.: Harvard University Press 1997).

Koniak, Susan P., "When the Hurlyburly's Done: The Bar's Struggle with the SEC," *Columbia Law Review* 103: 1236–80 (2003).

Kramer, Matthew H., *Objectivity and the Rule of Law* (Cambridge: Cambridge University Press 2007).

Kronman, Anthony T., *The Lost Lawyer: Failing Ideals of the Legal Profession* (Cambridge, Mass.: Harvard University Press 1993).

Kruse, Katherine R., "The Human Dignity of Clients," *Cornell Law Review* 93: 1343–64 (2008).

Kruse, Katherine R., "Beyond Cardboard Clients in Legal Ethics," *Georgetown Journal of Legal Ethics* 23: 103–54 (2010).

Kunen, James S., *"How Can You Defend Those People?": The Making of a Criminal Lawyer* (New York: Random House 1983).

Lahav, Alexandra D., "Portraits of Resistance: Lawyer Responses to Unjust Proceedings," *UCLA Law Review* 57: 725–87 (2010).

Langevoort, Donald C., "The Epistemology of Corporate-Securities Lawyering: Beliefs, Biases, and Organizational Behavior," *Brooklyn Law Review* 63: 629–76 (1997).

Leiter, Brian, "Legal Realism," in Dennis Patterson, ed., *A Companion to Philosophy of Law and Legal Theory* (Oxford: Blackwell 1996), pp. 261–79.

Levin, Yuval, *The Great Debate: Edmund Burke, Thomas Paine, and the Birth of Right and Left* (New York: Basic Books 2014).

Locke, John, *Second Treatise of Civil Government* (1690), ch. IV, sec. 22. C. Macpherson, ed. (Indianapolis: Hackett 1980).

Loo, Dennis D., and Ruth-Ellen M. Grimes, "Polls, Politics, and Crime: The 'Law and Order' Issue of the 1960s," *Western Criminology Review* 5: 50–67 (2004).

Luban, David, "Paternalism and the Legal Profession," *Wisconsin Law Review* 1981: 454–93 (1981).

Luban, David, "The Adversary System Excuse," in David Luban, ed., *The Good Lawyer: Lawyers' Roles and Lawyers' Ethics* (Totowa, N.J.: Rowman & Allanheld 1983), pp. 83–122.

Luban, David, "The Lysistratian Prerogative: A Response to Stephen Pepper," *American Bar Foundation Research Journal* 1986: 637–49 (1986).

Luban, David, *Lawyers and Justice* (Princeton: Princeton University Press 1988).

Luban, David, *Legal Ethics and Human Dignity* (Cambridge: Cambridge University Press 2007).

Luban, David, "Lawfare and Legal Ethics in Guantánamo," *Stanford Law Review* 60: 1981–2026 (2008).

Luban, David, "The Conscience of a Prosecutor," *Valparaiso University Law Review* 45: 1–31 (2010).

Lyons, David, *Ethics and the Rule of Law* (Cambridge: Cambridge University Press 1984).

MacIntyre, Alasdair, *After Virtue* (Notre Dame, Ind.: University of Notre Dame Press, 2d edn., 1984).

Margulies, Joseph, *Guantánamo and the Abuse of Presidential Power* (New York: Simon & Schuster 2006).

Markovits, Daniel, *A Modern Legal Ethics* (Princeton: Princeton University Press 2008).

Marmor, Andrei, *Philosophy of Law* (Princeton, N.J.: Princeton University Press 2011).

Merryman, John Henry, *The Civil Law Tradition* (Stanford: Stanford University Press, 2d edn., 1985).

Mitchell, John B., "The Ethics of the Criminal Defense Attorney – New Answers to Old Questions," *Stanford Law Review* 32: 293–337 (1980).

Mitchell, John B., "Reasonable Doubts Are Where You Find Them," *Georgetown Journal of Legal Ethics* 1: 339–61 (1987).

Morris, Herbert, "Persons and Punishment," *The Monist* 52: 475–501 (1968).

Muller, Ingo, *Hitler's Justice: The Courts of the Third Reich* (Cambridge, Mass.: Harvard University Press 1992).

Murphy, Mark C., *Natural Law in Jurisprudence and Politics* (Cambridge: Cambridge University Press 2006).

Nagel, Thomas, "The Fragmentation of Value," in *Mortal Questions* (Cambridge: Cambridge University Press 1979), pp. 128–41.

Neiman, Susan, *Evil in Modern Thought* (Princeton, N.J.: Princeton University Press 2002.

Nussbaum, Martha C., *Sex and Social Justice* (Oxford: Oxford University Press 1999).

Ogletree, Charles J., Jr., "Beyond Justifications: Seeking Motivations to Sustain Public Defenders," *Harvard Law Review* 106: 1239–94 (1993).

Olson, Edgar O., "Is Rent Control Good Social Policy?," *Chicago-Kent Law Review* 67: 921–45 (1991).

Parker, Christine, and Adrian Evans, *Inside Lawyers' Ethics* (Cambridge: Cambridge University Press 2007).

Pennington, Nancy, and Reid Hastie, "A Cognitive Theory of Juror Decision Making: The Story Model," *Cardozo Law Review* 13: 519–57 (1991).

Pepper, Stephen L., "The Lawyer's Amoral Ethical Role: A Defense, A Problem, and Some Possibilities," *American Bar Foundation Research Journal* 1986: 613–35 (1986).

Pitkin, Hanna, "Obligation and Consent – I," *American Political Science Review* 59: 990–99 (1965).

Plato, "Crito," Hugh Tredennick, trans., in Edith Hamilton and Huntington Cairns, eds., *Plato: The Complete Dialogues* (Princeton, N.J.: Princeton University Press 1961).

Postema, Gerald J., "Moral Responsibility and Professional Ethics," *New York University Law Review* 55: 63–89 (1980).

Rawls, John, *A Theory of Justice* (Cambridge, Mass.: Harvard University Press 1971).

Rawls, John, *Political Liberalism* (New York: Columbia University Press 1993).

Rawls, John, "Legal Obligation and the Duty of Fair Play," in Samuel Freeman, ed., *John Rawls: Collected Papers* (Cambridge, Mass.: Harvard University Press 1999), pp. 117–29.

Raz, Joseph, *The Authority of Law* (Oxford: Oxford University Press 1979).

Raz, Joseph, "Rights-Based Moralities," in Jeremy Waldron, ed., *Theories of Rights* (Oxford: Oxford University Press 1984), pp. 182–200.

Raz, Joseph, *The Morality of Freedom* (Oxford: Oxford University Press 1986).

Raz, Joseph, "Authority, Law, and Morality," in *Ethics in the Public Domain* (Oxford: Oxford University Press 1994).

Raz, Joseph, "Incorporation By Law," *Legal Theory* 10: 1–17 (2004).

Reath, Andrews, "Kant's Moral Philosophy," in Roger Crisp, ed., *The Oxford Handbook of the History of Ethics* (Oxford: Oxford University Press 2013), pp. 443–64.

Regan, Milton C., Jr., *Eat What You Kill: The Fall of a Wall Street Lawyer* (Ann Arbor: University of Michigan Press 2004).

Rhode, Deborah L., *In the Interests of Justice: Reforming the Legal Profession* (Oxford: Oxford University Press 2000).

Ross, W. D., *The Right and the Good* (Oxford: Oxford University Press 1930).

Ross, Ysaiah, *Ethics in Law: Lawyers' Responsibility and Accountability in Australia* (Chatswood, N.S.W.: Butterworths, 10th edn., 2010).

Sarat, Austin, "The Profession Versus the Public Interest: Reflections on Two Reifications," *Stanford Law Review* 54: 1491–99 (2002).

Sartre, Jean-Paul, "Existentialism Is a Humanism," (Philip Mairet, trans.) in Walter Kaufmann, ed., *Existentialism from Dostoevsky to Sartre* (New York: Meridian 1957), pp. 287–311.

Scanlon, T. M., *What We Owe to Each Other* (Cambridge: Harvard University Press 1998).

Schauer, Frederick, *The Force of Law* (manuscript, forthcoming).

Scheffler, Samuel, ed., *Consequentialism and Its Critics* (Oxford: Oxford University Press 1988).

Schwartz, Murray, "The Professionalism and Accountability of Lawyers," *California Law Review* 66: 669–98 (1978).

Shaffer, Thomas L., *On Being a Christian and a Lawyer* (Provo, Utah: Brigham Young University Press 1981).

Shapiro, Scott J., "Authority," in Jules Coleman and Scott Shapiro, eds., *The Oxford Handbook of Jurisprudence and Philosophy of Law* (Oxford: Oxford University Press 2002), pp. 382–439.

Shapiro, Scott J., "The 'Hart-Dworkin' Debate: A Short Guide for the Perplexed," in Arthur Ripstein, ed., *Ronald Dworkin* (Cambridge: Cambridge University Press 2007), pp. 22–55.

Shapiro, Scott J., *Legality* (Cambridge, Mass.: Harvard University Press 2011).

Shiffrin, Seana Valentine, "Promising, Intimate Relationships, and Conventionalism," *Philosophical Review* 117: 481–524 (2008).

Simmons, A. John, *Moral Principles and Political Obligations* (Princeton, N.J.: Princeton University Press 1979).

Simmons, A. John, "Associative Political Obligations," *Ethics* 106: 247–73 (1996).

Simmons, A. John, *Political Philosophy* (Oxford: Oxford University Press 2008).

Simon, William H., "The Ideology of Advocacy: Procedural Justice and Professional Ethics," *Wisconsin Law Review* 1978: 29–144 (1978).

Simon, William H., "Ethical Discretion in Lawyering," *Harvard Law Review* 101: 1083–1145 (1988).

Simon, William H., *The Practice of Justice* (Cambridge, Mass.: Harvard University Press 1998).

Simon, William H., "Authoritarian Legal Ethics: Bradley Wendel and the Positivist Turn," *Texas Law Review* 90: 709–26 (2012).

Singer, Peter, "Famine, Affluence, and Morality," *Philosophy and Public Affairs* 1: 229–43 (1972).

Smith, Abbe, "Defending Defending: The Case for Unmitigated Zeal on Behalf of People Who Do Terrible Things," *Hofstra Law Review* 28: 925–61 (2000).

Smith, Abbe, and Monroe H. Freedman, *How Can You Represent Those People?* (New York: Palgrave MacMillan 2013).

Smith, Clive Stafford, *Eight O'clock Ferry to the Windward Side: Seeking Justice in Guantánamo Bay* (New York: Nation Books 2007).

Smith, M. B. E., "Is There a Prima Facie Obligation to Obey the Law?," *Yale Law Journal* 82: 950–76 (1973).

Susskind, Richard, *The End of Lawyers? Rethinking the Nature of Legal Services* (Oxford University Press, 2008).

Tenbrunsel, Ann E., and David M. Messick, "Ethical Fading: The Role of Self-Deception in Unethical Behavior," *Social Justice Research* 17: 223–36 (2004).

Thomson, Judith Jarvis, "The Trolley Problem," *Yale Law Journal* 94: 1395–1415 (1985).

Tigar, Michael E., "Defending," *Texas Law Review* 74: 101–110 (1995).

Tigar, Michael E., "Litigators' Ethics," *Tennessee Law Review* 67: 409–24 (2000).

Tuck, Richard, "Hobbes," in *Great Political Thinkers* (Oxford: Oxford University Press 1992).

Unger, Roberto Mangabeira, *Knowledge and Politics* (New York: Free Press 1987).

Vaughan, Diane, *The Challenger Launch Decision: Risky Technology, Culture, and Deviance at NASA* (Chicago: University of Chicago Press 1996).

Vischer, Robert K., *Martin Luther King Jr. and the Morality of Legal Practice* (Cambridge: Cambridge University Press 2013).

Waldron, Jeremy, "A Right to Do Wrong," *Ethics* 92: 21–39 (1981).

Waldron, Jeremy, "Two Sides of the Coin," in *Liberal Rights* (Cambridge: Cambridge University Press 1993), pp. 1–34.

Waldron, Jeremy, "Rights," in Robert E. Goodin, Philip Pettit and Thomas Pogge, eds., *A Companion to Contemporary Political Philosophy* (Chichester: Wiley-Blackwell, 2d edn., 2012), pp. 745–54.

Walker, A. D. M., "Political Obligation and the Argument from Gratitude," *Philosophy and Public Affairs* 17: 191–211 (1988).

Walzer, Michael, *Spheres of Justice* (New York: Basic Books 1983).

Webb, Duncan, *Ethics, Professional Responsibility and the Lawyer* (Wellington: Butterworths 2000).

Weber, Max, "Bureaucracy," in H. H. Gerth and C. Wright Mills, ed. and trans., *From Max Weber: Essays in Sociology* (Oxford: Oxford University Press 1946), pp. 196–244.

Wendel, W. Bradley, *Lawyers and Fidelity to Law* (Princeton, N.J.: Princeton University Press 2010).

White, James Boyd, *Heracles' Bow: Essays on the Rhetoric and Poetics of the Law* (Madison: University of Wisconsin Press 1985).

Wilkins, David B., "Legal Realism for Lawyers," *Harvard Law Review* 104: 468–524 (1990).

Williams, Bernard, *Ethics and the Limits of Philosophy* (Cambridge, Mass.: Harvard University Press 1985).

Williams, Patricia J., "The Pain of Word Bondage," in *The Alchemy of Race and Rights* (Cambridge, Mass.: Harvard University Press 1991), pp. 146–65.

Wishman, Seymour, *Confessions of a Criminal Lawyer* (New York: Times Books 1981).

Wolff, Robert Paul, *In Defense of Anarchy* (New York: Harper & Row 1970).

Wolff, Robert Paul, "The Conflict Between Authority and Autonomy," in Joseph Raz, ed., *Authority* (New York: New York University Press 1990), pp. 20–31.

Woolley, Alice, *Understanding Lawyers' Ethics in Canada* (Markham, Ont.: LexisNexis 2011).

Woolley, Alice, et al., *Lawyers' Ethics and Professional Regulation* (Markham, Ont.: LexisNexis 2008).

Young, Iris Marion, *Justice and the Politics of Difference* (Princeton: Princeton University Press 1990).

Zimbardo, Philip, *The Lucifer Effect: Understanding How Good People Turn Evil* (New York: Random House 2008).

Ziv, Neta, "Lawyers Talking Rights and Clients Breaking Rules: Between Legal Positivism and Distributive Justice in Israeli Poverty Lawyering," *Clinical Law Review* 11: 209–39 (2004).

Index